TO MY WIFE AND SON,
HAZEL AND JOHN

Action Before Westport, 1864

ACTION BEFORE WESTPORT

1864

REVISED EDITION

Howard N. Monnett

Introduction by John H. Monnett

UNIVERSITY PRESS OF COLORADO

Published by the University Press of Colorado
5589 Arapahoe Avenue, Suite 206C
Boulder, Colorado 80303

The University Press of Colorado is a cooperative publishing enterprise supported, in part, by Adams State College, Colorado State University, Fort Lewis College, Mesa State College, Metropolitan State College of Denver, University of Colorado, University of Northern Colorado, University of Southern Colorado, and Western State College of Colorado.

The paper used in this publication meets the minimum requirements of the American National Standard for Information Sciences—Permanence of Paper for Printed Library Materials. ANSI Z39.48-1992

Library of Congress Cataloging-in-Publication Data

Monnett, Howard N.
    Action before Westport, 1864 / Howard N. Monnett ; introduction by John H. Monnett. — Rev. ed.
      p.   cm.
   ISBN: 0-87081-413-3 (alk. paper)
     1. Westport (Kansas City, Mo.), Battle of, 1864.   I. Monnett, John H.
   II. Title.
E477.16.M6   1995
973.7'37 — dc20

95-20496
CIP

10 9 8 7 6 5 4 3 2

Preface to the Original

On January 5, 1888, General Joseph Orville Shelby wrote to a friend about some rumors concerning General Sterling Price's last raid into Missouri during the closing months of 1864. After a lengthy defense of the conduct of the Confederate invaders and of General Price's management of the expedition, General Shelby concluded his letter by writing: "Some time I will tell you a heap about that expedition that would astonish many people in this state."

If the dashing Shelby ever revealed his knowledge, no record of it exists today. No doubt he did possess astonishing information, for this was a most astonishing raid—in its conception, in its execution, and in its culmination. It began on August 4, 1864, and came to an end on December 2, 1864. It was a cavalry raid, covering 1,488 miles of Trans-Mississippi territory and encompassing forty-three engagements. The problems of logistics involved were tremendous; property damage in the state of Missouri alone was enormous. Its climax came during the action before Westport where both blue and gray became fighters of prodigious, untaught valor.

The results of the expedition were widespread. It jeopardized General George H. Thomas' Union army at Nashville due to the delayed arrival of General Andrew Jackson Smith's infantry corps. It saved Mobile, Alabama, to the Confederacy for several months. In a letter to William T. Sherman, September 10, 1864, General U. S. Grant stated that "had it not been for Price's movements General Canby would have sent twelve thousand more men to Mobile" who, in cooperation with a force sent from Sherman's army at Atlanta, would have been sufficient to take that vital city. The expedition drew, according to the official Union reports, not less than 22,650 troops from the Federal armies east of the Mississippi—an example of what could have been accomplished by a full-scale invasion with all the forces of the Confederate Department of the Trans-Mississippi.

But above all else, the climactic action before Westport brought to an end the Civil War on the Missouri-Kansas border. For ten years that borderland had known the fullest meaning of Civil War. During those years it had seethed with hatred and known the most bitter antagonisms. It had experienced constant violence and strife and had been wracked with internecine war.

To most of the public and too-many historians, the Civil War was fought in Virginia and the neighboring states, with but a few skirmishes west of the Mississippi. Even a cursory examination of the official records, however, will reveal that Missouri and Arkansas and Kansas suffered battles just as devastating and a good deal more bitter than those in the east.

Little has been written of General Price's invasion of Missouri in 1864. What records do exist often reveal widely differing Confederate and Union versions, very often actually contradicting each other. In preparation for the writing of this account of Price's Expedition a sincere effort was first made to collate them. In this book certain limits have been imposed upon the scope of the material covered. In point of time, only the operations of the action before Westport (October 19-23, 1864) are reported in detail. However, in order to clarify the background and aftermath of that action, short discussions of the events leading up to the combat and following it have been included.

The action before Westport came at a time when the eyes of both the Union and the Confederacy were focused on the gigantic struggles before Atlanta and Petersburg. With the fall of Vicksburg on July 4, 1863, the Trans-Mississippi became an isolated region with most of its eastern ties severed. It came during the closing months of a long Civil War when few were interested in what happened "out West." It attracted very little attention from statesmen, journalists, soldiers, and citizens in the east. "After all," wrote one easterner, "those westerners have been fighting for a decade now. It was their Old John Brown who started the whole mess anyhow."

To be sure, the action before Westport was neither a Gettysburg nor a Chancellorsville, but men fought and died there before Westport just the same. They fought and died for a principle and an ideal just as much as did those who fought and died at Gettysburg and Chancellorsville. They, too, deserve to be remembered for their moment in history.

HOWARD N. MONNETT

Overland Park, Kansas
January 1, 1964

Acknowledgments

MANY PERSONS have contributed in varying degrees to the preparation of this book. I am particularly indebted to E. B. Long of Oak Park, Illinois, for his interest in this project and for the time spent with me in searching the battlefield of Westport. It was because of his encouragement that this work was completed. To Jay Monaghan, consultant for the Wyles Collection of Lincolniana at the University of California in Santa Barbara, go sincere thanks for putting me on the track of much unknown material. To James W. Patton, director of the Southern Historical Collection, University of North Carolina Library, I owe a debt of gratitude for placing in my hands invaluable manuscript material.

I want to thank Mrs. Dana O. Jensen, editor of the *Bulletin of the Missouri Historical Society*, for permission to use two of my articles which first appeared in that journal—"The Origin of the Confederate Invasion of Missouri, 1864" (October, 1961 issue), and "The Confederate Advance to Lexington, 1864" (April, 1963 issue). Her interest in Price's Raid has been most encouraging.

Sincere thanks go to William M. E. Rachal of the Virginia Historical Society, Misses India Thomas and Eleanor Brockenbrough of the Confederate Museum, Victor Gondos of the National Archives, Dr. Allan Nevins of the Huntington Library, James Anderson of the Native Sons of Kansas City, Howard

Turtle of the *Kansas City Star*, and Mrs. Russell Needham of the Kansas City, Missouri, Junior College. All have aided either in the search for materials or by valuable suggestions, advice and encouragement.

The staffs of the following institutions were most generous in meeting requests and making available the facilities in their respective libraries: Kansas State Historical Society, Missouri Historical Society, State Historical Society of Missouri, Iowa Department of History and Archives, State Historical Society of Iowa, the Confederate Museum, Vanderbilt University Library, University of Texas Library, University of Arkansas Library, Duke University Library, the Library of Congress, the University of North Carolina Library, Virginia Historical Society, South Carolina Historical Society, the National Archives, the Harry S. Truman Library, the New York Public Library, and the Kansas City, Missouri, Public Library.

I am deeply indebted to George Barnett for permission to use his four paintings of Price's invasion of Missouri and Kansas as illustrations in this book.

Scores of persons in Missouri, Kansas, and Arkansas have been most helpful in making their family records and documents available to me. All are sincerely appreciated. Especially do I acknowledge the help of material given me by E. Taylor Campbell of St. Joseph, Missouri, Jeanette Klinge of Marshall, Missouri, and Doris Jean Mabry of Kansas City, Missouri, and the many letters supplied me by the members of the United Daughters of the Confederacy.

I must also thank my comrades in the Kansas City Civil War Round Table, the Kansas City Posse of the Westerners, and the Native Sons of Kansas City. Principal among these who have inspired me by their interest, aided me in searching out materials, or tramped the battlefields with me, are: Dr. Bert Maybee, Arthur Beyer, Richard Byrne, L. E. Seymour, Frank Pexton, Lester Wright, Clinton Kanaga, Robert Jones, Tom Hooper,

Acknowledgments

Alan Farley, W. H. Edwards, John M. Gregory, and Norton Adler.

I shall ever be grateful to Conrad L. Eckert, the Westport Historical Society, and Arthur E. Lowell and S. K. Lowell for their deep interest in Westport history. Because of their efforts this record of the action before Westport in 1864 is published.

To two people, long dead but very much alive in my memory, I owe a special debt of gratitude. Mrs. John B. Wornall first told me the story of the battle of Westport and Colonel John F. Philips, who led a brigade at Byram's ford, took me on my first tramp over the battlefield. That was a half century ago. It was then that this book began.

Howard N. Monnett

Contents

Introduction

ON A WARM AUGUST AFTERNOON in 1917, two brothers began digging a hideout cave near an old, crumbling limestone fence at the corner of Wornall Road and what is today Gregory Boulevard in Kansas City, Missouri. As the rich soil turned under their shovels, the younger boy, aged ten, stopped to examine an unusual-shaped piece of lead that he uncovered. Soon the digging yielded several other lead balls as well as an encrusted portion of an old musket and a rusty sword.

The next day the boys took their trophies to show a neighbor, an elderly woman of pioneer stock, Mrs. Roma Wornall. Certainly she would know their origin. On an October day in 1864, members of Mrs. Wornall's family had huddled in the same house where she still lived in 1917, as the Battle of Westport—the largest land engagement of the Civil War west of the Mississippi River in terms of the number of men engaged—raged outside. Her vivid memory of those events was still fresh enough after half a century to entice the boys with tales of the battle fought along the wooded hillsides where they played. For the younger lad, Howard Norman Monnett, Mrs. Wornall's stories were sufficient to spark his interest in the Battle of Westport and the Civil War.

Howard Monnett was descended from prominent Kansas City pioneers. His great-grandfather, Thomas Jefferson Vanderslice, came to the region in a covered wagon in 1847. During the late 1860s Vanderslice served as representative from the first district in the Kansas State legislature. During Howard Monnett's youth, an uncle for whom he had been named, Howard Vanderslice—one of the early and prolific benefactors of the Kansas City Art Institute—donated to that city the Pioneer Mother statue in Penn Valley Park, today a well-known symbol of that great midwestern metropolis. The statue sits on a prairie grass knoll in stark contrast to the city skyline, a visual bonanza, artfully depicting the transformation of the prairies into modern civilization by pioneer ancestors. The sculptor, A. Phimster Proctor, used portraits of Howard Monnett's great-grandmother as a model for the statue.

Monnett's boyhood home on Greenway Terrace in the heart of Kansas City stood near the sites of heavy fighting during the Battle of Westport. The same summer that he and his brother Robert found the relics, Howard Vanderslice took him on a tour of the old neighborhood battlefield accompanied by Judge John F. Philips of the U.S. District Court. The judge, as a colonel in the 7th Missouri (Union) Cavalry, had led an assault at Byram's Ford during the height of the battle on October 23, 1864.

In later life Monnett still remembered Colonel Philips from that day so long ago. "He was an old man with a shaky voice," he would tell his family. "But I can still thrill to the memory of him walking over that battlefield and saying, more to himself than to those about him, "This is the spot where poor Coombs was shot . . . I put Thurber's guns over there . . . I found Blair dead behind this stump . . . Dale was killed right there.'"[1]

On that afternoon in 1917, Howard Monnett touched the past. While Roma Wornall had perked his interest, Judge Philips instilled in him a passion for researching every aspect of the battle. That research began when Howard was an undergraduate at the University of Kansas. It went with him to graduate school at the University of Colorado and eventually into the Kansas City, Missouri, public schools and junior college where he taught before his appointment as dean of faculty and eventually, interim president.

The result was the publication by the Westport Historical Society and the Lowell Press in 1964 of his book, *Action Before Westport, 1864*. Reaching scholars and the public for the one hundredth anniversary of the battle during the height of America's Civil War Centennial, *Action Before Westport* received critical acclaim nationally and was heralded as a definitive scholarly work on the subject. The major contribution of the study was Howard Monnett's meticulous reconstruction of the sequential events of the actual fighting. There are places in the text where the reader can almost hear the reports of artillery, feel the rush of the cavalry charge, and smell the acrid aroma of spent black powder hanging in the crisp autumn air.

For me, the next generation of the Monnett family, the realization of Dad publishing such a book was overwhelming. At the time, I was an undergraduate at the University of Kansas. I went on to major in history, and three academic degrees later made it my life's profession.

Thus, old Colonel Philips, whose memory reached back to the Civil War, touched the Monnett family in a way that, with a little luck, will extend into the twenty-first century. But for now, the news is the republication of *Action Before Westport*, edited with a new introduction by the next generation of Monnett historians.

As my father was by far my chief mentor and role model, a part of me feels totally unworthy of updating his highly successful book and spearheading its release; and another part of me knows better than to use introductory space in a scholarly publication to say, "Thanks, Dad for everything," a tribute I did not have the chance to pay when my father was alive. Still, it is a gesture I wish to express. Although I am primarily a western historian, my father's interest in the Battle of Westport has become my own.

Some time after *Action Before Westport* went out of print, I began seeking a publisher interested in reprinting the book. Much of this effort was at the urging of Howard's friend and mine, Fred Lee, a long-standing Kansas City journalist and historian. Through his encouragement and that of Gil Bergman and Orvis Fitts, of the Kansas City Civil War Roundtable, that desire finally has become reality. It is quite fitting that the University Press of Colorado, located in Boulder, where Howard Monnett did his graduate work, has enthusiastically undertaken the project.

Although *Action Before Westport* has been unavailable for some time now, the interest it generated in the battle has continued through the years. Shortly after the arrival of the book, my father encouraged a citywide tour of the battlefield sites each year, on a weekend near the anniversary date. In 1977, the tour became official under the auspices of the Kansas City Civil War Roundtable and the Westport Historical Society. In 1994 plans were underway to revive the tour after a hiatus of several years. During the 1970s, Laurance C. Phister, an active member of the roundtable, suggested that the group undertake the project of soliciting funds for placing permanent historical markers along the site of the battlefield tour. The result was the inception of the Monnett Battle of Westport Fund, a repository for proceeds to mark the important sites. Today, the effort of the Monnett Fund continues after having made great strides during the 1970s and 1980s.[2]

Not only did *Action Before Westport* inspire superior preservation efforts, it launched additional research into the 1864 campaign as well.

Shortly after *Action Before Westport* appeared, two regional publications were added to the popular literature of the Price Raid and the Battle of Westport. In 1976 the Westport Historical Society published Fred Lee, Ed., *The Battle of Westport.* This book contained several accounts of the battle as well as the order of battle detailing the units that fought there. The major importance of Lee's book is the detailed description of the Battle of Westport tour sites. For years, it has served as a guidebook for hundreds of Kansas City residents traveling along the historical paths of that community's only major Civil War battlefield.

In 1977, the Lowell Press of Kansas City published Lumir F. Buresh, *October 25th and the Battle of Mine Creek,* which details the Union rout of Confederate general Sterling Price's army following its defeat at Westport. A retired army officer, Buresh's most significant contribution was his research of the fighting units actually in Missouri and Kansas during the autumn of 1864. Such specific details continue to fascinate and puzzle Civil War aficionados to the present day.

From a broad historical perspective, however, the Battle of Westport was one of those tremendous Civil War engagements that probably should never have been fought. As Howard Monnett points out, by the autumn of 1864 the "Confederacy was being strangled to death and desperate remedies were very much in order."[3] With Lee's Army of Northern Virginia immobilized along the Petersburg-Richmond line, and General John Bell Hood's Confederate forces defeated in bitter fighting around Atlanta, the Price Raid into Missouri was little more than a risky strategic diversion to relieve pressure on Confederate forces in the eastern theater of combat.[4]

Tactically, the Price Raid was all but a major blunder from the start. Buoyed by his success in May in the so-called Red River Campaign, General Edmund Kirby Smith, commanding the Confederacy's Trans-Mississippi Department, hoped to draw off Union forces from the east to meet an invasion of Missouri by Confederate raiders moving up from Arkansas. Smith's most able commander, Major General Richard Taylor, unable to further tolerate his commander's argumentative temper, requested transfer back east. Smith thus settled for the titular political head of secessionist sentiments in Missouri, Major General Sterling Price, an overly optimistic politician with questionable military ability, whom Smith personally regarded as cast-off material.

Apparently reconciled if not seduced by Price's promise to recruit at least 30,000 volunteers in Missouri for the cause of the South, Smith ignored the fact that sporadic cavalry raids into that state from Arkansas during the previous two years had met with something less than spectacular success. His choice of Price as commander of the expedition would ensure that this trend would continue.[5] In short, the Price Raid was intended to move up eastern Missouri to St. Louis, then across the state to Kansas City and the rich military stores at Fort Leavenworth, Kansas. The design was unrealistic in its objectives, and it justly deserves the title Howard Monnett gave it in his second chapter, "This May Seem a Wild Plan." Compounding the impossible tactical odds against it was Price's predictable inability as a commander.

Throughout the campaign, Price failed to organize and utilize to the optimum the abilities of competent subordinates and fighting units like General Jo Shelby's Iron Brigade, commanded in the field by Brigadier General M. Jeff Thompson, not to mention the single-most-effective weapon of terror he had at his disposal, the guerrilla units that had wreaked havoc in western Missouri during the summer of 1864. Indeed, Price went out of his way *not* to wield a heavy hand on the civilian population of Missouri. Undoubtedly such a policy was intended to encourage cooperation and enlistments among those friendly to the South. This is puzzling in light of the recent and hated Union "Order Number Eleven," forcing civilians in Jackson and Cass counties from their homes. Revenge against Unionists in surrounding counties would have been a more natural course of action given the Confederacy's circumstances at that point in the war.

Indeed, 1864 was a time for desperate measures for the Confederacy. With General William T. Sherman practicing total war against Confederate civilian populations back east, and Union forces in western Missouri suspending the Constitution to control alleged guerrillas among the civilian populace, this was no time for Confederate invasion forces to waste precious time in enemy-occupied territory practicing Southern chivalry.

Strategically, the inappropriateness of the Confederate's decision to invade Missouri in 1864 is glaringly apparent in retrospect. By autumn, the tidal wave of Union industrial output had grown so enormous, and Union regiments continued to replace casualties from their significantly higher population base at such a tremendous rate, that the war-depleted South could no longer keep up.

The always meager and inferior industrial resources of the Confederacy, which probably doomed it early in the war, were so exhausted by the autumn of 1864 that nothing short of full-scale European interven-tion on behalf of the Confederacy could have saved the "lost cause." And that forlorn hope had died two years previously on the field of Antietam and subsequently in the corridors of the capital city of Wash-ington, where President Lincoln made the fateful decision to issue a proclamation of emancipation for slaves in occupied Confederate terri-tory. In short, it is arguable that an overwhelming Confederate victory at the Battle of Westport would have done little to help the Confeder-acy survive an extra month, or for that matter, even an extra day.

So the Battle of Westport must inevitably be approached, examined, and remembered for its broad regional significance rather than the neg-ligible impact it had on the strategic outcome of the Civil War. Indeed, its regional importance outlasted that particular conflict by decades and reaches far beyond the Missouri-Kansas border. Because its campaigns were generally smaller than the events east of the Mississippi, the west-ern theater of war has often been treated as an isolated, comparatively peripheral segment of the Civil War.

But once scholars look beyond the actual fighting to the broader events of western development during the 1860s, the Missouri-Kansas borderlands and the entire West emerge as an important slice of the far-reaching *effects* of the Civil War, both regionally and for national unity and development.

Until recently, the Civil War has been scrutinized by scholars mainly as a pivotal watershed for the massive industrial surge of the northeast during the second half of the nineteenth century, the neglect of the South during the same period, and the cultural impact of the changes wrought by the war on race relations reaching far into the twentieth century. Rarely have the effects of the war been examined in relation to the other great phenomena of the late nineteenth century, western expansion, and territorial development.

As a graduate student living in Palo Alto, California, in the late 1960s and early 1970s, I could not help but be influenced by the sweeping changes in the social attitudes of that time. Recently, many scholars trained during that period of the American experience have been applying new interpretations to the history of the West as well as examining new ways in which the West has impacted the national mainstream and how the nation, in turn, has impacted the West. One of these new areas of endeavor has been the West and the Civil War.

Though many of these new studies are primarily military in scope, topics of broader scope are also expected to emerge.

Nevertheless, as a western historian I cannot help but be impressed by some of these recent military studies examining the influences of the Civil War on the region. Works concluded during the early 1990s alone deserve attention by Civil War enthusiasts and western historians alike. Leading the way is Alvin M. Josephy, Jr., *The Civil War in the American West* (New York: Alfred A. Knopf, 1991). Josephy, a past president of the Western Historical Association (1994), has undertaken a major study of the Trans-Mississippi theater of war, melding its diverse peoples, events, and subregions in such a way as to illustrate their relevance to the entire nation with respect to the Civil War and its effects. The work will likely become the standard reference.

A recent scrutiny of the literature from the past two or three years reveals a wealth of new studies on the Civil War in the West. Among the more scholarly endeavors is William L. Shea and Earl J. Hess, *Pea Ridge: Civil War Campaign in the West* (Chapel Hill: University of North Carolina Press, 1992), detailing one of the more decisive conflicts in the Missouri-Arkansas borderlands. Thomas W. Cutrer, *Ben McCulloch and the Frontier Military Tradition* (Chapel Hill: University of North Carolina Press, 1993), is a major biography of one of the West's most important Confederate commanders, while Joseph H. Parks, *General Edmund Kirby Smith, CSA* (Baton Rouge: Louisiana State University Press, 1992), explores the career of the Confederacy's commander of the Trans-Mississippi Department.

Laurence M. Hauptman, *The Iroquois in the Civil War: From Battlefield to Reservation* (Syracuse: Syracuse University Press, 1993), expands on the early themes of Annie Abel and Angie Debo by examining the intricate role of Native Americans in the Civil War, while Douglas Hale, *The Third Texas Cavalry in the Civil War* (Norman: University of Oklahoma Press, 1993), deals with more traditional military themes popular during the centennial years by examining the history of a single regiment.

David Paul Smith, *Frontier Defense in the Civil War: Texas Rangers and Rebels* (College Station: Texas A & M Press, 1991), and Jerry D. Thompson, *Desert Tiger: Captain Paddy Graydon and the Civil War in the Far Southwest* (El Paso: Texas Western Press, 1992), explore little-known topics of the Civil War West. Although lacking somewhat in historical method, Robert Scott's *Glory, Glory, Glorieta: The Gettysburg of the West* (Boulder: Johnson Books, 1992) is a detailed popular account of one of the more famous engagements in the West, the Battle of Glorieta Pass.

In addition to the appearance of new works, such traditional western history publishing bastions as the University of Nebraska Press and the University of Oklahoma Press are now reissuing important studies of the Civil War in the West, not the least of which is Jay Monaghan's standard reference work, *Civil War on the Western Border, 1854-1865*, first published in 1955, now available as a Bison Book from the University of Nebraska Press. Not to be outdone, Albert Castel and Herman Hattaway, Eds., and the University of Oklahoma Press have reissued O. S. Baron's 1914 classic, *Three Years with Quantrill: A True Story Told by His Scout John McCorkle* (1992).

An important clearinghouse for the printing of new books dealing with the Civil War in the West is the Kansas Heritage Press. By offering reprints from a variety of publishers like the Press of Camp Pope Bookshop in addition to their own reprints, a treasure trove of western Civil War books, like John Newman Edwards' *Shelby and His Men* (Cincinnati: Miami Printing, 1867) and William Forse Scott's *The Story of a Cavalry Regiment: The Career of the Fourth Iowa Veteran Volunteers from Kansas to Georgia 1861–1865* (New York: G. P. Putnam's Sons, 1893), are once again available to researchers in addition to the previously mentioned newer works and reprints of recent twentieth-century studies by such western Civil War scholars as Albert Castel and Donald R. Hale.

The explosion of interest in the Civil War in the West is not limited to books. Scholarly periodicals have also shown renewed interest in the topic. One of the more recent studies is Richard W. Hatcher III and William Garrett Piston, Eds., "Kansans Go to War: The Wilson's Creek Campaign Reported by the Leavenworth Daily Times," *Kansas History* v. 16, nos. 3 & 4 (1993–1994). Marvin R. Cain and John F. Bradbury Jr., "Union Troops in the Civil War in Southwestern Missouri and Northwestern Arkansas," *Missouri Historical Review* 88 (October 1993), William L. Shea, "The Road to Pea Ridge," *Arkansas Historical Quarterly* 52 (Autumn 1993), and Daniel E. Sutherland, "Guerrillas: The Real War in Arkansas," *Arkansas Historical Quarterly* 52 (Autumn 1993) all deal with new interpretations of the war on the Arkansas-Missouri-Kansas border.

Other recent titles of interest include Gary L. Cheatham, "'Desperate Characters': The Development and Impact of Confederate Guerrillas in Kansas," *Kansas History* 14 (Autumn 1991) and James M. McPherson, "From Limited to Total War: Missouri and the Nation, 1861–1865," *Gateway Heritage* 12 (Spring 1992). Mary Jane Ward, "Now the Wolf Has Come: The Civilian and the Civil War in the Indian Territory," *Chronicles of Oklahoma* 71 (Spring 1993) and L. Boyd Finch, "Arizona in Exile: Confederate Schemes to Recapture the Far Southwest," *Journal of Arizona History* 33 (Spring 1992) are examples of excellent articles by revisionist scholars dealing with events that occurred in territories farther west.

In the popular market, a recent article of interest addressing the Price Campaign and the Battle of Westport is Scott E. Sallee, "Missouri! One Last Time: Sterling Price's 1864 Missouri Expedition, 'A Just and Holy Cause,'" *Blue & Gray Magazine* 8 (June 1991). Indeed, a plethora of literature—both books and periodicals—has inspired a recent renaissance of interest in the Civil War Trans-Mississippi West. The literature presented here is merely a sampling of the fine studies available. They represent works of particular interest to me.

It is highly likely that future research will stress more than ever the relationships between the *effects* of the Civil War and the development of the West and the relationships of the war's impact in the West on national development. In addition to military alteration of western populations, some questions for future inquiry might be: Is it possible to examine meaningfully popular sovereignty as a "laboratory of democracy" rather than to merely recount its failures? Can we measure the influence and impact of the war on easterners' decisions to migrate west during the conflict and afterward? Can we interpret the ironic juxtaposition of western gold and silver rushes as cultural melting pots with the concept of the expansion of slavery? Did Native Americans play a greater role in shaping events in the West because of the Civil War than we previously thought? How, if any, did these events shape territorial politics in such newly organized places as Colorado and Arizona? In essence, given the wave of current revisionism in western history, the Civil War will never again be viewed as an "eastern" event affecting for great lengths of time after 1865 only populations east of the Mississippi. I believe we will soon determine that this greatest of American conflicts did not merely touch the West in varied remote hot spots like Kansas, but rather it helped to shape huge regions of the West and its people in very distinctive ways.

Consequently it is fitting that exhaustively detailed studies like *Action Before Westport* be made available, once again, to researchers. Although Howard Monnett concerned himself primarily with the human drama of the battle itself, such specific details are essential ingredients, the very tools of the interpretive scholar in search of broader meanings.

But *Action Before Westport* is also a vivid and thrilling story that has appealed greatly over the years to readers with nonscholarly interest in the Civil War and western history. Traditional Civil War buffs, for example, will view here the little-known late war exploits of such famous Union personalities as William Starke Rosecrans, major general of volunteers, banished to the Trans-Mississippi front as commander of the military Department of the Missouri, after his crushing defeat at Chickamauga. Then there is Major General Alfred Pleasonton, like Rosecrans, exiled to the Department of the Missouri. Pleasonton had run afoul of the Lincoln administration in February 1864 for opposing the so-called Kilpatrick-Dahlgren Raid against Richmond, an abortive maneuver that accomplished nothing except for the compilation of a long casualty list. Coupled with the new general-in-chief U.S. Grant's determination to place Philip Sheridan in command of the Cavalry Corps in the Army of the Potomac's final operations, Pleasonton found himself in Missouri, fighting at the Battle of Westport.[6]

Students of western history quickly will recognize the commander of the Confederate invasion forces, Major General Sterling Price, for his activities in New Mexico in January 1847 during the war with Mexico. Price was colonel of the 2nd Missouri Infantry of Stephen Watts Kearny's Army of the West after Colonel Alexander W. Doniphan's departure to Chihuahua. Following New Mexico's annexation from the Mexican republic in August 1846, it was Price who, as military governor of New Mexico, utilized a devastating artillery barrage to ruthlessly suppress the "Taos Rebellion" of Hispano and Indian patriots in the San Geronimo church in Taos Pueblo.[7]

Indeed, Missouri in 1864 was alive with an impressive cast of characters who would write their names in the annals of western history. Here is "Bloody Bill" Anderson and William Clarke Quantrill, guerrilla scourges of the Kansas-Missouri border. Lieutenant Colonel Frederick

W. Benteen of the 10th Missouri (Union) Cavalry also fought at Westport. Of course his fame, or infamy, is well-known to every follower of Custer's 7th Cavalry at the Battle of Little Bighorn. Benteen, who always had a reputation for being a disgruntled "sniveler," even during his early career in the Civil War, took charge when the chips were down at the Battle of Westport, just as he would do on a windswept hill in Montana in 1876, when he reinstated order to Major Marcus Reno's shattered command. Only at Westport had he the advantage of the offensive.

During a Union assault on October 23, 1864, Colonel E. F. Winslow, commanding the Fourth Brigade of Pleasonton's Provisional Cavalry Division, was hit by a Confederate ball. Assuming command of the wavering lines of the Fourth Brigade, Benteen drew his saber and pressed the charge. As Howard Monnett writes: "Suddenly there were no more lines. . . . A ragged surf of gray broke from the melee, formed in tight desperate knots that were engulfed, shattered, and swept away. General [John Sappington] Marmaduke's [Confederate] division was in retreat."[8]

One of the more endearing stories that has emerged from the Battle of Westport, a story with legendary status that cannot be completely substantiated in fact, are the alleged roles played in the fight by James Butler (Wild Bill) Hickok, and his close friend and comrade in arms, William F. (Buffalo Bill) Cody. According to official records, Cody, at age eighteen, enlisted into Company F, 7th Kansas Cavalry on February 19, 1864. Later he claimed his enlistment was the result of drinking too much whiskey and that he could never remember the circumstances under which he actually enlisted. The 7th Kansas and its commander, Colonel. C. R. Jennison, had gained a reputation as the scourge of the Missouri Bushwhackers. The men of the regiment called themselves Jennison's Jayhawkers. The 7th Kansas was attached to Brigadier General John McNeil's brigade. Although the muster rolls list Cody as a private, he later claimed that he was a scout for McNeil's brigade at the time of the Battle of Westport.

Another member of that brigade was Cody's friend, William Butler Hickok. Cody had known Hickok since 1856 when Hickok was the constable of Monticello township in Johnson County, Kansas. Later the pair worked together for the freight company of Russell, Majors, and Waddell of Pony Express fame.

According to Cody's tale, which he related in later life, General McNeil sent Hickok, a man named Dave Tutt, and a third unidentified companion into the Confederate lines as spies a month before the Battle of Westport. Two days after the battle, while Sterling Price's army retreated toward Fort Scott, Kansas, and the 7th Kansas skirmished with the Confederate rear guard, Cody met Hickok as he dashed back into the Union lines dressed as a Confederate officer. The unidentified companion had been killed during the battle. Allegedly, however, Dave Tutt had turned traitor. The next year Hickok caught up with him on a street in Springfield, Missouri, and killed him with a single rifle shot.[9]

Another intriguing story has linked Howard Monnett directly to a legendary western personality who fought at the battle of Westport. In early October, preceding the battle, Confederate general Jo O. Shelby's famous Iron Brigade rested briefly in Boonville, Missouri. During this respite Shelby went to a photographer's studio and had his picture taken. Although survivors of his brigade often told of seeing copies of the photo at reunions after the war, those copies completely disappeared by the turn of the century. For years, researchers had only photos of Shelby taken in later life. No photo existed of him at the time of the Battle of Westport—until 1971.

On a hot summer day in that year, my father salvaged an old box of papers from a decrepit building in Tombstone, Arizona—the "town too tough to die"—the home of Wyatt Earp, Doc Holliday, the outlaw Johnny Ringo, and a host of other legendary western characters, some of whom fought it out one bright October day in 1881, at the legendary gunfight at the OK Corral. Inside the old box, he discovered a brittle yellowed copy of the Boonville photograph of Jo Shelby. What was more interesting, however, was the inscription on the reverse side:

> General Joseph Shelby—
> My general, I rode with him
> in Missouri in 1864.
> —*John Ringo*

My father's discovery was the first indication that the infamous Arizona desperado had fought at the Battle of Westport. Although Ringo's presence apparently had no effect on the outcome of the Battle of Westport, my father felt he had touched the past once again on that day in 1971. It was always his wish to include the little anecdote in a new printing of *Action Before Westport*. It is with pleasure that I include it on these pages now. But alas, the elusive photo has disappeared once again, this time from the papers among Howard Monnett's estate—no doubt through complete fault of my own.[10]

A special interest for many students of the Civil War in the West has been the impact the conflict had on Indian populations. Living and working in Colorado I have always been fascinated how events there during the Civil War era impacted events in the Kansas-Missouri borderlands. I am equally amazed how events in the two locations are usually examined separately as if there were no interrelationships. This is apparent, for example, in the case of the Union commander at the Battle of Westport, Major General Samuel Ryan Curtis.

At the Battle of Westport, Curtis was commander of the Army of the Border, organized to meet the Price invasion. The Army of the Border consisted primarily of Kansas regiments and militia. But Curtis also had a prior role as commander of the army's military Department of Kansas, which included the eastern portion of Colorado Territory. Since his victory at Pea Ridge in 1862, one of Curtis' major objectives was to protect white settlers and gold seekers in western Kansas and eastern Colorado from the developing Indian war with the Southern Cheyenne and Arapahoe.

Students of western history know all too well the circumstances of the climax of that war. How on the dawn of November 29, 1864, one month after the Battle of Westport, elements of the 1st and 3rd Colorado volunteer regiments under the command of Colonel John M. Chivington brutally attacked the peaceful village of Cheyenne chief Black Kettle at Sand Creek, killing mostly noncombatant women and children and mutilating their bodies. Although federal congressional investigating committees later brandished the Sand Creek affair as an unwarranted "massacre," and although some scholars will argue that pondering historical "ifs" is relatively meaningless, the question to be raised here is nonetheless intriguing: Would the Sand Creek Massacre have resulted in such brutality had the Price Raid and the Battle of Westport never have happened? Indeed, would it ever have even taken place?

Certainly any understanding of Major General S. R. Curtis, commanding the department where Sand Creek occurred, reveals his priorities. Understandably, his chief concern in the autumn of 1864 was

Confederate invaders. Two of the units in his army were the 2nd Colorado Volunteers, commanded by Colonel J. N. Smith, and the Independent Battery of Colorado Volunteers, commanded by Capt. W. D. McLain. Indeed, the 2nd Colorado, at the pleading of Colorado territorial governor, John Evans, were under orders by General Rosecrans, in whose Department of the Missouri they had originally been attached, to return to Colorado that summer to protect the frontier from the Cheyenne.

With Price's invasion, however, the 2nd remained on the Kansas-Missouri border and fought valiantly at Westport, even losing Colonel Smith who was then replaced by Major J. H. Pritchard following the action on the Little Blue River. Colorado Territory was left in the hands of a few troops of the Colorado 1st and the newly recruited Colorado 3rd Regiment, one-hundred days enlistees gathered in part from the saloons of Denver and, many of them, along with their commander, Colonel John M. Chivington, avowed Indian haters.[11]

Certainly General Curtis was not sympathetic to the grievances of the Cheyenne and Arapahoe. "I want no peace till the Indians suffer more," Curtis told Chivington in the summer of 1864.[12] Always politically astute since his days as an Iowa congressman, Curtis knew full well that Congress had authorized the raising of the Colorado "Bloodless Third" regiment because of his urging that another unit was needed on the Colorado frontier to fight the Cheyenne and Arapahoe. If he made peace with the Indians, it would appear to Congress that he had made a mistake and put the government to useless expense on the frontier, at a time when huge expenditures were needed for the last offensives against the Confederate capital at Richmond.[13]

Chivington took Curtis at his word. With Curtis' attention focused almost obsessively on General Sterling Price, Chivington used his "freedom" to attempt genocide against Black Kettle's Cheyenne with what he thought was his department commander's blessing.

Like everyone else, Curtis later did not support Chivington's action at Sand Creek. It is doubtful, however, that Curtis would have condoned Chivington's actions at the time of the affair. It is unlikely the militia officer would have committed such barbarities had Curtis been even slightly less concerned with Confederates and more genuinely attuned to military developments in the western portion of his regular army jurisdiction during the autumn of 1864.

So in 1865, Congress commissioned Curtis as one of the ranking officers to negotiate new peace treaties with the plains tribes in a futile attempt to patch up the mess created by the Sand Creek Massacre. Indeed, the true irony of the events transpiring on the border in October and November 1864 is that the smaller, more isolated, and at the time more peripheral incident at Sand Creek had far-reaching and devastating consequences for settlers on the central-southern plains, while the massive clash of cavalry and artillery at the Battle of Westport turned out to be but a temporary travail for citizens along the Kansas-Missouri border and had virtually no effect whatsoever on the outcome of the Civil War.

Although the causes and circumstances of the Sand Creek Massacre are complex and controversial, few can argue that the event was a major watershed in dealings by the American government with the plains tribes, resulting in part in the clash of the army and the Indian Bureau for control of Indian affairs. The effects of the incident kept the frontier and policy makers in Washington in a state of turmoil for years to come. Back in Missouri, Sterling Price's renowned subordinate, Major General John Sappington Marmaduke, was elected governor in 1884, while Jo Shelby became a U.S. marshal for western Missouri nine years later, following his self-imposed exile in Mexico. He died in Adrian, Missouri, in 1897 and was buried in Kansas City in one of the most spectacular and well-attended funerals that city had ever witnessed.[14] Major General Samuel Ryan Curtis died on duty in December 1866, never living long enough to realize the full impact of his command decisions.

Over the years historians and Civil War buffs have advanced the knowledge of both the Price Raid and the Battle of Westport. Commendably, they have pointed out several minor factual errors in *Action Before Westport*. Most of these are antiquarian, dealing either in mistaken geographic locations of some of the specific events of the battle or with newly discovered details pertaining to the composition or identities of certain fighting units present. We know now, for example, that an eastern unit fought at Westport. The 2nd New Jersey Cavalry, composed of three companies (225 men) and at least one company of the 19th Pennsylvania Cavalry (est. 75 men), commanded by Captain Michael Gallagher, constituted part of a battalion of General Karge's brigade. It fought alongside Winslow's-Benteen's brigade at Westport.[15]

In the text I have indicated errata with an asterisk. The corresponding footnotes appear at the end of this introduction. Unless otherwise noted, this new information was discovered through the research of the late Lumir F. Buresh as he prepared his book, *The Battle of Mine Creek* (1977).

Perhaps the most significant development found in this new printing of *Action Before Westport* will prove to be the fine-tuning given to the "Regiments and Batteries at the Battle of Westport" (Appendix). Through the fine efforts of Fred Lee, who first updated the listing in his *Battle of Westport* (1976, 1982), and additional investigation conducted by Gil Bergman of the Kansas City Civil War Roundtable, whose ancestor fought in the battle, this new printing contains the most up-to-date listing available of the order of battle in western Missouri for October 21–23, 1864, both Union and Confederate. I extend my sincere gratitude to these gentlemen and to Orvis Fitts of Kansas City, who pointed out to me much of the new information uncovered by Lumir F. Buresh. They have, through the years, kept the spirit of the Battle of Westport alive for the people of Kansas City. Their efforts are worthy of significant praise.

I also wish to thank the historical societies of Kansas and Missouri for the fine photographs they have provided for this new printing. To the Civil War Roundtable of Kansas City, the people involved with the Monnett Fund, and the Westport Historical Society for their fine efforts in preserving the battlefield—your efforts are nothing short of monumental. To all those working behind the scenes at preservation, although I may not presently know your names, I thank you wholeheartedly for your dedication. Finally I wish to extend my appreciation to the people of Kansas City themselves, who, since the days of Roma Wornall, Judge Philips, and Howard Vanderslice, have kept alive their pride and interest in their regional history and in the Battle of Westport, right down to the eve of the twenty-first century. Without you, none of these efforts at preserving the field or writing the history would have happened.

JOHN H. MONNETT
Boulder, Colorado
1994

Introduction

Notes

1. *Kansas City Star*, April 19, 1961.

2. Fred L. Lee, Ed., *The Battle of Westport* (Westport, Mo.: Westport Historical Society, 1976), 52–53; *Kansas City Star*, July 21, 1993.

3. Howard N. Monnett, *Action Before Westport, 1864* (Kansas City: Westport Historical Society, 1964), 8.

4. Ibid., 9–17.

5. Scott E. Sallee, "Missouri One Last Time: Sterling Price's 1864 Missouri Expedition 'A Just and Holy Cause,'" *Blue and Gray Magazine* 8 (June 1991): 11–13.

6. Ezra J. Warner, *Generals in Blue: Lives of the Union Commanders* (Baton Rouge: Louisiana State University Press, 1964), 373.

7. Susan A. Roberts and Calvin A. Roberts, *New Mexico* (Albuquerque: University of New Mexico Press, 1988), 109.

8. Monnett, *Action Before Westport*, 115.

9. *Kansas City Star*, October 22, 1963; Joseph G. Rosa and Robin May, *Buffalo Bill and His Wild West: A Pictorial History* (Lawrence, Kans.: University Press of Kansas, 1989), 8–11.

10. Howard N. Monnett, "General Jo Shelby and Johnny Ringo," *Westport Historical Quarterly* 8, 3 (December 1971): 25–29.

11. Stan Hoig, *The Sand Creek Massacre* (Norman: University of Oklahoma Press, 1961), 70.

12. *Official Records of the War of the Rebellion*, Series I, 16, Part 3, 462.

13. Hoig, *Sand Creek Massacre*, 112.

14. Ezra J. Warner, *Generals in Gray: Lives of the Confederate Commanders* (Baton Rouge: Louisiana State University Press, 1959), 274.

15. Francis C. Kajencki, *Star on Many a Battlefield: Brevet Brigadier General Joseph Karge in the American Civil War* (Cranbury, N.J.: Associated University Presses, 1980), 117–118; George P. Walmsley, *Experiences of a Civil War Horse Soldier* (N.Y.: University Press of America, 1993), 107–117.

Corrections to First Edition

p. 54   Greer was actually two miles of the north to the Blue Mills Crossing.

p. 70   Samuel J. Reader of the 2nd Regiment, Kansas State Militia, was a quartermaster. As such, he held the rank of second lieutenant, not private.

p. 71   The identity of this battery should be the Independent Colored Battery, Kansas State Militia Light Artillery. The men were mustered as

Independent Battery, U.S. Colored Light Artillery on December 23, 1864, at Fort Leavenworth, Kansas, as a result of their exemplary performance at the Battle of Westport and the subsequent pursuit of Price's army. The battery was commanded by Captain H. Ford Douglas and was equipped with six 10 pdr. Parrot guns. *Official Army Register of the Volunteer Force of the U.S. Army for the Years 1861–1865,* v. 8 (Washington, D.C.: Adjutant General's Office, 1867), 168.

p. 93   The wagon train crossed the Big Blue River at Byram's Ford then moved south on the Harrisonville Road (west of the Big Blue River) to Russell's Ford.

p. 94   The Hickman Hills Road is actually east of the Big Blue River. The wagon train crossed at Byram's Ford to the west bank of the Big Blue River.

p. 108   Colonel James H. McGhee, McGhee's Arkansas Cavalry, was only wounded in this charge. He was subsequently wounded a second time on October 25, 1884, in the Battle of Mine Creek. John N. Edwards, *Shelby and His Men: Or the Civil War in the West* (Cincinnati: Miami Printing, 1867), 443.

p. 111   Composition of the Union batteries in action at Byram's Ford were one gun of Co. L, 2nd Missouri Light Artillery, commanded by Captain Charles H. Thurber and two guns of Co. H, 2nd Missouri Light Artillery, commanded by Lieutenant Philip Smiley. The section of Co. H was attached to the four guns of Co. L. All of the guns in both of these batteries were three-inch Ordnance rifles (aka "Rodman guns"). The misidentification of the two batteries is due to errors in Sanborn's reports.

p. 115   The battery should be Co. L (not H), 2nd Missouri Light Artillery.

p. 118   This route was on the east side of the Big Blue River.

p. 119   The Union battery with McNeil's Brigade at Russell's Ford was Co. H, 2nd Missouri Light Artillery. This was the remaining unit of that battery. It consisted of two three-inch Ordnance rifles and was commanded by Captain William C. F. Montgomery.

I. THE ADVANCE TO WESTPORT

1. Prelude to Battle

IT WAS CLOSE TO MIDNIGHT on a Saturday night, October 22, 1864 when some 30,000 Union and Confederate soldiers sank exhausted on the hills and prairies surrounding the little village of Westport, Missouri.[1]

For more than thirty days these men had struggled in a running fight from Pocahontas, Arkansas to the outskirts of St. Louis and thence across the width of Missouri itself. Major General Sterling Price and his 10,000 Confederate cavalrymen were aiming toward Fort Leavenworth and its rich storehouse of food and military supplies.[2] But on the next day at this tiny frontier town on the Santa Fe trail, they were to be caught in a vicious pincers movement initiated by the Federal Army of the Border and the Army of the Department of the Missouri. Here, at the gateway to the West, they were to fight one of the Civil War's largest land battles west of the Mississippi river—the climax of a Confederate cavalry raid which, from the standpoint of logistics, miles traveled and number of engagements fought, equaled or exceeded any other raid the Civil War produced, including General William T. Sherman's march from Atlanta to the sea.[3]

For more than ten years, ever since Kansas had been opened as a territory by the Kansas-Nebraska Bill of 1854, these prairies and hills had known the terrorizing conflict of border warfare —the warfare of John Brown, of Quantrill, of Todd and Bloody

3

Bill Anderson. And now on the morrow, Sunday, October 23, 1864, this battle before Westport was to end forever the Civil War in the west. It was to bring to a close a decade on the western frontier that would remain long in the memory of man.[4]

The air was frosty and the stars hung low in the blue-black sky of that autumn night in Missouri. Sporadic rifle fire ran red along the lines as pickets clashed in darkness. In the distance, over toward Independence, came the constant boom of artillery as the Yankees pounded the Rebel rearguard. Upon the bluffs south of Brush Creek Confederate campfires jeweled the night and the singing voices of Negroes entertained the weary men. North of the creek and its rising valley a few dim lights marked the Harris House in Westport where Federal officers came and went.[5]

The soldiers dozed restlessly on the cold ground. Sleep was elusive. The tension preceding the battle had been building up over too many days. Tomorrow's fighting would be decisive.

2. *"This May Seem a Wild Plan"*

THE LONG MARCH TO WESTPORT began in Meridian, Mississippi, on Saturday, July 23, 1864. It was a hot, humid day and the weather had done nothing to ease the desperate, frightened mind of Captain J. Henry Behan, C.S.A.

This thing he was going to do was an unprecedented act for an assistant commissary of subsistence. It could bring reprimands and reprisals. But these were desperate days demanding desperate measures. Captain Behan's world was falling apart, and he must do what he could do to save that world. The letter had to be written.

Sitting in the heat that enveloped the headquarters of the Department of Alabama, Mississippi, and East Louisiana, the Confederate Captain of Commissary began to write:

His Excellency Jefferson Davis
Richmond, Virginia

Sir: I take the liberty of communicating with you on a subject which probably I have no right to, but prompted by my desire for our speedy success and independence I am not reluctant in so doing. While the enemy have almost entirely withdrawn from the Trans-Mississippi Department, being compelled to do so by the many reverses they have met in Texas, Louisiana, and Arkansas, I would respectfully suggest that the armies of Generals [John B.] Magruder, [Richard] Taylor, and [Sterling] Price be massed under the command of Gen-

eral E. Kirby Smith . . ., and with this army go through Arkansas and Missouri, capturing Franklin and St. Louis, at
which point they can cross the Mississippi River into Kentucky, go along the Ohio River, subsisting on the rich country they will pass through, take Louisville, Ky., thence down
to Nashville, destroying the vast amount of commissary and
quartermaster stores at that place. From thence they can move
on Chattanooga, cutting off all of [William T.] Sherman's
supplies, and necessarily, with General [John B.] Hood in
front and this army in rear, we will be able to capture the
whole of the Yankee army under Sherman. This may seem a
wild plan, and if Your Excellency considers it too arduous for
infantry, the command can be mounted very readily in the
three states named, Texas, Arkansas, and Missouri, and recruited in Kentucky and Tennessee. Hoping that this will
meet with some consideration,

I am, very respectfully, Your Excellency's obedient servant,

J. HENRY BEHAN[1]

Captain Behan promptly dispatched his letter to the President
of the Confederacy and awaited results. The more he thought
about his "wild plan," however, the better he liked his invasion
idea, apparently, for on the following Monday, July 25, he hur-
riedly wrote Jefferson Davis a second letter:

I can, and will, if wished, forward to you my idea of the plan
of campaign, route of march, and all details as to mounting,
subsisting, and supplying the army in general.

Corn and forage will soon be ready and fit to feed to stock,
and by the time the army moves into North Arkansas and
South Missouri it will be hard enough to feed. I will await
Your Excellency's reply if this matter meets with your consideration.[2]

The impetuous Captain Behan had it all figured out! Would
the President adopt the plan?

With the passing of the hours the importance and magnitude
of his proposed invasion must have grown in the very active
mind of the Commissary Captain. He had a plan that would save
the Confederacy and win independence for the South. Jefferson

Davis must be made aware of its significance. Captain Behan swept all military protocol aside and on Wednesday of that week, July 27, wrote Davis a third letter! The tone was bolder. Behan's imagination was afire. He was a Napoleon planning grand strategy:

> I again write to urge my opinion in regard to an expedition through Arkansas, Missouri, etc., which I wrote you about on the 23d and 25th instant.
>
> If General Price can enter Missouri he can get at least from 10,000 to 15,000 men, if not more. All he will want will be arms, accouterments, etc., which are in St. Louis in abundance. One of the commands, General Magruder's or General Taylor's, can return for these, while the balance cross the river and conduct the campaign as proposed. I see no objection just now, being well informed in regard to the situation of that country at present. I hope my views will meet with some consideration from your Excellency, and that I may hear from you. Direct to me here, care of Capt. S. F. Pennington, depot quartermaster, as I may be ordered on duty in a few days, and he will forward them to me.[3]

With that letter Captain J. Henry Behan, C.S.A., vanished from history—but not his "wild plan."

Jefferson Davis, President of the Confederate States of America, was just as concerned about the future of the Confederacy as was his assistant commissary captain. There were neither reprisals nor reprimands. To the contrary, Davis was definitely interested in the plan. He endorsed Behan's letter, and, penning on it the notation "for his perusal and attention," sent it to his military adviser, General Braxton Bragg.[4]

General Bragg, instead of curtly reminding Captain Behan to attend to his procurement of rations and forage and leave the planning of grand strategy to the proper Confederate officials, "maturely considered" the plan, found it "very comprehensive," and returned it to Davis on August 18.[5] In his endorsement, General Bragg hinted that Behan's plan might "now be contemplated in the Trans-Mississippi Department," but stated that he was quite certain that such a plan would have very little chance of success.[6]

The Confederate President was still not satisfied. Two days later he sent Captain Behan's letter to the Secretary of War, James A. Seddon, with the notation that the latest word from the Trans-Mississippi Department indicated that the "very desirable results" of Behan's plan could not be attained.[7] There is almost a note of disappointment and desperation in Davis's words.

On August 23, 1864, the harassed Secretary Seddon returned Behan's letter to the President. The secretary must have studied the plan with the same serious consideration that Bragg and Davis had given it, for his endorsement of the document indicated that he would "advise the attempt to execute it" if the Department of the Trans-Mississippi found it impossible to operate its troops on the east side of the Mississippi river.[8]

Davis finally filed the correspondence on August 25 with the notation that things were moving in Arkansas and that those movements indicated that General E. Kirby Smith, commanding the Department of the Trans-Mississippi, was doing what he could in line with Captain Behan's plan.[9]

This amazing consideration of a commissary captain's daring strategic proposal by the highest echelon of Confederate command is certainly indicative of the desperate state of affairs in the Confederacy in mid-1864. General Robert E. Lee's Army of Northern Virginia was wedged deep in the Richmond-Petersburg lines, and General William Tecumseh Sherman, sidestepping his way south toward Atlanta, was approaching Peachtree Creek, opposed only by wily little General Joe Johnston. Guerrilla fighting, meanwhile, had exploded all over the back country of Arkansas and Missouri in brief clashes of smoke and flame, leaving men dead in obscure thickets.[10]

The Confederacy was being strangled to death, and desperate remedies were very much in order. The first remedy was tried on July 17 before Atlanta, when Jefferson Davis fired cautious

Joe Johnston and supplanted him with the immature and rash General John B. Hood. But that only made matters worse. Hood lashed out at Sherman with a poorly timed and badly planned attack at Peachtree Creek on July 20-21, only to be thrust back into the defenses of Atlanta. With its two largest armies under virtual siege—one at Petersburg, the other at Atlanta—it was to be expected that the Confederacy should turn for relief to its troops in the Trans-Mississippi.

On July 22, 1864, the day before Captain Behan wrote his first letter to Jefferson Davis, General Braxton Bragg was in Columbus, Georgia, sizing up General Hood's defeat of the day before. Recognizing the Confederacy's situation as one of extreme danger and demanding unusual measures, Bragg sent a dispatch to Lieutenant General Stephen D. Lee, temporarily in command of the Department of Alabama and Mississippi, stating that "the President orders a prompt movement of Lieutenant General Taylor and the infantry of his corps to cross the Mississippi."[11]

General Stephen D. Lee sent this dispatch and two other wires repeating the order to General E. Kirby Smith, Richard Taylor's superior, between July 16 and 23.[12] This order, of which Davis later denied having any record,[13] must have been issued in a moment of panic. Had Bragg given it careful thought, he would have realized the impracticability of such a movement. In addition to posing several logistic problems of great magnitude, it failed to recognize that the Federal Navy completely controlled the Mississippi river.[14]

The physical difficulties in getting a large body of troops across the river in the face of fire from Federal gunboats was not the only obstacle to the crossing. Confederate troop morale in the Trans-Mississippi was at low ebb. The men had not been paid in nearly a year and desertions were increasing each day.[15] In addition, the Trans-Mississippi soldier was a rugged individualist who possessed very little sense of national loyalty to the Confederacy. He wanted to fight in his own section of the country,[16] where he could get home to see the wife and children if they needed him.[17]

There was also prevalent in the Trans-Mississippi Confederacy a strange and nebulous feeling that if the eastern Confederacy should collapse, the Confederate states west of the river would be able to continue as an independent nation under the blessing of the French who were active in Mexico. In fact, soon after Gettysburg, Jefferson Davis had written General E. Kirby Smith about rumors of the Trans-Mississippi Department seceding from the Confederacy.[18]

In Arkansas the Confederate Governor Harris Flanigan, and the Confederate Senator Augustus H. Garland, presented a further obstacle to the crossing by taking a firm stand against the movement. Flanigan complained bitterly in a letter to Davis,[19] and Garland told Secretary of War Seddon that the Arkansas troops would throw down their arms before they would obey such an order.[20] Indeed, there was one open rebellion, but the ringleaders were quickly arrested, tried, and shot.[21]

Despite these obstacles, however, General Smith ordered Lieutenant General Richard Taylor to attempt the crossing, and then promptly washed his hands of the whole affair, probably because he understood the impossibility of such a movement, and because he and Taylor were not on very good terms.[22]

The day selected for the crossing was August 18, 1864, but on that day General Taylor declared the whole thing impossible of achievement. The only crossing finally made was by General Taylor himself, in a small canoe on a dark night a few days later.[23] Another plan to relieve the pressure on the two Confederate armies under siege east of the Mississippi had failed. But already General Kirby Smith had another scheme underway.

On August 21, 1864, from his headquarters in Shreveport, Louisiana, General Smith wrote a long letter to President Davis in which he reviewed the activities in the Department of the Trans-Mississippi since Smith had taken command in March, 1863.[24] In addition to describing his successes on the Red River and the reasons for failing to move troops to the east bank of the Mississippi, Smith made the statement that "there remained a third plan, viz., to push a large cavalry force into Missouri and support the movement by occupying my infantry in operations against Frederick Steele."[25] It was this plan of General Smith's which Jefferson Davis must have had in mind when he closed the file on Captain Behan's "wild plan," August 25, with the notation that Smith was moving in the direction outlined by the commissary captain.

Also in his letter to Davis, Smith pointed out that he had been putting the third plan into operation when he was ordered to attempt the Mississippi crossing. Had it not been for this, "my infantry would have been now in the Arkansas Valley and Price would have been entering Missouri," Smith wrote.[26]

When General Kirby Smith wrote this letter to the Confederate President, Major General Sterling Price had already left his Camden, Arkansas, headquarters to initiate his last great raid into Missouri. The long march to Westport had begun.

The final decision to employ Confederate troops in an invasion of Missouri was made by General Edmund Kirby Smith and Major General Sterling Price.

Handsome Kirby Smith was every inch a soldier, whose tragedy lay in the fact that he was forced, as commander of the Trans-Mississippi, to assume civil as well as military command of an area too large to be defended by the small number of troops he had available. Born in St. Augustine, Florida, in 1824, Smith graduated from West Point in 1845, twenty-fifth in a class of forty-one. Assigned to the infantry, he won distinction in the Mexican War with two brevets. Returning from Mexico, he taught mathematics at West Point for a short period before returning to active duty on the frontier. When he resigned from the United States army on March 3, 1861, he was a major in the famed 2nd United States cavalry.

Commissioned a colonel in the Confederate States cavalry, his rise to prominence was fairly rapid. At the battle of First Bull

Run, he commanded the Fourth Brigade in General Joseph E. Johnston's Army of the Shenandoah, and arrived on the field from the valley in time to influence the tide of battle. Recovering from a severe wound received at Bull Run, he added to his reputation by his invasion of Kentucky in 1862. For this campaign he was made a Lieutenant General, outranking Stonewall Jackson, William J. Hardee, and Leonidas Polk.[27]

In February, 1863, Smith was appointed to command of the Trans-Mississippi Department, which soon became isolated from the rest of the Confederacy with the fall of Vicksburg in July. Cut off from Richmond, Smith assumed almost autonomous command of the Confederacy west of the Mississippi. In February, 1864, Kirby Smith was made a full general because of his tremendous responsibilities, and thereby caused discontent among many of the Confederate high commanders, especially the hard-fighting James Longstreet.[28]

Forced to shoulder almost dictatorial powers because of having to do too much with too little, General Smith found his task "no bed of roses."[29] Never having the opportunity to direct a large army, he might have become one of the Confederacy's great combat generals had he been freed from his tremendous civil and political responsibilities.

Major General Sterling Price was fifty-five years old when he began his last raid into Missouri and fought the action before Westport. Just three years before, he had been a strikingly handsome man, six feet two inches tall, erect and of a commanding presence, with great dignity and courtesy of manner. In matters of dress he had been scrupulously neat and careful, and somewhat fond of display.[30] Long a controversial figure in the bitter partisan politics of Missouri and later of the Confederacy, he was, in late 1864, a far different man than he had been in 1861. Now fat and flabby, weighing very nearly three hundred pounds, his erectness and dignity were no longer part of him. His great weight prohibited his using a horse for any length of time, and compelled him to lead his troops in a four-mule carriage driven by a negro boy. His huge body size accentuated his unusually small hands and feet. His complexion was florid and ruddy, his hair a streaked white, his small eyes gray and faded, almost hidden beneath bushy, unkempt eyebrows. Neither bearing nor appearance bespoke the Virginia-Missouri gentleman he once had been.[31] Perhaps such companions as Quantrill, Anderson, Todd, and Jesse James, who were or had been in his forces, had subconsciously contributed to "Pap" Price's deterioration. Surely, however, the presence of such men in his company must have galled the old warrior, for he was still a man of high moral character, sincerely devoted to the cause of Missouri and the Confederacy.

Of much natural military ability, Sterling Price had gained some reputation as a brigadier general in the Mexican War. The hero of Lexington in 1861, he had commanded Missouri troops at Wilson's Creek and at Pea Ridge. Commissioned a major general in the Confederate army, he had fought well at Corinth, Iuka, and Helena, and had defeated Frederick Steele on the Red River. But "Pap" Price was a politician from first to last. A former legislator, congressman and governor of Missouri, his military outlook was completely colored by his political aspirations. The Missouri invasion was to prove no exception.

For some weeks now he had been comtemplating another raid into Missouri. His intelligence sources, which blanketed the state, indicated that Missouri was ripe for invasion.[32] In fact, Thomas C. Reynolds, Confederate Governor of Missouri in absentia, had written General Price on July 18 from Marshall, Texas, the exile capital of Missouri, pleading that he undertake such an expedition, for which "the President and Secretary of War are impatient."[33]

On July 22 Price answered Reynolds, concurring wholeheartedly in the proposal. "I have confidence of the happiest results from the expedition you suggest," he wrote.[34] And then, on the very same Saturday, July 23, 1864, that the commissary captain, J. Henry Behan, had written Jefferson Davis his proposal for a Missouri invasion, Major General Sterling Price took pen in hand and proposed the same thing to General Edmund Kirby Smith![35]

Writing from his headquarters in Camden, Arkansas, General Price told Smith:

> I am also assured that the Confederate flag floats over nearly all the principal towns of North Missouri, and large guerrilla parties are formed and operating in the southern portion of the State. These facts indicate the feelings of the people of the State, who fear that the increasing desire of the North for peace, and the unparalleled and continued successes of our armies, may bring about a cessation of hostilities and a negotiation for boundaries, without our army being in possession of any portion of the State. To give us this military possession, as well as to encourage our friends there, I respectfully but urgently suggest the propriety of making a move into the State for the purpose of concentrating and organizing these detached parties, which when brought together, the least sanguine seem to think will amount to not less than 30,000. What troops can be spared for this purpose is for you to say.[36]

In view of what was to transpire during the raid, one wonders if General Price did not let his political interests color the true situation in Missouri and elsewhere. He certainly misjudged the feelings of the people in his state, for the 30,000 never materialized, and the successes of Confederate arms elsewhere were far from being "unparalleled" and "continuing."[37]

General Price had received more direct news as to Jefferson Davis's interest in a Missouri invasion than that supplied by Governor Reynolds. This was in a letter dated July 20, 1864, and written to him by Colonel Thomas L. Snead, Confederate congressman from Missouri.

Congressman Snead, returning from a session of the Confederate Congress, wrote that he had "had long interviews with the President, Secretary of War, and General Bragg," Davis's military adviser, and had learned that Davis had "sent General [Simon Bolivar] Buckner to the Trans-Mississippi in view of a movement into Missouri, as he thought that his popularity with the Kentuckians (of whom the population of Missouri is largely composed) would make him a very useful participator in that campaign."[38] Snead went on to suggest that General Price place Buckner in command of all his cavalry, indicating that such an arrangement might quash the constant "intriguing" and "grumbling" of Generals John S. Marmaduke, James F. Fagan, and William L. Cabell, and at the same time "free your very best cavalry officer (Shelby) from the hampering influence of Marmaduke's incompetency and enable him to do great and splendid service."[39]

Generals Marmaduke, Fagan, Cabell, and Joseph O. Shelby were later to command units under Price in the proposed invasion, but despite the "hampering influence" Shelby would still do "great and splendid service."

If Congressman Snead was correct in his statement of Jefferson Davis's reason for sending General Buckner to the Trans-Mississippi, then the Confederate President must have been thinking of a much larger invasion of Missouri than that which was finally launched by Kirby Smith. Why then did Jefferson Davis not take steps through General Bragg or Kirby Smith to see that such an invasion was instituted? If General Kirby Smith wholeheartedly supported an all-out expedition, as his correspondence seems to indicate, then why did he not properly support General Price? From his procrastination, delay, and failure to support the movements of General Taylor across the Mississippi river and Price into Missouri, one might conclude that General Smith never meant to send troops in force to either place, and that there might be some basis for the insinuations that General Smith was setting up a nation of his own; Kirby Smithdom, it was called. However, in all probability, General Smith failed to support General Price because he had little faith in Price's generalship.

Although Sterling Price had been somewhat of a military hero in the public mind for some time, he was by no means popular with General Kirby Smith.

On January 15, 1864, Smith had written a Confederate senator, Robert W. Johnson of Arkansas, about the state of affairs in the Trans-Mississippi, and particularly the necessity for more able generals. Kirby Smith wrote:

> The Government must not send me any more castoff material. I want support, able support. [Major General Richard] Taylor is the only district commander in whom I can rely. . . . [Major General T. W.] Holmes is a true patriot . . . but a younger man should command the District of Arkansas, where boldness, energy, and activity, with prudence, are essential to success. Price is not equal to the command, and I would regard it unfortunate were he to succeed to it.[40]

General Smith did in fact make an effort to get rid of General Price by sending him to the eastern theater with General Taylor, but Taylor did not want him either. This matter was brought to the attention of the Confederate authorities by an aide-de-camp of General Braxton Bragg on August 12, 1864—eight days *after* Kirby Smith had placed Price in command of the Missouri invasion.

Captain Thomas Butler, the aide-de-camp, had been sent by General Bragg to Clinton, Louisiana, as liaison officer to observe the proposed Mississippi river crossing. In his report to Bragg, Captain Butler said:

> He [General Richard Taylor] also suggests that when the troops are brought from Arkansas, General Price be left in the trans-Mississippi Department. He thinks, unless ordered to remain, the general will be sent over, as General E. K. Smith is anxious to get rid of him.[41]

Relations between General Price and Jefferson Davis had been far from warm since they had quarreled two years before,[42] and Governor Reynolds was later to state that he had always had doubts as to General Price's suitability for the command of the invasion.[43]

Despite these objections, Sterling Price was placed in command of the Missouri invasion. The choice, in all probability, was due to the supposed influence which General Price had in the state of Missouri and to the fact that Kirby Smith was afraid not to name him in view of the terrific row that would have resulted.[44]

3. "In a Just and Holy Cause"

GENERAL STERLING PRICE'S ORDERS to invade Missouri were issued by General Kirby Smith on August 4, 1864.[1] The orders were brief and ambitious. Instructing Price to take all the cavalry of his district plus a brigade of Louisiana troops under Colonel Isaac F. Harrison,[2] Smith pointed out ways of organizing the invading army and reminded Price that his object was to raise men for the Confederacy.

> "You will scrupulously avoid all wanton acts of destruction and devastation," Smith wrote, "restrain your men, impress upon them that their aim should be to secure success in a just and holy cause and not to gratify personal feeling and revenge. Rally the loyal men of Missouri, and remember that our great want is men, and that your object should be, if you can maintain yourself in that country, to bring as large an accession as possible to our force."[3]

Then in two sentences General Smith sketched the plan of operations.

> "Make Saint Louis the objective point of your movement, which, if rapidly made, will put you in possession of that place, its supplies, and military stores, and which will do more toward rallying Missouri to your standard than the possession of any other point. Should you be compelled to withdraw from the State, make your retreat through Kansas and the In-

dian Territory, sweeping that country of its mules, horses, cattle, and military supplies of all kinds."[4]

Although General Smith urged a rapid movement, General Price moved slowly. It was not until September 6, more than a month after the issuance of his orders, that Price crossed the Arkansas river,[5] and another twelve days before he reached Pocahontas, Arkansas, where, having been joined by the dashing Jo Shelby, he organized his army.[6]

General Price took the greater part of four days to get his troops organized. He called them the Army of Missouri and when completed the force had three divisions, commanded by Generals James F. Fagan, John S. Marmaduke, and Joseph O. Shelby.

Major General Fagan's division was made up largely of Arkansas cavalry and comprised four brigades totaling twenty cavalry regiments, one battery, and one section of artillery.[7] James Fleming Fagan was thirty-six years old. A native of Arkansas, he had seen service in the Mexican War and dabbled in Arkansas politics. When Arkansas seceded from the Union, Fagan raised a regiment and was commissioned colonel of the 1st Arkansas Infantry regiment on May 6, 1861. Distinguishing himself at the battle of Shiloh, he became a brigadier general and was transferred to the Trans-Mississippi Department. On his native soil he fought brilliantly at Prairie Grove and defeated General Frederick Steele in the Camden expedition. For this achievement he was promoted to major general—but Fagan, as later events were to disclose, had fought himself out against the enterprising Steele.[8]

Major General Marmaduke's division consisted of two brigades, encompassing ten regiments of cavalry, one engineer company, and two batteries of artillery, one from Texas, the other from Missouri.[9] This division was predominantly Missourian. John Sappington Marmaduke, its leader, looked and acted the beau ideal he really was. A handsome, six-foot bachelor, he came from one of Missouri's aristocratic families. His father, a former governor of the state, sent his son to Harvard and Yale before securing for him an appointment to West Point. John graduated from the academy in the class of 1857, ranking thirtieth in a class of thirty-eight. When secession came, he was serving on the frontier, but resigned his commission as second lieutenant to offer his services to Missouri's pro-Confederate governor, Claiborne Fox Jackson. As colonel of the 3rd Missouri, Marmaduke also distinguished himself at the battle of Shiloh and rapidly secured a brigadier general's commission. Raiding in Arkansas and Missouri, he earned a reputation for hard fighting, and a promotion to major general. He was soon to fight hard again at Westport, Missouri, but his division would be the first to give way before the pursuing Federal cavalry.[10]

Brigadier General Shelby's division was made up of three brigades with thirteen Missouri cavalry regiments and one Missouri battery of artillery.[11] This division was a provisional one but it did contain Shelby's famous Iron Brigade, which was certainly the best combat outfit in Price's army, and probably the most famous military organization west of the Mississippi.[12]

Joseph Orville Shelby was a native of Kentucky and thirty-three years of age when he saved General Price's army at Westport from complete destruction. A wealthy rope manufacturer in Waverly, Missouri, Shelby was a slave owner and an active participant in the Missouri-Kansas border disputes of the late 1850's. He had entered the Confederate army as a captain of cavalry in 1861 and had fought with distinction at Carthage, Lexington, Wilson's Creek, and Pea Ridge. After the last-named battle he organized his famous Iron Brigade at Newtonia, Missouri, and soon gained a reputation for ruthless raiding in Missouri and Arkansas. Wounded in the attack on Helena, Arkansas, Shelby became a brigadier general in the Confederate army on December 15, 1863. His reputation as a skillful cavalry commander was further enhanced by his action against Steele just prior to General Price's invasion of Missouri. Flamboyant in dress, romantic in his speech, chivalric in his manner, he captured the imagination of both his followers and his enemies. But above all else, Jo Shelby was a tireless, slugging fighter. Major General Alfred Pleasonton, whom Shelby was to fight at Westport, once said of the Confederate cavalryman, "Shelby was the best cavalry general of the South."[13] General Pleasonton, commander of the Union cavalry at Brandy Station and at Gettysburg, should have known what he was talking about, for he had fought some of the best the Confederacy had to offer—J. E. B. Stuart, Wade Hampton, and Fitzhugh Lee. With the end of the war, Shelby led the remnant of his brigade into Mexico to support the Emperor Maximilian rather than surrender to the North.[14] He was always to be the "undefeated rebel."

By September 18, 1864, General Price's Army of Missouri was fully organized—at least on paper. Many of the units were mere skeleton outfits and many of the men were without arms and mounts. Shelby's Iron Brigade with 1,455 men had 278 unarmed and 48 dismounted, and Colonel S. D. Jackman's Brigade with 1,596 men had 1,155 unarmed and 133 dismounted.[15] The state of Missouri, with its rich storehouses of military supplies, was supposed to furnish the missing arms and horses—and it did.

On September 19, General Price entered Missouri with his forces "in fine health and spirits. We found the roads very rough and bad, but have not suffered much from that cause. Our strength is nearly 8,000 armed and 4,000 unarmed men."[16]

General Price had early determined to invade Missouri in three columns. General Fagan's division was to take the center route by way of Martinsburg, Reeves' Station, and Greenville; General Marmaduke was to march to the right of Fagan's route, by Bloomfield; and General Shelby's division was to move to the left of Fagan by way of Doniphan and Patterson. Intervals of twenty miles were to be maintained between the columns in so far as possible. The headquarters was to march with the center column, and all three divisions were to form a junction at Fredericktown, about twenty-one miles southeast of Pilot Knob. This marching arrangement was the best possible for utilizing available roads, quick frontal deployment, and the collection of maximum forage and supplies.

The three columns reached their rendezvous at Fredericktown on the 24th and 25th of September.[17] The march had been without incident except for a brief contact between a small Federal scouting party and some of General Shelby's troopers at Doniphan, Missouri, on September 20 and again on September 22 at Patterson, Missouri. Both encounters resulted in hasty withdrawals of the Federal militia.[18] As a result of the September 20 contact, the Confederate position became known at the Union fort in Pilot Knob where General Price was soon to meet the first organized Federal resistance.[19]

Meanwhile, at the Union headquarters in St. Louis, Major General William S. Rosecrans, commanding the Federal Department of the Missouri, had finally become convinced that much more than an ordinary Confederate raid was in progress. With his department depleted of troops, General Rosecrans found himself in a dangerous situation,[20] though by no means for the first time in his experience. As a former commander of the Army of the Cumberland, he had been in tighter corners at Stones River and at Chickamauga. Receiving word from General C. C. Washburn, Federal commander at Memphis, that General Andrew Jackson Smith with 6,000 infantrymen was being sent up the river to Sherman's army before Atlanta, General Rosecrans halted Smith's division at Cairo, Illinois.[21] After an exchange of messages with General Henry W. Halleck, Lincoln's Chief of Staff in Washington, Rosecrans succeeded in having Smith ordered to St. Louis where he arrived at Jefferson Barracks, below the city, on September 13.[22] These veteran infantry troops, with some cavalry, plus the remnant of his scattered department troops and the ten rather incomplete regiments of twelve-month volunteers which had been feverishly organized just previous to General Price's raid, were all that General Rosecrans could muster to halt the Rebel raiders.[23]

On September 26, General Price and his Army of Missouri swung westward toward Pilot Knob, the southern terminus of the St. Louis and Iron Mountain Railroad. Pushing sharply through the rugged hills, General Fagan's division led the advance, and by the following morning had closed in on Fort Davidson, which guarded the Federal supplies stored at Pilot Knob. The fort, mounting four 32-pounder siege guns and three 24-pounder howitzers, presented a formidable defense against infantry and cavalry, but because its hexagonal walls were almost completely surrounded by hills, it was extremely vulnerable to properly placed artillery.[24]

Fort Davidson was garrisoned by 1,051 soldiers and 150 armed civilians under the command of Brigadier General Thomas Ewing Jr., one of General Rosecrans' district commanders. General Ewing fully realized that the only veterans in his little band of defenders were the five companies of the 14th Iowa Infantry from General A. J. Smith's command which he had brought with him the day before—562 soldiers. The remainder of the garrison was an unknown and an unpredictable factor. Ewing, nevertheless, determined to delay the Rebel advance as long as he could, even though it would mean almost certain capture.[25]

The Confederate assault on Fort Davidson fell to the divisions under Generals Fagan and Marmaduke, General Shelby having taken his division on a wide sweep to the north of Pilot Knob in an effort to cut the railroad and thus discourage any Federal reinforcements coming from St. Louis. After a morning of desultory firing on the fort, General Price launched his attack about two o'clock in the afternoon of September 27, with General Fagan's division on the right and General Marmaduke's on the left. The assault, preceded by a few rounds from the field pieces in position on the left of the Confederate line, was uncoordinated.[26]

General Fagan's Arkansans poured down the rough slopes of Pilot Knob hill in misty rain and onto the three-hundred acre plain surrounding the fort. They were well in advance of General Marmaduke's Missourians who were gingerly picking their way down the rocky terrain of Shepherd's Mountain, and were the first to come under fire. About five hundred yards from Fort Davidson's walls, the stout Arkansans met a withering blast from the fort's defenders. For not more than five minutes could the bewildered men stand their ground. Breaking for the rear, the bulk of Fagan's division fled from the field.[27] The exception was the brigade led by Brigadier General William L. Cabell, which fought its way to the ditch surrounding the fort's parapet. This position they were soon forced to abandon, however, for lack of support, since the greater portion of Marmaduke's division had found a convenient dry creek bed at the foot of Shepherd's Mountain in which to take cover until darkness.[28]

Most of the Confederate losses in the assault on Fort Davidson were sustained by General Cabell in his withdrawal.[29] The repulse had been quick, decisive, and revealing—revealing in that Marmaduke's and Fagan's divisions, with the exception of Cabell's Brigade, showed a decided aversion to fighting. Confederate morale had been hard hit.

Inside the walls of Fort Davidson there was rejoicing amidst the confusion. General Ewing's casualties of approximately 200 were not excessive, but they were more than the small garrison could afford.[30] Convinced that the Rebels would renew their attack with the coming of daylight, and that this time they would have proper artillery support, General Ewing called a hurried council of war to consider evacuation.

Soon after midnight the general and his garrison crept silently over the drawbridge, which had been covered with tents to muffle the sound of the cavalry and six-gun battery. Two hours later, as had been arranged, the large magazine in Fort Davidson exploded, but by that time the gallant defenders had slipped between two of General Price's camps and were well on their way to Caledonia.[31]

During that day of setbacks for the Confederate raiders, General Shelby's division was operating near Potosi, where it had destroyed three railroad bridges of the Iron Mountain line, and torn up several miles of track. After his repulse at Fort Davidson, General Price began frantically to send messages to General Shelby, but the couriers never reached that dashing officer. As a result, Shelby was not in position to block General Ewing's retreat that night.[32]

It was almost noon the next day before the confused and befuddled General Price could get his pursuit under way. He had not realized until eight o'clock that morning that the Union garrison had evacuated.[33] He had supposed that the magazine explosion was an accident and that those Union defenders not killed in the blast would soon surrender.[34]

Finally organized, the Confederate pursuit was far from aggressive, and the Fort Davidson garrison, with very little delay, was able to reach Leasburg about sundown on September 29, having marched sixty-six miles in thirty-nine hours.[35] At Leasburg the Union boys found a trainload of rations and entrenching tools destined for the Federal garrison at Rolla. Filling their stomachs and then seizing the tools, they dug all night. When Generals Marmaduke and Shelby appeared early the next morning, the intrepid Yankees were already safely ensconced behind formidable earthworks crowned by railroad ties.[36] The Confederate pursuers, surveying the strong Federal position, disposed their forces as if for an assault but made no further demonstration. The next morning the Rebels were gone.[37]

While Marmaduke and Shelby were chasing General Ewing, General Price had taken Fagan's division and moved toward St. Louis. Although they advanced only to within forty miles of the city, they pushed that metropolis to the edge of panic.[38] But General Price had lost his nerve and now had no intention of taking St. Louis. If he had had such an intention, General Price must now have realized that in his rage at General Ewing's escape he had committed a colossal blunder in sending Shelby and Marmaduke after the wily Ewing. He did not now have sufficient troops with him to take the city.

On September 30 Price turned northwestward and passing through St. Clair and Union, marched in leisurely fashion toward Missouri's capital. The next day Shelby and Marmaduke rejoined Price and Fagan. By October 3 the combined forces had occupied Hermann, destroyed railroad bridges across the Meramec, Moselle, and Gasconade rivers, ripped up miles of track, burned innumerable depots, and captured a supply train loaded with clothing and 400 Sharps rifles.[39] The rifles were particularly welcome, for many of General Price's soldiers were still unarmed. The Rebels' wagon train and beef herd were also enlarged as the raiders moved westward. When they entered the state, General Price's forces had only about 300 not-too-full wagons. By the time the train reached Westport on October 23, it had grown to 500 wagons, all well filled.[40]

By October 6, 1864, the Rebel vanguard under Jo Shelby had reached the banks of the Osage river. Here General Shelby again met strong resistance and succeeded in forcing a crossing only after leaving Colonel David Shanks, commanding the Iron Brigade, severely wounded on the muddy banks of the river.[41] The next morning General Fagan's division took the advance and soon ran into trouble along Moreau Creek, a small stream near the outskirts of Jefferson City. Fighting here was furious for a short time, until the Federal troops fell back into the city's entrenchments. The Rebels now stood on the heights in full view of the capital.[42]

In the meantime General Rosecrans, "Old Rosy" his soldiers called him, finally lost his famous temper and swung into action. Recognizing that his problem was two-fold—to assemble enough cavalry to hit General Price's invaders and at the same time to protect Federal posts throughout the state from raiding guerrilla bands—the testy Rosecrans called out the state militia. At the same time he instructed his district commanders—Brigadier Generals John McNeil, Egbert B. Brown, Clinton B. Fisk, and John B. Sanborn—to leave enough of a force to provide safety for the posts in their various districts, and then to concentrate the remainder of their commands in Jefferson City. By October 6 this had been accomplished and General Fisk, by right of rank, assumed command of the combined troops.[43]

General Price and his Army of Missouri "gathered like a cloud of destruction about the capital of the state," and no one was more eager for its capture than Thomas C. Reynolds, Confederate Governor of Missouri in absentia.[44] From Marshall, Texas, the exile Confederate capital of Missouri, he had urged this invasion, and he had accompanied the expedition with the understanding that he would be inaugurated governor if Jefferson City was captured. But Reynolds was doomed to disappointment and bitterness.[45] The savage repulse at Fort Davidson was still fresh in Rebel memories, and General Price had lost all appetite for frontal assaults. By the morning of October 8, "Pap" Price and his gray cavalrymen had turned their backs upon Jefferson City and Governor Reynolds' ambition and were marching westward across the state to disaster.

General Rosecrans now ordered the veteran General A. J. Smith with 4,500 seasoned fighters to move out behind the invaders, but Smith's slower moving blue infantrymen were destined never quite to catch up with the Rebel cavalrymen. However, when "Old Rosy" hastily recalled his recently assigned district commander, Major General Alfred Pleasonton, from leave of absence in the East, the Federal Department of the Missouri went from the defensive to the offensive. General Pleasonton arrived in Jefferson City on October 8, soon after General Price and his army had departed. Things instantly began to happen.[46]

Alfred Pleasonton, former commander of the cavalry of the Army of the Potomac, was still smarting under the order that had sent him into exile in the Trans-Mississippi, and he was just waiting for an opportunity to get into a good fight. He had cause for resenting his transfer to Missouri. The highly successful Union cavalry which was rampaging in the Eastern theater of war under the colorful General Phil Sheridan, was in many respects the result of General Pleasonton's efforts. Now he was not with them to reap the awards and honor of his efforts, and another man, just as vain and just as pretentious, was garnering the harvest. Pleasonton had found a bitterness and a resentment that would never leave him as long as he lived.[47]

From the moment he graduated from West Point in 1844, Alfred Pleasonton was wedded to the United States Army. A confirmed bachelor, he devoted his time and energy to the service, driving himself and his staff unmercifully. He was a tall man, handsome, impeccable in his dress, a striking military figure, often wearing on his wrist a rawhide whip in lieu of a sword at his waist. In outbursts of temper he would shake the rawhide in the face of some unfortunate subordinate.

Now General Pleasonton reacted to his new task with characteristic decision. Finding approximately 4,100 horse soldiers in Jefferson City, he organized them into three provisional brigades led by General Rosecrans' three district commanders: Brigadier Generals Sanborn, Brown and McNeil. These brigades he placed under the temporary command of John B. Sanborn, with orders to proceed after Price as a corps of observation, and to harass and delay the raiders as much as possible until other Union forces could be brought up.[48]

General Sanborn immediately sent the First Brigade out the Springfield road toward Versailles and Warsaw, and the Second and Third Brigades along the railroad toward California and Tipton. By the morning of October 9, in the heavily timbered country east of Russellville, General Sanborn had engaged all three of the brigades in a delaying action with General Fagan's division, which was protecting the Confederate rear as the indefatigable Price swung sharply northwest and headed toward Boonville, the bastion of Missouri rebeldom.[49]

General Sanborn, however, did not give up. Pushed aside by General Fagan, the Yankee cavalryman hung on the Rebel flank, harassing and delaying the Rebel march. Through October 11 he kept up his aggressive tactics until General Price was forced to employ both Marmaduke's and Fagan's divisions in order to end them.[50]

General Sanborn withdrew to the south of the Petit Saline, but principally because his horsemen had been thirty-six hours without rations. Hoping to meet a subsistence train so that he could feed his troops and return to the harassment, he fell back to California, Missouri. Here he was able to procure four days' rations and a veteran cavalry brigade of 1,500 men.[51] This brigade, under the command of Colonel E. C. Catherwood, had been operating with General A. J. Smith's infantry.

By ten o'clock on the morning of October 13, General Sanborn had his command started back toward Boonville. Unfortunately, however, General Price and his army had completed their leisurely rest in friendly Boonville, and were again on the move westward.

The Army of Missouri had arrived in Boonville on October 10, and had been welcomed with enthusiasm, feted and ministered to like the liberating warriors Sterling Price really believed them to be. Between 1,200 and 1,500 farm boys, unarmed and ill-prepared, here joined the raiders, caught up in the glory that seemed always to ride with "Pap" Price.[52] Some of them, just a few days later, would see the elephant and meet death in the muddy streets of Independence. Here crafty and treacherous "Bloody Bill" Anderson, with a company of about 100 men, reported to the Confederate leader, and was hurried off with specific orders to destroy the North Missouri Railroad. And here, also, the ruthless and already legendary men of William Quantrill were dispatched to wreck the Hannibal and St. Joseph Railroad.[53]

Brigadier General M. Jeff Thompson, replacing the hapless David Shanks in command of the Iron Brigade, wrote of this stay in Boonville, "What was done and not done here in the next three or four days I do not propose to relate as I had only to try to control my own Brigade, to save their reputation from the demoralization which was seizing the army. The plunder of

Boonville nearly completed this demoralization for many officers and men had loaded themselves, their horses and wagons with 'their rights' and now wanted to turn Southward and save what they had."[54]

Time was beginning to run out for the Army of Missouri. Behind it was the enterprising General Sanborn, hanging on like a leech and stinging like a gadfly. Coming up on its flank were General A. J. Smith's infantry veterans, soon to be increased to 9,000 in strength by the arrival of 4,500 veterans under Major General Joseph A. Mower.[55] Moving up from the south were increasing numbers of state militia. Events were building rapidly to a climax.

At ten o'clock on the night of October 12, the Confederate army moved out of Boonville and marched eleven miles to Chouteau Springs. When it moved, so did General Sanborn and his blue-coated cavalry. Realizing that somehow he must delay the raiders until General A. J. Smith could bring his infantry and artillery to within striking distance, Sanborn divided his little command. A small contingent under Captain James M. Turley was left to hang on Price's rear while General Sanborn took the remainder of his cavalrymen and raced up the Georgetown-Lexington road. By the afternoon of October 15, he reached Cook's Store and was in position to attack the Rebel flank if the Confederate cavalry should make a rapid move toward Kansas.[56]

General Sterling Price, however, had not finished his work in Missouri. On October 13 he had sent Brigadier General John B. Clark, Jr., now in command of General Marmaduke's old cavalry brigade, across the Missouri river to attack Glasgow where it was rumored the Yankees had some 5,000 guns stored in the City Hall.[57] These weapons would more than take care of equipping the 1,500 recruits General Price had picked up in Boonville.

At daylight on October 14, General Shelby took a brigade of his division and a section of artillery and went to the aid of General Clark by attacking Glasgow from the west side of the river. This diversionary movement might have succeeded if Clark and Shelby could have coordinated their attacks, but General Clark's Brigade ran into difficulty getting across the river and was an hour late in launching its attack. The delay gave the Federal garrison sufficient time to burn some of the stores before it was forced to surrender.[58]

Meanwhile, General Price had taken the remainder of his army and pushed on to Jonesborough where he ordered General M. Jeff Thompson to take 1,000 men and a section of artillery and attack the Federal force at Sedalia, to the south and west. Such an assignment delighted the dashing and reckless Thompson. Riding at a gallop, the Rebels thundered toward their target. Sedalia was the western terminus of the Pacific Railroad and its capture would hinder General Rosecrans' supply efforts. Ten miles from their destination, the graycoats sighted a long column of Federal cavalry moving westward toward Lexington. Hiding in the woods and fields until the column had passed, General Thompson moved out again, picked up a few Union stragglers, and learned from them that this was General Pleasonton on his way to join General Sanborn. From friendly natives he also learned that Federal infantry was already on the La-Mine. Slipping between these two enemy forces, the Rebels raced on toward Sedalia, but only after General Thompson had sent a courier to General Price warning him that the energetic Pleasonton might now be ahead of the Rebel columns.[59]

Jeff Thompson's attack on Sedalia was direct and smashing. In a column of regiments his raiders galloped against the two redoubts defending the town. The Yankees broke and fled.[60] Restraining his troopers from wholesale looting, General Thompson succeeded in securing some horses, rations, and arms, and in paroling his prisoners. "Having secured all the weapons and horses, arms, and *soldiers goods*," General Thompson wrote later, "I prepared to leave the town. I called out the Prisoners and made a 'spread eagle speech' and paroled them *verbally*."[61] He had to work fast. There was grave danger of being trapped by the advancing Union infantry and cavalry. Within a very few hours he was marching out of the dazed town, leaving it still reeling from the whirlwind attack. In the darkness of night he slipped by General Pleasonton again and reached General Price near Waverly on October 18. That same day General Clark returned from his Glasgow expedition. With his forces reunited, General Price hurried on toward Lexington.[62]

The halcyon days of the Confederate invasion were over, however. At long last the Federals were upon General Sterling Price and the Army of Missouri. Early in the afternoon of October 19 they would meet in force and then would begin the five long days of action before Westport. The ill-fated Army of Missouri was marching into a trap. Behind it was General Pleasonton; on its right flank was the Missouri river; on its left were the infantrymen of Smith and Mower; and in front of it was Kansas and a shrewd, fussy old Union general who had won the battle of Pea Ridge back in 1862—General Sam Curtis.

II. THE ACTION BEFORE WESTPORT

1. "Kansas, Rally! To Arms, and the Tented Field"

THE FEDERAL DEPARTMENT of Kansas, which comprised the districts of Colorado, Nebraska, North Kansas, South Kansas, and Upper Arkansas, was under the command of Major General Samuel Ryan Curtis, United States Army.

The dour and crotchety General Curtis was by profession and training a soldier, civil engineer, and lawyer. He possessed the uncanny knack of combining his three professions into the one career of politician. A graduate of West Point in the class of 1831, he had served in the army for a brief time on the frontier and during the Mexican War. He had engaged in engineering and dabbled in law for short periods before getting himself elected to Congress where he was serving his third term as a representative from Iowa when the Civil War erupted. He reentered the military service as Colonel of the 2nd Iowa Infantry and rose rapidly to command of the Federal Army of the Southwest. He led this western contingent in successful operations along the Missouri-Arkansas border, culminating in the victory at Pea Ridge and the occupation of Helena. Appointed to command of the Department of the Missouri, he permitted his political inclinations to infiltrate his military job and thereby incurred the disfavor of Abraham Lincoln who was already plagued by too many political generals. President Lincoln promptly replaced General Curtis with the ambitious General John M.

Schofield and sent the engineering-lawyer-soldier to command the Department of Kansas.[1] There in "Bleeding Kansas," which had been a political cauldron for almost a decade, General Sam Curtis continued to dabble in politics when not chasing Indians and guerrillas, and all the time fussing and fuming in his frustration. In this last respect he was not unlike his brother officers —Generals Rosecrans and Pleasonton.

Considering the tremendous area which he had to contain, General Curtis had a pitifully small number of troops available for the task. His strength as reported for August, 1864, showed only 6,956 men present for duty[2] and these were scattered all over the western territory, protecting outlying settlements and pursuing marauding redmen. On September 17 when he first learned the details of General Price's invasion of Missouri, General Curtis just had returned to his headquarters at Fort Leavenworth from an extended operation against the Indians. Realizing that his troops were too far away to call back in time for action against the advancing Confederate cavalry, General Curtis immediately set to work to marshal what opposition he could. He sent word to his district commander, General James G. Blunt, who was off on an Indian chase, to break off pursuit and to come with all possible speed to Fort Leavenworth with whatever troops he could muster. Already stationed along the Kansas-Missouri line were the 2nd Colorado, the 15th Kansas, the 16th Kansas, and the 11th Kansas Regiments of Volunteer Cavalry, together with a portion of the 3rd Wisconsin Cavalry. These were all the troops General Curtis could scrape together in time to meet the raiding graybacks, possibly 4,000 soldiers. More simply had to be found. There was only one place to find them—in the Kansas State Militia. General Curtis promptly wired the Kansas governor, Thomas Carney, for help.[3]

In his telegram of September 17, 1864, General Curtis told Governor Carney all he knew concerning the Confederate movement and warned him that the militia might be needed to check the invaders. Having issued his warning, General Curtis immediately armed the field-works already established along the eastern Kansas border and constructed others so as to secure Fort Scott, Paola, Lawrence, and Olathe against guerrilla raids. Heavy siege guns were well placed at strategic locations from Fort Scott to Fort Leavenworth.[4]

On September 20 General Curtis again warned Governor Carney of the Confederate threat against Kansas and requested him to notify the militia "to be ready to co-operate against the foe."[5]

The governor's reaction to Curtis' warnings was certainly not one of alarm. Not completely convinced that the Confederate invasion implied danger to the state, the Kansas executive exacted a promise from General Curtis not to use the militia in the field and to employ them only in garrison duty in so far as possible.[6] However, through the co-operation of the governor, the Federal commander was able to gather and distribute arms and equipment to a large part of the militia.[7]

General Curtis' difficulty in arousing the state to arms can be attributed primarily to the national and state elections of 1864. The Kansas governor was so embroiled in a factional fight for power within the Kansas Republican party that he had time for little else. The Carney and Lane factions were slugging it out in a bitter election campaign that bid fair to become a war within a war. Democrats and Radical Democrats were merely present as the two Republican groups fought for the United States Senate seat as well as political control of the state.[8]

By the end of the first week of October General Curtis was almost frantic in his efforts to arouse the governor. But it was all to no avail. The executive could not be convinced that Kansas was in danger. This was just a device on the part of the general to get the militia mobilized and thus keep these Kansas citizen-soldiers away from the polls on election day.

All day October 8 telegrams raced back and forth between the Department of Kansas and the Department of the Missouri. From his headquarters in Fort Leavenworth General Curtis pelted Governor Carney with news of the Confederate advance across Missouri with pleas to "Hurry out the militia."[9]

Governor Carney had gone to Leavenworth City to meet General George Deitzler who commanded the state militia. Shortly after nine o'clock that night, Carney informed Curtis at the Fort that when General Deitzler arrived from Lawrence the next morning they would meet with General Curtis concerning the situation. However, by midnight Governor Carney at last committed himself to General Curtis, "I shall call [the militia] as you desire."[10]

The next day, nevertheless, the governor again had his doubts about the necessity for mobilizing the Kansas militia. Still not quite trusting the politically-minded Curtis, Governor Carney wired General William S. Rosecrans in St. Louis—"Are we in danger here from Price? Inform me." By five o'clock that evening, Carney had his answer. "I think no effort should be spared to secure yourselves from Price who will move west," wired "Old Rosy," and he used such phrases as "marauding parties" and "plundering Kansas."[11]

That did it. Governor Carney called out his Kansas militia and issued a proclamation which he had written the day before. He might have hesitated in issuing it, but he spared no words in urging his fellow Kansans to arms. He proclaimed:

"The State is in peril. Price and his rebel hosts threaten it with invasion. Kansas must be ready to hurl them back at any cost . . . Kansans, rally! You will do so, as you have always promptly done when your soil has been invaded. The call this time will come to you louder and stronger because you know the foe will seek to glut his vengeance upon you. Meet him, then, at the threshold and strike boldly; strike as one man against him. Let all business be suspended. The work to be done now is to protect the State against marauder and murderer. Until this is accomplished we must lead a soldier's life and do a soldier's duty. Men of Kansas, rally! One blow, one earnest, united blow will foil the invader and save you. Who will falter? Who is not ready to meet the peril? Who will not defend his home and the State? To arms then! To arms, and the tented field until the rebel foe shall be baffled and beaten back!"[12]

The next day, October 10, General Sam Curtis in an effort to bolster the proclamation declared martial law throughout the state. He ordered all men, white and black, between the ages of eighteen and sixty to temporary military service. General George Deitzler as commander of the Kansas State Militia established his headquarters in Olathe and promptly designated rendezvous points along the border from Atchison in the north to Fort Scott in the south. "Let each man come with such arms as are at hand and a full supply of ammunition," he ordered. "As this campaign will be a short one, no change of clothing will be necessary."[13]

Even now Governor Carney still had his doubts. The declaration of martial law bothered him. Was this essentially a political maneuver on the part of General Curtis? Was the general conniving with the governor's political opponents? Some newspapers were convinced of it. One editor declared the whole business to be a political trick engineered by General Curtis.[14] Another accused Curtis of entering into conspiracy with Senator Jim Lane to remove the men of Kansas from the polls at election time.[15]

Governor Carney and General Deitzler called upon Curtis on October 10 to find out if the general really intended to take the men from the state. "They also informed me," wrote General Curtis of this visit, "that expressions of some of my officers had led them to distrust the whole matter of the militia movement, supposing it might be a political scheme gotten up by some around me to transport the people beyond the convenient exercise of their elective franchise, which would come off early in the next month. These were shocking enunciations."[16]

They were indeed, but crusty old Sam Curtis was more indignant than he was shocked. Calling upon his skill as a lawyer, he shamed the two Kansans and apparently convinced them that no political chicanery was going on. "My manner and matter

39

appeared to assure these officers," General Curtis declared.[17]

Governor Carney's proclamation and General Curtis' declaration produced the required effect. The response was electrifying. The word swept from one end of the state to the other and the men, black and white, poured toward the points of rendezvous within a few hours. Business virtually ceased to exist. Farms and shops were deserted. Harvesting stopped abruptly and the roads were filled with men, horses and wagons, streaming toward the eastern border as if on a gala holiday.[18]

By Tuesday, October 11, 1864, 3,300 militiamen were marching toward Leavenworth. At 6 a.m. Wednesday morning, 1,000 from Douglas County marched into Lawrence and that evening were joined by an additional 800 from Jefferson County and 700 from Shawnee County. By Saturday morning 17,000 men had reported for duty and 15,000 were assembled along the state line ready to meet the Confederate invaders.[19] General Curtis had his reserves. He was now ready to operate against General Price and the Army of Missouri with the few regular troopers he had at hand. Numbers were immaterial; the Confederate advance to Westport had to be stopped.

2. A Dark and Dangerous Man

THE FEDERAL CAVALRY COLUMN, four hundred strong, was threading its way slowly down the Pawnee, six days out of Fort Larned, when the courier caught up with it. The tired troopers had spent those six days chasing a war party of 1,500 Cheyenne and Arapahoe warriors north toward the Smoky Hill. The blue cavalrymen had overtaken their prey on Pawnee Fork. For four hours they had engaged the redmen in savage combat before the Indians broke off the engagement and fled up the Pawnee. The troopers had pursued them for two days and nights. But the horses could endure no more. The chase was abandoned and the weary cavalrymen turned back toward Fort Larned. It was then that the courier came seeking the blue column's commander, General James G. Blunt.[1]

The dispatch bearer was from General Curtis and bore orders for General Blunt to make haste to Fort Leavenworth. Sensing the urgency in his commanding officer's message, Blunt turned over command of the column to his subordinate and raced toward Leavenworth, riding day and night.

Major General James Gilpatrick Blunt was in many respects a strange and contradictory person. A native of Maine, he was a seaman turned horse soldier on the dry and dusty plains of Kansas. A medical doctor by profession, he was an ardent abolitionist by avocation. While practicing his profession he was as gentle as a woman; while pursuing his avocation he was ruthless, hard, and vicious. He was not a tall man, but the thick body and almost leonine head gave him stature. It was the face and eyes that marked him as a fanatic—a dark and dangerous man. The eyes were sharp and black, set deeply in the head below shaggy brows. The man's countenance was made more grim by the stubby black mustache and goatee. Never jovial, seldom genial, he was on one day much what he was on another—except on battle days.

James Blunt was by nature a hard fighter. In the shock of battle he became the aggressive leader, sure of himself and his actions, never doubting for a moment his ability to achieve victory. It was then that the fanaticism came into its own and the man became another John Brown of Kansas, scornful of God and man. It was then that the disease which was to claim his life in an insane asylum in 1879 tainted the emotions and mentality of the man.

James Blunt was a determined man, not to be shaken from his purpose. He was lawless, lewd, coarse and unscrupulous. He was a hard drinker and a braggart, but he was a born soldier with a flair for cavalry tactics and the employment of light artillery. Early in the war he had ridden with James H. Lane, Kansas' Grim Chieftain, and rose rapidly in rank. He had fought brilliantly at Cane Hill and Prairie Grove and now in the action before Westport he was to rise to the zenith of his military career.[2]

General Blunt galloped into Leavenworth late on October 8, the day all telegraph wires were cut east of Pleasant Hill.[3] General Curtis and the Army of the Border were gradually losing contact with General Rosecrans and the Department of the Missouri. Despite the hour, General Blunt picked up Senator Jim Lane in the village and rode out to the Fort to report to Curtis.[4] General Curtis briefly apprised General Blunt of the military situation in Missouri and ordered him to proceed immediately to Olathe and upon his arrival to wire Curtis for further orders.

On October 10 General Blunt rode into Olathe, contacted General Curtis, and was ordered to relieve Major General George Sykes of command of the District of South Kansas.[5] Blunt did as directed, immediately shifted his headquarters to Paola, and set about organizing the few volunteer Federal troops in his district and getting them in shape for immediate combat.

At one o'clock in the morning of October 13 General Blunt was awakened by his orderly who handed him a telegram from General Curtis. It was an order directing Blunt to take all his cavalry and his artillery and move without delay to Hickman Mills, Missouri. By daylight the eager Blunt, sensing approaching battle, was on the move. He arrived at the Mills shortly before noon October 14 and on the next day found his little force substantially increased by the arrival of additional cavalry and Kansas Militia. The cavalry troops were mostly veterans under command of the notorious Colonel Charles R. Jennison of "Kansas Redlegs" fame and the dependable Colonel Charles W. Blair. The militia, mostly infantry, were under command of their militia officers, Brigadier General W. H. M. Fishback and Colonel James D. Snoddy. The two militia officers were later to prove most difficult for the fire-eating Blunt.

Prior to General Blunt's move to Hickman Mills, General Curtis had sent a portion of the 2nd Colorado Cavalry under its colonel, James H. Ford, to reconnoiter toward Independence. It did not take Colonel Ford long to discover that he was in unfriendly territory and that the local population and guerrillas operating there had received positive orders from General Price not to destroy any forage in the neighborhood.[6] It appeared that Sterling Price intended to move his Army of Missouri that way. After sending two companies to Independence as an extreme outpost, Colonel Ford and the 2nd Colorado Cavalry returned to Hickman Mills in time to join General Blunt who was organizing and brigading his forces.

General Blunt's final organization produced three brigades. The First Brigade commanded by Colonel Charles R. Jennison consisted of the 15th Kansas Cavalry under Lieutenant Colonel

George H. Hoyt, the 3rd Wisconsin Cavalry Battalion of five companies under Captain Robert Carpenter, and a battery of four twelve-pound mountain howitzers under Lieutenant H. L. Barker.

The Second Brigade was under the leadership of the efficient, hard-fighting colonel of the 11th Kansas Cavalry, Colonel Thomas Moonlight. Moonlight's Brigade was made up of the 11th Kansas Cavalry now commanded by its pompous Lieutenant Colonel Preston B. Plumb, and Company L of the 5th Kansas Cavalry and Company D of the 16th Kansas Cavalry. The former company was ably led by Captain James H. Young and the latter by Captain W. H. Kendall. Later Company M of the 5th Kansas and Company A of the 16th Kansas were added to the brigade. Colonel Moonlight's artillery consisted of one battery of four twelve-pounders manned by Company E of the 11th Kansas Cavalry. This little brigade was to do some of the most effective fighting of the campaign as it resisted the Confederate advance on the Little Blue river.

The Third Brigade was to prove most difficult to General Blunt. It was placed under the leadership of Colonel Charles W. Blair of the 14th Kansas Cavalry. Colonel Blair was a small man but with a driving energy and a readiness for rough fighting that gained him great respect. Blair's Brigade consisted almost entirely of Kansas Militia except for Company E of the 14th Kansas Cavalry under Lieutenant W. B. Clark, Captain James H. Dodge's 9th Wisconsin Battery, and Captain W. D. McLain's Independent Colorado Battery of six rifled field-pieces. The militia forces comprised the 4th, 5th, 6th, 10th, and 19th Kansas State Militia regiments, Lieutenant D. C. Knowles' two-gun 2nd Kansas State Artillery Battery, and Captain John Wilson's Independent Scouts.[7]

These militia forces of the Third Brigade were placed under the immediate command of Brigadier General W. H. M. Fishback of the Kansas Militia who in turn was under orders from the brigade commander, Colonel Blair. In thus creating a brigade within a brigade General Blunt ran into trouble. General Fishback deeply resented taking orders from a colonel and likewise contended that the militia forces should receive orders that were transmitted only through the hands of state authorities, indicative again of the state's distrust of General Curtis' intentions. Without General Blunt's or Colonel Blair's knowledge, General Fishback commanded Colonel J. S. Snoddy to take his 6th Kansas Militia back to Kansas to assist in that state's protection.[8]

Colonel Snoddy, only too willing to cooperate, and his 6th Kansas were well on their way when Blunt and Blair learned of the movement. General Blunt's violent temper exploded. Ordering the 15th Kansas Cavalry in pursuit of the defecting column, General Blunt raced ahead and, in person, stopped the regiment. His anger had mounted with the miles. He placed General Fishback and Colonel Snoddy under arrest, sent them to Paola under guard, and marched the column back to Hickman Mills himself.[9]

The men of the 6th Kansas Militia returned willingly, cheering General Blunt as they marched along. On their return to camp they promptly elected as their colonel James Montgomery who had formerly been with the 3rd Kansas Volunteer Infantry and only recently had distinguished himself in South Carolina and Florida as a leader of the 2nd South Carolina Colored Volunteers.[10]

The United States Senator from Kansas, Samuel C. Pomeroy, currently serving as a volunteer aide on General Curtis' staff, learned of Fishback's plight and immediately interceded for his influential Kansas constituent. Securing a vague explanation of the action from Fishback that seemed to satisfy the proprieties, Senator Pomeroy persuaded General Curtis to release the militia officer. Although he was returned to the Third Brigade, General Fishback did not continue to command the militia in that brigade. Colonel Snoddy remained a prisoner at Paola until after the retreat of the Confederate army from Westport had begun.[11]

In the meantime, General Curtis with the assistance of General

George Deitzler and General M. S. Grant of the Kansas Militia had completed organization of the state forces and had concentrated the main body at Shawnee and along Turkey Creek beyond Shawnee. A depot for ordnance, subsistence and quartermaster stores was established at Wyandotte.[12]

These Kansas farmers and storekeepers turned soldiers were still in a holiday mood as they lounged in their camps along the state line. A less soldierly army was probably never gathered together since the days of the American revolution. Horse-play, card-playing, and political arguments were the militia's pastimes. On occasions the activity was a bit more elevated for one militia company boasted a brass band always willing to perform.[13] Newspapers were eagerly consumed and although their news was often unreliable they did provide fuel for many arguments, the chief being whether there really was a Confederate invasion moving toward Kansas. Many of the local sheets still declared emphatically that the whole story of General Sterling Price and his invading army was a complete myth fabricated for political purposes.[14]

During these hectic days, Generals Curtis and Deitzler labored to bring the militia into fighting trim. They saw that the men were well fed and equipped with proper arms, most of them being given new Enfield rifles.[15] Nothing could be done about the issuance of regulation uniforms, however. This bothered General Curtis for he knew that Confederate uniforms in the Trans-Mississippi were in most instances no uniforms at all but the same type of everday clothing the Kansas militiamen were wearing. Serious difficulties could arise if these men of his went into combat indistinguishable from General Price's Rebels. Curtis therefore ordered all members of the militia not in uniform to wear on their coats some kind of a piece of red material. The majority of the men solved the problem by adorning themselves with the flaming leaves of the sumach, which blazed in every thicket in Kansas during these mid-October days. Because of these distinguishing badges the men good-humoredly called themselves "The Sumach Millish."[16]

General Curtis now felt that the Army of the Border was as near ready to move out against Price and the Army of Missouri as it ever would be. The Federal objective would be Lexington, Missouri, which the doughty Curtis hoped to occupy before the Rebel raiders. His plan of movement toward the town was simple. Major General George Deitzler was to take the left wing of the army from its camps around Shawnee and proceed by way of Independence, Missouri. The right wing, under General Blunt at Hickman Mills, was to approach Lexington by way of Warrensburg. General Curtis would thus be assured that no unfriendly militia units or guerrilla bands were operating in his rear. He issued the necessary orders for the advance from his headquarters in Wyandotte, Kansas.

The movement immediately ran into trouble. Many of the Kansas militiamen refused to cross the state line. They would defend Kansas but they were not willing to fight for Missouri. General Grant with the 19th and 4th Kansas Militia regiments was ordered to join Colonel Ford and the 2nd Colorado Cavalry who were now holding Independence. Reaching the state line, the 19th Kansas refused to cross. After passionate appeals from Generals Deitzler and Grant the men finally consented to move as far as Independence but no farther. Other militia units moved up to the Big Blue river, while those concentrated at Mound City, Paola, Fort Scott, Shawnee, and Wyandotte remained at their stations in the event General Price and his invaders should suddenly swing south from Lexington.[17]

At seven o'clock on the evening of October 16 following the unhappy episode with Fishback and Snoddy, General Blunt with the First and Second Brigades moved out of Hickman Mills toward Pleasant Hill. General Blunt's force consisted of 2,000 cavalry and eight mountain howitzers. Before daylight the next morning they marched into Pleasant Hill where Blunt halted the troops for a brief rest.

Pushing on toward Holden, the advance was slowed by repairing of the telegraph lines and a meeting with Major Emory S. Foster and his cavalry battalion of Missouri volunteers, an irregular militia and citizens' group from Warrensburg. General Blunt sent the citizens with the ailing Major Foster back to Warrensburg and attached the remainder of the battalion under the command of Captain George S. Grover to Colonel Jennison's Brigade.[18] By noon General Blunt and his force reached Holden where they went into bivouac.

At Holden General Blunt learned that General A. J. Smith's infantry was at or near California, and that General John Sanborn was some twelve miles northwest of Sedalia, hanging on the Confederate flank. General Blunt immediately wired General Curtis this information and requested that the Third Brigade, which had been left in Hickman Mills, together with the 16th Kansas Cavalry and the 2nd Colorado Cavalry be sent to his support.[19] General Blunt intended to rendezvous with them on the Independence-Lexington road. With these reinforcements Blunt hoped to form a junction with General Sanborn and General Smith and move to an attack upon General Price.[20]

After completing his telegraphic communications, General Blunt pulled out of Holden after dark. By marching all night he was able to reach Lexington with his advance brigade, Colonel Moonlight's, by ten o'clock the next morning, October 18. He had beaten General Price to the town. Only a small band of guerrillas occupied the place and most of these were killed or captured by the fast-moving Colonel Moonlight.[21]

While General Blunt was advancing upon Lexington, General Curtis had wisely decided that since it was virtually impossible to move the Kansas Militia as a unit to Lexington, the next best thing was to hold them together at the most available line of defense. This he determined to be the Big Blue river.

Moving his headquarters from Wyandotte to Camp Charlot in Kansas City, General Curtis sent Colonel Blair and the Third Brigade to the Big Blue river with orders to work with the engineers in fortifying that line. The men fell to work with a will and soon formidable abatis, breastworks and rifle pits were constructed along the west bank of the river at fords and other salient points.

At Kansas City martial law was declared and rigidly enforced. That town was undergoing the same confusion and alarm that had previously swept St. Louis and Jefferson City. Home Guards were quickly activated under the command of Colonel Kersey Coates. The city's mayor, Colonel R. T. Van Horn, promptly issued a proclamation requesting all businesses to close at four o'clock in the afternoon and all able bodied men to come to the courthouse for drill. Colored troops, the citizen guards, lawyers, doctors, divines and merchants joined the service or labored on the fortifications that were thrown up south and east of the town's limits.[22]

Long after dark on October 18 General Curtis received dispatches from General Blunt announcing the occupation of Lexington and pleading for reinforcements. General Jo Shelby, leading the Confederate advance, was reported moving out of Waverly on the road to Lexington. General Price with the remainder of the invaders was near Marshall and pushing up the river rapidly. A collision of Blunt and Shelby was only a few hours away.

Dejected and discouraged, Sam Curtis was forced to inform Blunt that reinforcements were impossible—the Kansas Militia was unwilling to venture so far away from Kansas.[23]

General Blunt with his 2,000 horsemen and his eight cannon was entirely on his own.

3. "This Is the Place to Make the Fight"

THE LATE OCTOBER DAWN was a bleary dilution of night in which the blackness above the treetops faded to desolate gray. An early breeze, cold and raw, riffled through dry leaves and thickets, and seemed discouraged by the heavy growth.

As the grayness increased General James G. Blunt's little command began to stir in its camps. Out on the Fair Grounds, south of Lexington, the First Brigade built its fires and cooked its rations. Upon the hill near the Masonic College buildings the men of the Second Brigade were also moving about. Their sleep had been fitful that night. Too many dark and disturbing memories were connected with the ground on which they slept for this was where the ill-fated Colonel James Mulligan had made his bloody stand against General Price in 1861.

Three miles out on the Dover road Captain H. E. Palmer of the 11th Kansas Cavalry squatted by his small fire and tried to eat his hardtack and bacon. He was so weary he could hardly bring the food to his mouth. He had felt just as exhausted the night before when General Blunt had ordered him to take about 250 men "and to go out on the road to Dover, say three miles, and hold that position as long as you can. Don't mind the fight anywhere else. You are to hold the Dover town road until ordered to retreat. I shall depend upon you, Palmer."[1] Somehow he had managed to obey that command. Now in the grayness of dawn as the men finished their breakfast, Captain Palmer searched for the strength to set the troopers to work clearing a field in front of them in which to fight.

A like distance out on the Warrensburg road Captain Louis F. Green, with Company B of the 11th Kansas Cavalry and Company A of the 16th Kansas Cavalry, commanded the picket and was engaging his men in similar duty.[2]

Even before the first gray of daylight General Blunt was astir. With his two aides, Senator James H. Lane and Lieutenant Colonel John T. Burris, he had ridden through the town inspecting every approach and thoroughly studying the ground over which he might be compelled to fight. Returning to his headquarters, he issued a field order placing all of Lafayette County under martial law and directing every able bodied male of Lexington between fifteen and sixty, white or black, to report with spade or pick to work on the fortifications.[3] They were to assemble with the mayor at two o'clock that afternoon. That time never arrived. By eleven o'clock that morning General Blunt's pickets met the advancing Confederates and the long action which reached its climax at Westport had begun.

General Sterling Price had received information of General Blunt's seizure of Lexington and also of General A. J. Smith's presence near Sedalia. Fearing that the two Union forces might join, General Price made a flank movement to the left and thus intercepted the Federal line of march. The Army of Missouri was then in position to approach Lexington in three columns by the Dover, Salt Fork, and Warrensburg roads.[4] General Jo Shelby again took the advance by the middle road and first made contact with General Blunt's pickets. The boys in blue fell back slowly, stubbornly contesting every foot of the road. The pressure increased; so did the resistance. Now firing was heard along the Dover and Warrensburg roads.

Back in camp General Blunt heard the first shots. Now in the grip of battle fever he began shouting orders. Suddenly he was everywhere he was needed. In matters of minutes he had his two brigades in battle line south and east of the town where open and gently rolling country gave him the opportunity to move freely and to observe quickly any flanking movements that might develop. Likewise he had the Independence road to his rear, a line of retreat if that became necessary. His eight mountain howitzers he placed in strategic locations behind his line.

Slowly the pickets along the Salt Fork and Warrensburg roads were pushed back toward General Blunt's battle line. But still they resisted. The Confederate advance swept forward again and again against Blunt's line. Three o'clock came and the Union line still held, but with each hour the attacking Confederates grew stronger as more of them poured up the two roads. The howitzers proved most effective in stemming the advance. However, General Price would soon have his larger guns up and in action. General Blunt knew he could not hold much longer. Quickly he withdrew the Second Brigade and hastily formed a second line.[5]

Out on the Dover road Captain Palmer was having his troubles. Here the contest was more evenly matched for awhile. The Confederate cavalry coming down the road numbered no more than 500. Palmer, with his 250 boys in blue, had been reinforced by Captain Grover with some of Foster's Cavalry Battalion and felt confident that he could hold his own.[6] All afternoon the two forces skirmished along the Dover road. Three times the Yankees drove the Confederate cavalry back to the timber along the Tabo.

All of the time Captain Palmer was conscious of the mounting sounds of battle two miles to his right. He sent a message to General Blunt stating that he was holding the Dover road but could see no use in staying where he was. "Could I not do better service elsewhere?" he inquired. No answer came back. Captain Palmer continued his skirmishing.[7]

About five o'clock the sound of musketry and cannonading suddenly ceased. Then after a long period of silence there came the faint echo of scattered firing miles away. Captain Palmer and his skirmishers were cut off—but they had held the Dover town road.

By late afternoon General Blunt realized he could resist no longer. The main body of General Price's army was very near and John Sanborn and A. J. Smith were still far away. Initiating a withdrawal down the Independence road, General Blunt ordered Colonel Moonlight to take the 11th Kansas Cavalry and four howitzers and cover the retreat. He could not have selected a better man for the task. Falling back over six miles, Colonel Moonlight made four successive stands within that distance. His last line was on a ridge which afforded him an opportunity to utilize his four guns to maximum advantage. Here the 11th Kansas Cavalry stood and held off the Rebel advance until darkness enveloped the field.

With the coming of night the Confederate cavalry went into bivouac. General Blunt, however, continued his march toward Independence until two o'clock in the morning when he finally ordered a halt near the banks of the Little Blue river. The boys in blue dropped exhausted to the ground, unaware of the damp coldness but keenly conscious that tomorrow's fighting would be even more severe.

With the advent of daylight General Blunt was up and about, surveying the banks of the river for a position he could hold. He liked what he saw and immediately sent word to General Curtis in Independence that he would fall back west of the Little Blue river and secure the first good position he could find. He asked that ammunition be sent to him at once.[8] General Blunt was ready for another fight.

General Curtis' reply was rushed back to Blunt. The Kansas Militia would move no farther forward than the Big Blue river. There the main line of battle must be established, not on the Little Blue. Curtis instructed General Blunt to leave Colonel Moonlight with 400 men and two howitzers at the crossing of the Little Blue river and to come back to Independence with the remainder of his division. Colonel Moonlight was not to bring on a battle but simply delay the Rebel approach as long as possible.[9]

Upon receipt of these instructions, General Blunt again wrote to General Curtis urging him to fight it out along the Little Blue. "This is the place to make the fight," Blunt urged. "I would suggest that you come down and examine the position if you have time."[10]

General Curtis did not have the time. He was too busy establishing the Kansas Militia along the Big Blue. Reluctantly General Blunt bid Colonel Moonlight goodbye and withdrew to Independence.

Colonel Thomas Moonlight, left with the 11th Kansas Cavalry and four howitzers, accepted his tremendous responsibility with characteristic energy. He set up his headquarters on the Lexington-Independence road near the wooden bridge that spanned the Little Blue river. He knew the stream was very shallow and easily fordable at most any spot and that to prevent Confederate cavalry from crossing was almost an impossible task. The fact that the banks were steep and lined with heavy timber was of some comfort to him. The timber and broken ground extended for two miles west of the river and there were numerous fences and walls affording points of resistance. The low range of hills back from the stream Colonel Moonlight vowed to possess. He placed Major Martin Anderson with two companies at the bridge itself and instructed him to hold it as long as possible but if forced to fall back to do so only after he had burned the structure. Captain Greer with Company I was sent two miles south down the river to hold the ford at that point. Captain Huntoon with Company H was stationed at a ford four miles distant. Heavy pickets were thrown out on the east bank along the Lexington road. The howitzers were placed to cover the bridge. All day the rest of the command was employed in abatis work, felling trees to block the road and fords.

That was all the colonel could do. Now he must wait for

the Rebel advance and hope that General Rosecrans and the Federal cavalry from St. Louis were not too far behind the Confederate raiders.

Colonel Moonlight was not the only one speculating about General Rosecrans' whereabouts. That same day at his headquarters in far-away City Point, Virginia, Lieutenant General Ulysses S. Grant was writing his chief of staff, General Henry W. Halleck, "Has Rosecrans yet come upon Price? If he has not he should be removed at once. Price is in a country where he supports his army without difficulty, and there is no reason why our forces should not move without delay . . . Anybody . . . will be better than Rosecrans."[11]

The autumn afternoon wore on. No gray cavalrymen appeared. The tension among the Union pickets grew almost unbearable. The early twilight dropped raw and cold and still the Lexington road remained empty. Darkness shrouded the little command but all through that long night the pickets never relaxed their vigilance.

Long after dark a telegraph operator with an instrument and a ground wire to tap the line reported to Colonel Moonlight. He had been sent from Independence by General Blunt.[12] The colonel and the 11th Kansas Cavalry were no longer completely isolated. With increased confidence Colonel Moonlight waited for the coming of daylight.

4. "They Fought Us on the Blue Grass Ridges"

THE CONFEDERATE ARMY OF MISSOURI was astir long before daylight on October 21. Quietly but efficiently the men in gray prepared to move out. Fresh fires winked from the Rebel positions where all manner of food that had been foraged in this rich countryside was being cooked to give the lean brown raiders a meal to fight on.[1] Work details moved back and forth to the supply wagons. Water details moved to creeks and springs and came back and orderlies rushed through the wan light of first daylight. Assembly blew and companies formed. Officers crisply shouted, swinging the companies into regimental line. The gray column began to move, darkly through a grayer morning. The horses, sensing the excitement, blew smoke vapor in the cold air. Their hoofs thudded dully on the frost-hard road.

General John Marmaduke's division took the advance with General Clark's Brigade in the lead. Captain D. R. Stallard with Company D of the 5th Missouri Confederate Cavalry was thrown out in front as skirmishers. General Shelby's division followed in close support of General Marmaduke while General Fagan remained in the rear with the Confederate wagon train.[2]

The gray of the morning had hardly dispelled the darkness when Captain Stallard came upon Colonel Moonlight's pickets a mile east of the Little Blue river.[3] Dismounting his men the Captain deployed his troopers in skirmish order and started for the timber where the Yankees were hidden. It was then the trees seemed to come apart with flashing fire. Every tree turned into a rifle and smoke drifted sinuously above the frost-stained grass. A third of the company went down in the first burst. The remainder continued their charge toward the blue skirmishers. More died or fell on the way. Bullets chopped into the horse holders before they could swing to the rear, and struck their charges with the solid, sodden impact of lead against flesh. Some of the mounts ran wild.

Onward toward the timber rushed the remnants of Company D. Suddenly a small and ragged line of blue figures detached itself from the trees and ran toward the river, turning now and then to fire into the low-lying haze of smoke that seemed to be following it. Finally the figures stopped shooting altogether and ran doggedly for the bridge that spanned the river.[4]

Rapidly General Marmaduke developed his advance. Pressing in behind Captain Stallard came Colonel Robert R. Lawther with the 10th Missouri Confederate Cavalry and Colonel Colton Greene with the 3rd Missouri Confederate Cavalry. They hit the slope toward the east bank of the river and had to slow down. Their gray cavalrymen were tumbling by the dozen as all along the thicket-crested west bank Yankee rifles began to shoot with quickening tempo, rising to drumbeat roll as more blue cavalrymen went into action. The Rebel line was ragged, broken here and there, crumbling as it stumbled forward. Some of the Confederates dropped to cover and began firing. Rifle balls slammed against the rocks of the river banks and whined away.

The hapless Captain Palmer of the Dover road fight was trying to sew up a rip in his only pair of pants when the Rebel advance hit Colonel Moonlight's force. Isolated during the fighting at Lexington, Captain Palmer had only succeeded in reaching the Union lines the preceding evening. This morning he had intended to devote to such domestic duties as getting his scattered gear in order and repairing his pants. But that was not to be. He scarcely had time to leap into his saddle and join his men in line of battle. The ripped pants he threw across his horse's back and went into the fight in his drawers.[5]

Colonel Moonlight's defense of the Little Blue crossing was violent and chaotic. It was vicious, hurly-burly fighting, charge and counter-charge, volley and saber. It was a wild melee of soldiers and horses slashing and stamping, shooting and shrieking. Men in blue, gray or butternut died on slopes, in gullies, in the river, on the bridge, beside bullet-scarred trees along the banks of the Little Blue river. And, in ceaseless, violent requiem, the roaring howitzers clouded the bright October morning.

Relentlessly, however, the Confederates pushed Colonel Moonlight's line back to the bridge. But here again the boys in blue were ready. Major Anderson, defending the bridge, had prepared a wagon-load of hay the evening before and had hauled it to the west end of the bridge. Now under sharp fire his troopers rolled the vehicle onto the wooden structure and ignited the hay. Within minutes the flames were eating the dry timbers of the bridge. The conflagration temporarily halted the Confederate advance and the concentrated fire from the Yankees' Martin-Henry breech loading rifles with which the Union cavalry was equipped drove Lawther, Greene, and the remnants of Stallard's skirmishers to take cover on the east bank.[6]

General John B. Clark, Jr., commanding the Confederate brigade coming upon the scene, immediately sent Captain Stallard back to the burning bridge to see if the fire could be extinguished. Colonel Lawther with the 10th Missouri Confederate Cavalry was ordered downstream to secure the ford one-half mile below the bridge. Lieutenant Colonel Preston with the 4th Missouri Confederate Cavalry was sent to take the ford one mile above.[7]

This movement by General Clark necessitated the further dispersal of Colonel Moonlight's small force and as a result Captain Stallard was able to get several pieces of artillery across the stream before the bridge collapsed. Lawther and Preston had very little difficulty in forcing the fords and General Clark soon sent the remainder of the brigade swarming across the river. Colonel Freeman's Brigade of Marmaduke's division poured in behind General Clark.[8]

Colonel Moonlight recognized that this rapid deployment and the increasing strength of the Rebels would soon flank and completely surround the 11th Kansas Cavalry. The intrepid Colonel rose to the occasion. He ordered all men to dismount and the horses sent to the rear. Then taking advantage of every stone wall, tree, and ravine, he began a slow withdrawal to the high bluegrass ridges west of the river. The 11th Kansas kept up a steady and rapid fire as it retreated and employed the four howitzers to excellent advantage. So destructive was its fire that the regiment was able to reach the heights with very little loss. But Marmaduke's division, still mounted, was now entirely across the Little Blue river and General Shelby was dismounting his division preparatory to wading the stream.[9] Colonel Moonlight and the 11th Kansas were face to face with disaster. It was now nine o'clock and for two hours the blue cavalrymen had fought magnificently. Their stubborn resistance had badly blunted the Confederate advance.

When the pickets had first clashed that morning and the bridge had been set afire, Colonel Moonlight had utilized his telegraph operator and sent a wire to General Blunt informing him that the 11th Kansas Cavalry was resisting but falling back. General Blunt had spent the preceding evening in Independence trying to persuade General Curtis to allow him to remain with Colonel Moonlight and make a stand on the Little Blue river. He had received General Curtis' approval of his request that morning and was just preparing to move out when the telegram from Colonel Moonlight arrived. In addition to the troops he had brought with him to Independence, General Blunt had succeeded in securing a fourth brigade under the command of Colonel James H. Ford of the 2nd Colorado Cavalry. This brigade was made up of Major J. Nelson Smith's 2nd Colorado Cavalry, and the remainder of the 16th Kansas Cavalry under Major James Ketner. Captain

W. D. McLain's Independent Colorado Battery of six rifled field-pieces was shifted over from the Third Brigade which General Blunt had left behind in Hickman Mills. This added about nine hundred men and six guns to General Blunt's force.[10]

Rapidly General Blunt's horse soldiers filed through the streets of Independence and then raced at full speed toward the Little Blue river. They arrived just as Colonel Moonlight and the 11th Kansas Calvary now joined by Companies I and H, which had been defending the fords, reached the heights about a mile west of the river.

General Blunt lost no time in sizing up the situation. His orders were quick and exact as he formed his division in line of battle. The 11th Kansas Cavalry held the left of the Yankee line. On the right of the 11th, General Blunt placed the now re-united 16th Kansas Cavalry under Lieutenant Colonel Sam Walker. McLain's Colorado Battery of six rifled guns held the center of the line. On its right was the 2nd Colorado Cavalry. Then continuing toward the right of the line came the 3rd Wisconsin Cavalry and the 15th Kansas Cavalry. Barker's Battery of five mountain howitzers supported the right of the Union line and Colonel Moonlight's four guns supported the left.[11]

After forming his line, General Blunt dismounted his troopers, sending the horses to the rear with every fourth man. Then the line moved forward toward the river and the advancing gray raiders. The battle lines met and erupted. The Rebels, also dismounted, rolled up to the line by the hundreds, colors flying high and taut throats shrilling their wild battle cry. The firing increased in volume. It was now heavier than ever. It came from the left, from the center, and then from the right rear.

Somehow the Yankees seemed to sweep to meet them. The solid blue mass broke into segments, no longer ranks but individuals. Contorted faces made a mottled, uneven frieze. Repeating rifles barked and snapped in unending clatter. Thin sabers glinted and flickered as they were shifted in the sunshine.

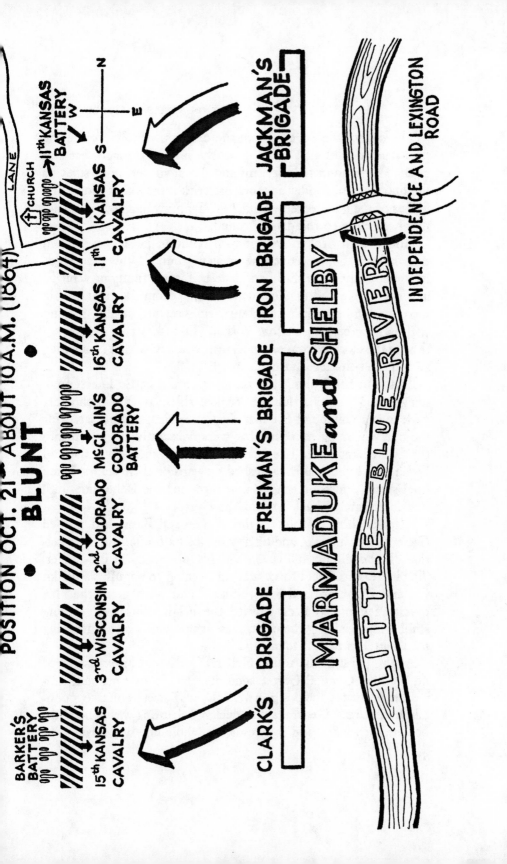

POSITION OCT. 21ᵗʰ ABOUT 10 A.M. (1864)

● BLUNT

BARKER'S BATTERY

15ᵗʰ KANSAS CAVALRY

3ʳᵈ WISCONSIN CAVALRY

2ⁿᵈ COLORADO CAVALRY

McCLAIN'S COLORADO BATTERY

16ᵗʰ KANSAS CAVALRY

11ᵗʰ KANSAS CAVALRY

11ᵗʰ KANSAS BATTERY

CHURCH

LANE

N
W   E
S

CLARK'S BRIGADE

FREEMAN'S BRIGADE

IRON BRIGADE

JACKMAN'S BRIGADE

MARMADUKE and SHELBY

LITTLE BLUE RIVER

INDEPENDENCE AND LEXINGTON ROAD

The cannonade began. From the center of the line came the slam-slam of McLain's rifled guns; the reports clanged, flat and clear. The cannon thunder, up and down and on both sides of the line, became louder as more batteries went into action. The flashes of the guns reflected like heat lightning against the smoke that held close to the damp ground.

Horses with broken legs or torn tendons, jerking free from their holders, hobbled over the uneven ground. Others ran wildly to get away from this man-made hell, some plunging straight into the smoke and rags of flame coming from the trees. A big sorrel with a bullet in its hind quarters screamed shrilly, pawing with its forefeet in an effort to rise. The calks of its shoes were tearing the clothes from a cavalryman who lay with a broken leg and a bullet-shattered arm.[12]

Back and forth along the rising slope the battle line surged, uneven and broken. But the Yankee riflemen ripped the turf with such a volume of fire that they more than compensated for the overwhelming numbers that were constantly being fed into the Confederate line. The men in blue flung themselves flat and began to fire ahead as they pushed forward on their bellies. They fired steadily into the smoke that shrouded the Rebel line until that line crawled back toward the river.[13]

After an hour of close fighting, General Blunt had pushed Generals Marmaduke and Shelby back a half mile. But this position Blunt could not hold even with his supremacy of fire-power. The increasing Rebel force was threatening to engulf his flanks. General Blunt ordered a withdrawal and once more the blue cavalrymen pulled back toward the heights but still resisting stubbornly. Gaining the crest, they again made a stand, utilizing their batteries to full advantage.[14]

At this point in the action General Curtis and his staff arrived on the line. General Curtis, according to his own account, immediately shifted the position of McLain's Battery and two mountain howitzers.[15] General Blunt declared that this was done without his knowledge and as a result his whole line was thrown into confusion.[16] That he was correct in his declaration, there can be no doubt. In moving the two mountain howitzers to an open and recently ploughed field, General Curtis exposed them to the enemy's sharpshooters who soon began to play havoc with the gunners and the horses. In order to help the situation, Major R. H. Hunt, chief of Curtis' artillery, ordered the additional two howitzers of the 11th Kansas Cavalry in support. All four guns, together with McLain's Colorado Battery, were then supported on the right by Colonel Ford and the 2nd Colorado Cavalry. However, their left was entirely unsupported.[17]

The guns immediately opened on the advancing Rebels with canister and spherical case. The range was short and the gray cavalrymen were driven back, but not for long. As more and more of General Shelby's division poured into the Rebel battle line, the pressure on the Union line increased and the exposed left flank of McLain's Battery and the four howitzers was soon discovered. General Shelby sent Colonel Jackman's Missouri Cavalry regiment under Lieutenant Colonel C. H. Nichols against that flank.[18]

Major Hunt saw General Shelby's attack forming on the left of the guns and frantically searched about him for help. Major Edmund Ross of the 11th Kansas Cavalry happened by at that instant and Major Hunt begged him to send Colonel Moonlight and the retreating 11th Kansas Cavalry to his aid.[19] Major Ross passed the word to his colonel and within seconds that nearly exhausted regiment came pressing back. The trouserless Captain Palmer wrote of that effort: "The rebel advance was within 400 or 500 yards of the battery. Quick work must be done to save the guns, worth a thousand men to us. Colonel Moonlight . . . came galloping down the line to my company . . . He ordered me to countermarch and charge the enemy with my eighty-eight men in a column of eight front. We charged down the road, passing the Little Blue church, straight for the enemy . . . As we reached the brow of the hill, a thought flashed through my mind that the first line, in which

I was riding, with seven soldiers to my left, would be shot as soon as we came in sight. I clutched the pommel of my saddle and threw myself almost flat on the horse. The volley of bullets came as I expected. I felt my horse going down, swung my feet clear of the stirrups, and fell on my horse's neck, unhurt. Geo. W. Edwards . . . fell on my back, dead. My men saw me fall and thought I was killed. They retreated back into the hollow. I jumped up and ran after them, a perfect hail-storm of bullets buzzing past me. I ordered the men to dismount. Every man left his horse in the road. We then jumped the fence into an orchard and charged the brick house, and took it, driving the enemy out; then charged the stone fence and took that."[20]

As Captain Palmer's company together with the rest of the 11th Kansas Cavalry pushed toward General Shelby's line, they were joined by the 2nd Colorado Cavalry under Major J. Nelson Smith. This western outfit was well-known to Shelby and his men because the Colorado troopers were mostly mounted on white horses and were "always at the front in a fight."[21]

The Colorado boys came charging to the batteries' rescue in a gallop and yelling at the top of their lungs. The gallant Major Smith was in the lead, shouting his encouragement and brandishing his saber, presumably forgetful of the premonition of death which he had experienced the evening before.[22]

General Shelby's gray horsemen, once more mounted, converged upon the guns but they were still yards away when the 2nd Colorado Cavalry hit them. Major Smith didn't quite make it. Seconds before the two lines of cavalry crashed together, the major fell from his white horse, a Rebel bullet in his heart. The fight was short and mean. It was horse against horse, man against man, a wild nightmare of chopping sabers, flashing guns, and smashing hoofs. As suddenly as the two lines came together, they thinned out and parted, leaving behind them a churned field that showed clearly what had been done. The loud indignation of gunfire passed and the trampled dead lay gray and blue and filthy, their anger gone and their smashed weapons and kicked hats cluttering the ploughed field. The guns had been saved and were hastily hauled to the rear as the 2nd Colorado and 11th Kansas formed anew to cover the retreat.[23]

General Curtis, seeing now that General Price and the Army of Missouri could not be held at the Little Blue river until General Pleasonton came up, hurried back to his headquarters in Independence. General Blunt declared: "He soon after [the charge of the 2nd Colorado Cavalry] left the field and gave me no further trouble during the day, except, on his return to Independence, he ordered back my ammunition wagons which I had ordered to the front, which circumstances came near proving disastrous to the whole command. My entire available force did not exceed three thousand men, with which to contend against Price's entire command, and my purpose now was to fight for time, that Rosecrans' forces might come up in the enemy's rear, and to enable the militia of Kansas to concentrate on the border."[24]

The shortage of ammunition for both men and batteries was acute. The 11th Kansas Cavalry, which had been fighting continuously since daylight, was almost entirely without ammunition. Colonel Moonlight held it in line, however, by having the men cheer lustily and defiantly and singing, "Rally round the flag, boys."[25]

On the right of the Union line Colonel Jennison with the First Brigade was likewise hard pressed. Here with the 15th Kansas Cavalry and a detachment of the 3rd Wisconsin Cavalry and Lieutenant H. L. Barker's Battery of five guns, he had been holding off a large segment of General Marmaduke's division.[26] Here also the fighting had been close and severe. Private James H. Campbell of the 14th Missouri Confederate Cavalry wrote of the fight on this part of the field: "The Union boys had dismounted and were fighting on foot and came out from their well concealed positions and fought us on the blue grass ridges with but little protection and came within thirty yards of our line where both sides fought like demons . . . I had occasion to go over the battle ground after the battle and in front of our battalion men lay in piles two or three across each other where they had fallen . . . My brother, at my left, received a minie ball through his hips . . . so I took him, as he was younger and smaller than myself, and carried him under my right arm with my gun under my left and marched through a shower of bullets 30 or 40 yards where we got protection from a log house and Gen. Marmaduke was sitting there on his horse and I afterwards understood that he had had two horses killed from under him in that engagement. I succeeded in carrying my brother off of the field and after seeing our doctor dress his wounds . . . I mounted my horse and rode over the field and every wounded and dead man had whiskey in his canteen and I have always thought this accounted for their desperate charge and this desperate fighting that Friday afternoon."[27]

General Blunt's actions since his arrival on the field had been characteristic of the man when consumed by the excitement of battle. He was everywhere on the front, always at the particular spot where he was needed most. Cheering the men, he encouraged them not only by his words but also by his actions and leadership. Seemingly reckless of his own life, he was fearless, cool and inspiring. Issuing the right orders at the right time, "he was the animating spirit of the battle."[28]

In his retreat to Independence, General Blunt dismounted his command and formed it into two lines. While one line was fighting the other would fall back through it to the horses, mount, and then take a new position from which to fight. The artillery was divided equally between the two lines, but Major Hunt remained continually with the front line batteries.[29]

Alternating his lines, General Blunt made a stand at the Massey farm two miles west of the Little Blue river, then another at the Saunders farm three miles west of Massey's.[30] It was four o'clock in the afternoon and the short October day was rapidly drawing to a close. The pressure of the Rebel army had abated somewhat and General Blunt's retreat slowed down. Blunt formed his last line of battle on the eastern outskirts of Independence and awaited General Price's attack.

When five o'clock came and still no Confederate attack, General Blunt pulled all troops of his command out of the line except the 16th Kansas Cavalry and marched them in column to General Curtis' entrenchments on the Big Blue river.[31] They arrived there long after dark, exhausted and hungry. The 16th Kansas Cavalry had orders to hold the line until the 11th Kansas Cavalry could be supplied with ammunition and sent back to relieve it.

General Shelby had now assumed the advance of the Rebel army. He soon discovered that General Blunt was evacuating Independence and immediately ordered his division to press forward. Colonel Walker and the 16th Kansas Cavalry stubbornly resisted Shelby's advance but fell back slowly into the fringes of the town. Here Colonel Walker found his ammunition exhausted and the 11th Kansas Cavalry waiting to relieve him. Almost immediately the Confederate advance entered the town. Sections of Rebel cavalry, a few mounted, the remainder dismounted, peeled off, one toward the railroad bridge, the others toward the principal streets of the town leading into the square. The horses' hoofs made smacking sounds in the packed dirt of the streets. Then other sounds came through the gathering dusk —the squeak of leather fast-ridden, the jingling of bits and curb chains and sabers, the pounding tread of charging regiments— sounds that seasoned soldiers never forget.

The 11th Kansas Cavalry, still ready for a fight, stood to its task in the streets of Independence. One of Colonel Moonlight's howitzers thundered, smothering all sounds, and the horses rippled with nervous movement—a fearful hesitation, a primitive uncertainty. Again the gun roared and the vibration in the streets became almost continuous, slamming with the intensity of mortar fire. Suddenly the town was filled with rushing horses and dismounted cavalrymen plunging and swarming and there sounded the steady flatting of carbines punched through with answering rifle fire. It all became tight and wicked, troopers charging in fours to get into the loosely spread Rebels and gun-flashes dancing along the mist of twilight and horses crashing together, whickering. There were the blunt, ugly sounds that bullets make when they strike into human flesh and a horse shrieked in bowel-torn agony and there came a falsetto screech of shattered bone. The melee surged back and forth through the streets, spilling out into the alleys, smashing windows, breaking awning posts and bringing them crashing down to the board walks. The skirmish pushed through the town, was renewed again at the railroad bridge and then ceased altogether as darkness became complete.[32]

Through the blackness of the night, the weary and battle-worn 11th Kansas Cavalry made its way toward the Big Blue river. It was midnight before it entered the Union lines. Back in Independence the Confederate Army of Missouri took over the town.

5. "I Can Stop Price at This Crossing"

AFTER GENERAL SAM CURTIS ordered the evacuation of Independence, he immediately set to work putting his lines along the Big Blue river in readiness to meet an attack which he felt sure would come early in the morning. Since October 15 he had been preparing the entrenchments along the west bank of the stream. Abatis had been placed to block the fords, and hastily erected dams deepened the water at several points favorable to crossing. The west bank of the Big Blue river was in the main much steeper than the east bank and was covered extensively with thick brush and timber. The east bank was relatively clear of vegetation.

The Federal position along the Big Blue extended from the river's mouth southward for about fifteen miles to Russell's ford near Hickman Mills. The left or north end of the line which extended from the main ford to the mouth of the river was placed under command of General Deitzler. Here at the main ford where the Independence-Kansas City road crossed, General Curtis made his headquarters. The right or south end of the Union line which extended from Russell's ford to the main ford was placed under General Blunt's command. All day Friday, while Colonel Moonlight and General Blunt were fighting along the Little Blue river and in Independence, Kansas Militia units were pouring into the Big Blue entrenchments. Governor Thomas

Carney as well as General Deitzler were frantically hurrying all available regiments into the line.[2]

Private Samuel J. Reader of the 2nd Regiment, Kansas State Militia, was typical of the many Kansas boys who willingly crossed the state line to take position along the Big Blue river.* Since October 17 he and his companions had been idling in Camp Grant in Johnson County, Kansas, and just itching for a good fight with the Johnny Rebs. When orders came to move that Friday morning of October 21, Private Reader eagerly gathered up his blankets and gun and mounting his own horse, Fox, rode toward Missouri and the advancing Rebels. That night he wrote in his diary: "We crossed into Mo. in a few miles march. Three men wouldn't cross at first of our Reg't. & lots of the 3rd. Thro' Westport & between two stone wall fences where our boys were killed last year. We went on to the Big Blue & camped ½ mile N. West of the stream in a grove of blackjack saplings, covered with dead leaves."[3] The next day Private Reader would have his fight and meet disaster.

In his tent near the main ford that same night, General Sam Curtis found his pessimism of the past few days giving way to optimism. As an engineer and a general he was proud of his fortified line along the Big Blue. He wired General Rosecrans: "I am confident I can stop Price at this crossing and hope you will come up in his rear and left so he cannot get out by Hickman Mills. If you can get that position we bag Price, if I succeed, as I hope to do. My losses have been considerable, but my troops are in good order, and ready to make a stand at this place."[4]

General Blunt, dark anger still rising within him because of General Curtis' interference with the disposition of troops along the Little Blue river that day, was not nearly so optimistic. He argued with his superior, contending that General Sterling Price would not move directly along the Kansas City-Independence road and against General Curtis' strong fortifications at the main ford. Rather the wily Confederate commander would make only a feint at the crossing and then flank the Union right at one of the upper fords.[5] Time was to prove Blunt correct.

The argument, however, was to no avail. General Curtis remained strong in his conviction, his optimism not the least shaken. General Blunt could do no more. He deployed his regiments as best he could at strategic spots along the right of the Union line.

By midnight General Curtis had 15,000 men in line along the west bank of the Big Blue river. His main line, which was the Union left and center, extended for six miles to the mouth of the Big Blue where a small steamboat was anchored guarded by two hundred fifty troopers of the 19th Kansas State Militia under Colonel A. C. Hogan. North of the Kansas City-Independence road as it crossed the main ford was the 6th Kansas State Militia under Colonel James Montgomery, together with six hundred colored volunteers, well-mounted and trained. Immediately behind Colonel Montgomery's cavalry was Captain Dodge's 9th Wisconsin Battery, a section of the 2nd Kansas Battery under Lieutenant Hicks, and two Parrotts under Lieutenant Minor, a highly educated negro. These last two guns were a part of the 2nd United States Colored Battery which was to win national fame in the action before Westport. These guns at the main ford were supported by the 5th Regiment Kansas State Militia, Colonel G. A. Colton commanding, and Lieutenant Eves' Battalion from Bourbon County, Kansas. Before morning these troops at the main ford were further augmented by the arrival of the 10th and 23rd Kansas State Militia regiments from Wyandotte and Kansas City.

Above the main ford as the road passed over the high bluffs of the west bank, Captain McLain's Independent Colorado Battery was in position to sweep the crossing. Colonel Ford's Fourth Brigade together with the 12th Kansas State Militia supported it. The 2nd Colorado Cavalry picketed the eastern approach to the crossing with one post advanced to Rock ford, four miles from Independence. Six companies of the 2nd Colorado under Captain Green were also thrown out as skirmishers.[6]

Two miles south of the main ford was another crossing of the Big Blue river known as Simmons' ford and three miles beyond that still another called Byram's ford. Secondary roads from Independence crossed at these fords and ran west to Westport, Kansas City and towards the state line. These were the two crossings General Blunt feared the Rebel army would use to flank the Union right. To prepare against this contingency General Blunt placed the 10th Kansas State Militia regiment under Colonel William Pennock and a section of the 2nd Kansas Battery at Simmons' ford. Long after midnight Colonel Moonlight with the remainder of the Second Brigade moved the battle-weary 11th Kansas Cavalry there and assumed command.

Colonel McCain with a mounted battalion of the 4th Kansas State Militia held Byram's ford. By nine o'clock Saturday morning he was joined by Colonel Jennison with the First Brigade, who took command there.[7]

But General Blunt had made a fatal error in deploying his troops. He had overlooked another crossing of the Big Blue —a relatively obscure cattle ford known to the farmers round-about as Hinkle's ford. Within a few hours that oversight would prove to be the undoing of the Army of the Border and General Curtis' fortified line.

Farther upstream from Byram's ford was still another ford sometimes called the Hickman Mills Crossing but more often referred to by the local residents as Russell's ford. Colonel George W. Veale with the 2nd Kansas State Militia and remnants of the 3rd Kansas State Militia had arrived there on the morning of October 21. They were later joined by Colonel Sandy Lowe with the 21st Kansas State Militia. These combined forces totaled 1200 men. They were supported by one piece of artillery, a twenty-four pound howitzer under command of Captain Ross Burnes of the 2nd Kansas. They went into camp near the ford to await the arrival of General M. S. Grant with additional militia cavalrymen. Among Colonel Veale's troopers was Private Sam Reader of the 2nd Kansas with his carefully

72

kept diary and his horse Fox. Young Reader made himself comfortable in a grove of blackjack saplings.[8] Little did he know that on the next day he and his comrades would be compelled to give up their position at this ford and in doing so would meet tragedy.

Although General Curtis had received a telegram from General Rosecrans on Friday, October 21, he had had no communication with General Pleasonton or General A. J. Smith. In fact, he had not been in touch with them since before the fight at Lexington.[9] To allow them additional time to come up in the Rebel rear had been a factor in General Curtis' decision to hold as long as possible along the Little Blue river. Now that the Army of the Border was secure in its main defense line along the Big Blue river, it was more than ever imperative that Generals Pleasonton and Smith hurry forward if the Rebel army was to be trapped. Somehow contact had to be made with them. A way was found in Daniel W. Boutwell, a scout from the 2nd Kansas State Militia regiment.

Dan Boutwell was no novice to war. He had seen prior military service as a member of the 6th Kansas Cavalry and had but recently been discharged from the service. A patriotic Kansan he had promptly responded to Governor Carney's call to arms and joined the 2nd Kansas for the emergency. Now he volunteered to reach General Pleasonton.

General Deitzler gave Boutwell verbal instructions. At seven o'clock that Friday night, dressed in Federal blue and without arms or papers, the scout left the general's tent on his mission. He rode his horse to Kansas City where he commandeered a skiff and started down the river. The night was dark and cold and the river was low. For several miles Boutwell made good time and then before he quite realized it he found himself securely lodged on a bar. Nothing he could do would budge the skiff.

Abandoning the craft, the scout struggled to shore and climbed up on the bank, wet and muddy. The coldness demanded vigorous movement and he hurried through the brush regardless of the noise he was making. He had gone but a short distance when he ran into Rebel pickets and was fired upon. A ball sang close to his head but he ran on and successfully eluded the guards in the thick underbrush.

Stealthily he worked his way around Independence, carefully avoiding all roads and houses where pickets might be posted. He crossed a small stream on some fence rails but half way across slid off and found himself wallowing in three feet of thick and slimy mud. All around him was encamped the rear of the Confederate army. Making use of the heavy timber, he made his way through the Rebel lines and long after daylight reached General Pleasonton's pickets. They conducted him immediately to the general's tent on the banks of the Little Blue river.

Daniel Boutwell was a sorry spectacle as he stepped into the neat quarters of the meticulously attired Pleasonton. To add to the scout's further embarrassment he found himself not only in the presence of one general but three. Generals McNeil and Sanborn were there also. The astonished scout was able to ask General Pleasonton if he would accept a verbal message from a very muddy soldier. The general replied that he would and Boutwell passed on to him General Deitzler's information.[10]

After carefully examining and cross-examining the messenger, General Pleasonton accepted Dan Boutwell's message and immediately dispatched couriers to Generals Curtis and Rosecrans informing them that the Provisional Cavalry of the Department of the Missouri would press forward energetically.[11]

General Pleasonton's movement behind the Confederate Army of Missouri up to the morning of Saturday, October 22, did seem to be particularly slow and on the surface appears to offer grounds for criticizing Pleasonton and Sanborn. However, General Pleasonton claimed that he held back because he feared he might move before General Curtis had time to organize the militia.[12]

General Alfred Pleasonton had caught up with the

Provisional Cavalry division at Dunksburg, Missouri, on October 19, and upon assuming command reorganized it into four brigades. The First Brigade he placed under the command of General John Sanborn, the Second Brigade under General Egbert Brown, the Third Brigade under General John McNeil and the Fourth Brigade under Colonel Edward F. Winslow.[13] The latter consisted of veteran cavalrymen from the Seventeenth Army Corps whom General Pleasonton had brought with him from St. Louis. To each of his four brigades the general had added a section of artillery.

On the same day the newly organized cavalry division moved out of Dunksburg. By midnight it had entered Lexington, just a few hours behind General Blunt. From Lexington General Pleasonton moved at daylight to Waverly and from there to Fire Prairie and thence to the crossing of the Little Blue river where he arrived at 5 a.m., Saturday morning, October 22. It was here, about noon, that the begrimed Dan Boutwell contacted him. With the addition of Colonel Winslow's cavalry brigade, General Pleasonton's division now numbered about 7,-000 men.[14]

On October 21, while General Blunt was making his determined stand on the Little Blue, General Rosecrans with General A. J. Smith's infantry moved into Lexington. The tired foot soldiers, however, were not to rest. General Rosecrans was in great fear that the Confederate army would slip off to the south around General Curtis and the jaws of the Federal trap would be evaded.[15] A. J. Smith and his infantry were started immediately for Chapel Hill. From there they were to proceed to Lone Jack and thus be in position to block a Confederate retreat.

Footsore and weary, the infantrymen had found the way across Missouri to be very hard. Only yesterday they had marched through snow. But the cold, damp weather did not bother them nearly so much as the wild rumors that ran through the ranks and the fact that most of them had not been paid in almost a year.[16] When Daniel Boutwell was making his report to General Pleasonton and General Curtis was facing General Price across the Big Blue river that Saturday morning, General A. J. Smith's infantry was closing in on Chapel Hill. The infantrymen were approaching a position where they could make history by capturing an army. But a misjudgment on the part of General Pleasonton was to pull them out of line long enough for the prize to escape. All the glory that remained for these weary foot soldiers they would find during a fatal December day on the hills surrounding Nashville, Tennessee.[17]

6. *"Death Was Everywhere—"*

SATURDAY MORNING, October 22, 1864, was a windy, raw morning with a coldness that was sharp and penetrating.[1] The sun rose brilliantly but it brought very little warmth for with it came a gusty northeast wind that only served to increase the biting cold. From his headquarters in Independence, General Sterling Price, perfectly confident that he could manage the Union forces converging upon him, set his three divisions in motion early that morning.

General Price saw the task before him as threefold. First, he must force a crossing of the Big Blue river and defeat the Army of the Border before Generals A. J. Smith and Pleasonton could come to Curtis' aid. Second, he must hold General Pleasonton and the Yankee Provisional cavalry at bay until General Curtis was defeated. Third, he must bring his heavily-laden wagon train up from the rear to the middle of his army to prevent its capture by General Pleasonton.

To the first task General Price assigned the divisions of Shelby and Fagan. The job of moving the wagon train up from the rear was also given to General Fagan. General Marmaduke's division had orders to hold Pleasonton's cavalry at sufficient distance to allow Shelby to take care of the Army of the Border.

The pressure against General Curtis' fortified line began at 9 o'clock that morning. General Shelby ordered Colonel Sidney

Jackman's Brigade to proceed toward the main crossing of the Big Blue river, to drive in General Curtis' pickets, and make a feint at the ford.[2] Jackman did not have far to go before making contact with the Yankee guards and within a matter of minutes had sent them racing back across the ford. General Curtis countered by having Colonel Ford send a battalion east along the road to skirmish with Jackman. The skirmishing continued in a dilatory fashion for half an hour. General Curtis became alarmed at the half-hearted manner in which Colonel Jackman was pressing toward the main crossing. It was then that General Sam Curtis realized the principal Confederate attack against his fortified line would come, not at this main ford across the Big Blue where he had made such elaborate plans, but at some other crossing upstream.[3] General Blunt had been right in his surmise last night.

Frantically General Curtis dispatched a message to Hickman Mills where General M. S. Grant had taken command at Russell's ford that morning. "Look out for your position," warned the harassed Curtis. "Send scouts out on road toward Pleasant Hill, and also toward Independence, to see if he [Price] is moving on my flank. Send me report every thirty minutes."[4]

General Curtis also sent two of his aides racing to give warning to General Blunt. Then he promptly moved his headquarters west along the road to the intersection of the Hickman Mills road. There he found a better position to watch all enemy movements along the Big Blue river.

In the meantime General Shelby had taken General M. Jeff Thompson's Brigade and had begun methodically to feel out the right of General Curtis' line. Colonel Jackman continued his feint at the main crossing until the wagon train had been brought up from Independence and headed down the Little Santa Fe road. Then breaking contact, Jackman rejoined General Shelby near Byram's ford.[5]

As General Jeff Thompson's cavalrymen probed the right of the Union line, they were unable to find a favorable crossing point. It was now well past eleven o'clock in the morning and General Shelby could delay no longer. He would have to force a crossing of the river and he determined on Byram's ford as the place for a breakthrough. It would be no easy task for Colonel Jennison with the First Brigade and a contingent of Colonel Blair's militiamen were favorably positioned for a stiff defense.

At Byram's ford the south fork of the Independence road crossed the Big Blue river and ascended a sharply rising hill on the west bank. Here on the road, as it made its ascent, Colonel Jennison placed the five howitzers of Lieutenant H. L. Barker's battery so that the guns commanded the east bank.[6] The ford itself had been filled with felled timber. The road was narrow and strewn with abatis. The banks of the river were steep and lined with a thick growth of trees and underbrush. Behind the guns the 15th Kansas Cavalry, the 3rd Wisconsin Cavalry and detachments of various Kansas State Militia units were dismounted and ready for any Rebel assault on the ford. General Shelby's task would be extremely difficult if the attack had to be entirely frontal.

Colonel Sidney Jackman, supported by M. Jeff Thompson, dismounted a part of his brigade and began the movement on the ford. It was slow going and the Union guns rendered the road across the ford impassable for massed troops. Still the Confederate attack persisted, a rush forward and then a mad dash back to the east bank amid the roar and pound of the Yankee artillery. Again and again Colonel Jackman lashed out only to be thrown back in confusion.[7]

By two o'clock in the afternoon General Shelby was convinced that Byram's ford could not be forced by a frontal attack. Instructing Colonel Jackman to continue pressure at the ford, General Shelby sent Colonel Frank B. Gordon with the 5th Missouri Confederate Cavalry upstream to find a crossing and Lieutenant Colonel Alonzo Slayback's Missouri Confederate Cavalry Battalion to seek one downstream. Neither had gone very far before accomplishing the mission. Colonel Slayback

79

easily found the little used Hinkle's ford which General Blunt had left unguarded. Men and horses splashed across the river in a wild dash and thundered south toward Colonel Jennison's unsuspecting left flank.

Colonel Jackman was charging Byram's ford with all his available force when Colonel Slayback hit Jennison's flank. It was too much for the bluecoated cavalrymen. The Yankee line rolled back and buckled. The Confederate flanking movement had succeeded and new gray columns came moving in at a right angle. Down logs blocked the artillery and General Shelby paused to see the way cleared for his guns. The wild ardent yell of the Rebel charge had begun up ahead again. Fragrant smoke from a burning thicket on the right mingled with the dark acrid smoke of the cannon, shutting out the sun, creating a murky twilight among the trees which crowded the narrow road as it crossed the ford. General M. Jeff Thompson with the Iron Brigade was coming up from the rear, and there was a smell of victory in the air. General Curtis' Army of the Border was crumpling. His sacrifice of men on the Little Blue so that this fortified line along the Big Blue river could be manned and completed was all for nothing. One more push from General Shelby's screaming veterans and General Curtis' line would be broken. The push was not long in coming.

General Blunt, on hearing Jennison's artillery fire that afternoon, had ordered Colonel Moonlight to abandon his position at Simmons' ford and to proceed southward in support of Colonel Jennison. However, Colonel Moonlight arrived at Hinkle's ford shortly after Colonel Slayback had made his crossing and therefore was in no position to assist Colonel Jennison who was now in full flight westward across the prairie. Colonel Moonlight, instantly comprehending what had occurred, ordered the Second Brigade at top speed toward Westport, hoping to reach the state line before Colonel Jennison and his pursuers could arrive there. Colonel Moonlight would then be in position to support Jennison and together the two of them might be able to prevent General Shelby from entering Kansas.[8]

Colonel Jennison with his ragtag force of cavalry and militia, completely out-flanked, had found his position at Byram's ford untenable. Momentarily scattered by Colonel Slayback's Rebel cavalry, the Yankee force nevertheless reunited and held long enough for Lieutenant Barker to pull out his battery. Then falling back steadily the blue cavalrymen continued to resist General Shelby's pursuit.

Colonel Gordon, going south along the river, had also found a ford suitable for a cavalry crossing soon after Colonel Slayback went across at Hinkle's. This was not too far north of the Hickman Mills crossing, the extreme right of General Curtis' line. Fording the river, Colonel Gordon and his 5th Missouri Confederate Cavalry found themselves squarely between two Yankee forces—Colonel Jennison's which was collapsing at Byram's ford and General M. S. Grant's militia force at the Hickman Mills crossing. However, the latter force was not in any better condition than Colonel Jennison's.

When General Grant received General Curtis' dispatch that Saturday morning warning him that General Price was going to try for a river crossing on the right of the Union line, General Grant had immediately sent large reconnoitering parties in all directions. As a result the militia general soon scattered his command and lost control of his troops.[9] When the breakthrough occurred at Byram's ford, General Grant was in no position to come to Colonel Jennison's aid with any appreciable number of militiamen. Colonel Veale with his 2nd Kansas State Militia, remnants of the 3rd Kansas State Militia, and two battalions from the 23rd Kansas State Militia under Lieutenant Colonel Guilford and the 13th Kansas State Militia under Lieutenant Colonel Johnson were all of General Grant's command available for action. These troops fell back rapidly in an effort to contact Colonel Jennison. They had arrived at the Mockabee farm on the Harrisonville road when Colonel Gordon with the

5th Missouri Confederate Cavalry, now reinforced by Colonel Jackman with a regiment and battalion of cavalry, hit them.[10]

The fight at the Mockabee farm was short but fierce, in many respects the fiercest of the many scattered engagements that took place that Saturday along the Big Blue river. Hastily forming his line in front of the old brass twenty-four pound howitzer which Captain Ross Burnes and his twenty artillerymen had hauled across the prairie, General Grant made his stand. Like seasoned veterans the Kansas farmers held their position and returned the Rebel fire. With their line finally broken in some confusion, the militiamen hastily reformed and returned to their deadly task.[11]

Captain Burnes, although under heavy fire, managed to get unlimbered. There was a moment of frantic activity about the gun and then a great wall of pallid, yellow smoke seemed to push out against the oncoming gray horsemen. The piece cracked and bellowed with thunder. The militiamen cheered and fired their rifles as the old cannon tore gaps in the Rebel ranks. Yet again the Kansans' line was broken and again it was reformed, one end resting in the Mockabee orchard, the other parallel to the lane leading from the Harrisonville road. But the Confederates had about all of this they could endure. Apparently exasperated by the deadly and stiff resistance of these raw Kansas farmers turned soldiers—pitifully few in numbers, with their old brass cannon, yet fighting like seasoned veterans—Colonels Jackman and Gordon arranged their lines and artillery for a final charge.[12] Every Confederate trooper was to become engaged. This would be a fight to the finish.

The Kansans saw the charge forming, but they did not waver. About the brass howitzer Captain Burnes drew his twenty gunners. Behind them Colonel Veale placed a battalion in support. The whole militia line was drawn in like a knot, strong and determined. Then lifting eerily in the hazy autumn air rose the Rebel yell. Abruptly it ended and in grim silence the gray horsemen galloped toward the waiting Kansans. "The prairie shook,"

"Death Was Everywhere—"

wrote General Shelby's adjutant, "the trampled grass, cut and whirled into yellow dust, rose up in clouds of smoke and minute particles. Not a shout, nor yell, nor battle-cry as the men neared the blue spot, coiled and massed like a group of rattlesnakes. Down went the Federal infantry to a man, rear rank and front rank, and a forest of bayonets seemed growing there and waving in the weird twilight. Death was everywhere, but no one saw him. Only the gaping guns vomiting grape—only the infantry and cavalry heating the air with bullets were before the eyes of the fierce Missourians. One swift, short, hungry yell now and no more. The Federal cannoneers were devoted soldiers and deserved a better fate; the supports beyond fought well at first, but in the murderous pistol combat they were no match for the Missourians, and rushed away toward Westport, disorganized and broken."[13]

The Rebel charge lasted but a very few minutes. When it was over General M. S. Grant no longer had a command. More than one hundred Kansas farmers lay dead in line. A larger number lay wounded. One hundred and two were held captive. The loss of horses was tremendous. Colonel Veale in his small battalion of 250 men lost twenty-four killed, an equal number wounded, eighty-eight taken prisoner, and one hundred horses destroyed.[14] All twenty artillerymen, along with Captain Burnes, lay dead or wounded, their old brass cannon in enemy hands.

Private Sam Reader of the 2nd Kansas State Militia was among the captives. That night he wrote of the event in his diary: "A Sanguinary field. Hot enough for anybody . . . Cap't. Burns fired 24 pounder cannon. It made an awful roar. Fox tried to break away. I lead him back to the road. I saw Judge Greer wounded in the leg, and I got him on Fox, and saw him ride toward the rear. I went to the right of the cannon. A rebel line came in front of us in the field & shot at our flag. I shot my carbine at them. Reloaded. I went with the boys in the orchard, and I shot my Springfield at the rebels, coming in a long line, yelling. We ran out in the lane, and I crossed in the field . . .

On looking back I saw the Rebels within 40 yards and their bullets flying around me, so I dropped down on my face."[15]

General Grant with remnants of his command escaped by a circuitous route to Olathe. Some of the 2nd and 23rd Kansas State Militia made their way to Wyandotte that night and then on the next day went to Kansas City. Colonels Jackman and Gordon, having rounded up their prisoners, and making arrangements for the care of their wounded and dead, moved out toward Westport to join the rest of General Shelby's division.

While the fight at the Mockabee farm was raging, General M. Jeff Thompson was having his troubles with the wily Colonel Jennison. The old Jayhawker was refusing to panic. His retreat toward Westport had been slow and stubborn. Time and again he lashed back at the pursuing Thompson. Because of Jennison's resistance Colonel Moonlight was able to join the First Brigade near the state line, a few miles south of Westport. Quickly deploying into line Jennison and Moonlight turned on General Jeff Thompson. Within a few minutes fighting with small arms had developed all along the line. The weary Rebel cavalry wavered and then began to fall back. Rapidly Colonels Jennison and Moonlight pressed their advantage and advanced the Yankee lines.

It was almost dark and General M. Jeff Thompson and the Iron Brigade had had enough. Breaking contact with the stubborn Yankees, the Rebel cavalrymen fell back two miles to the cover of some timber. Colonels Jennison and Moonlight were only too glad to cooperate with them. Maintaining their lines until darkness had fallen, the bluecoats then withdrew to Westport.[16]

With his right wing completely shattered, General Curtis had no recourse but to abandon his fortified line along the Big Blue river. General Blunt, learning that his line had been flanked at Byram's ford, immediately ordered General Deitzler with the left wing of the Army of the Border to fall back to Kansas City.[17] This the efficient militia general was able to do in fairly good order. Colonel A. C. Hogan with the 19th Kansas State Militia was designated as rear guard. As the colonel prepared to pull out of the line, he was sharply attacked by a detachment of five hundred cavalrymen from General Fagan's division. The skirmish was brief and vicious, a part of it being fought in the river. Colonel Hogan repulsed the attack and the Rebels fled leaving twelve dead in the stream and ten prisoners in the colonel's hands.[18]

General Deitzler completed his withdrawal before sunset and saw his militiamen safely stationed in the newly dug entrenchments around Kansas City. General Curtis, moving his headquarters to the Gillis House in Kansas City, had now pivoted back on his left and faced his line south instead of east. The unhappy General Blunt, having made certain of General Deitzler's safe withdrawal, rode to Westport, arriving there about the same time as Colonels Jennison and Moonlight. Blunt found Colonel Ford's Fourth Brigade in the town and immediately ordered it back to the Kansas City entrenchments along with McLain's Independent Colorado Battery. The 2nd Colorado Cavalry was left in Westport and the 16th Kansas Cavalry was ordered to hold the picket lines south of the village. Colonel Jennison's First Brigade was bivouacked north of Westport and Colonel Moonlight's Second Brigade just east of the Shawnee Mission.[19]

This same eventful Saturday also saw the long-awaited General Pleasonton and the Provisional Cavalry Division of the Department of the Missouri finally come up in the rear of the Confederate Army of Missouri. After General Pleasonton received Private Dan Boutwell's information that General Curtis was ready for combat, the dapper cavalry commander moved fast. Hastily constructing a temporary bridge over the Little Blue river to replace the one Colonel Moonlight had burned the previous day, Pleasonton crossed his troops, train, and artillery in a short period of time by utilizing that structure and a cavalry ford one-half mile downstream.[20]

General John McNeil of the Second Brigade took the advance with the 13th Missouri Union Cavalry, Colonel E. C. Catherwood commanding, and the 17th Illinois Cavalry, Colonel J. L. Beveridge commanding. They had not galloped far along the road to Independence before they bumped into General Price's rear guard, which was composed of Cabell's and Slemons' Brigades of General Fagan's division.[21]

The two Confederate brigades holding the eastern approaches to Independence had deployed in line of battle to await General Pleasonton's attack. A strong line of skirmishers supported by Captain W. M. Hughey's Arkansas Confederate Battery of Parrott guns was thrown out across the Independence road. General McNeil on making contact deployed his troopers and advanced against the Confederate skirmishers pressing them back upon the main body. General McNeil's advance was slow due to the well-directed fire from Captain Hughey's Parrott guns.[22] However, the Union pressure never ceased and gradually General Fagan was pushed from position to position. On the outskirts of Independence Confederate resistance stiffened and General McNeil called for additional troops. General Sanborn with the Third Brigade was immediately advanced to his aid as well as the veteran 7th Kansas Cavalry, Major F. M. Malone commanding. This regiment belonged to McNeil's Brigade.

Most of General Fagan's rear guard action up to this point had been done by Colonel W. F. Slemons' Brigade which was making a desperate effort to hold back General Pleasonton until the Confederate wagon train and beef herd had cleared Independence. The train and herd had been escorted to the Little Santa Fe road by a part of General W. L. Cabell's Brigade which was now returning to aid Colonel Slemons.[23]

It was three o'clock in the afternoon and Generals Sanborn and McNeil, now on the eastern outskirts of Independence, grouped their regiments for a movement through the town.

86

They hoped to clear the streets of the community in one grand charge and to push the retreating Rebels into the Big Blue river. Forming a close column of companies, General McNeil placed the 13th Missouri Union Cavalry in the vanguard and supported it with the 7th Kansas Cavalry and the 17th Illinois Cavalry. These units were to enter the town directly from the east at a gallop and with drawn sabers.[24] It was hoped that their momentum would carry them through the town.

General John Sanborn with the 2nd Arkansas Union Cavalry, Colonel John E. Phelps commanding, in the forefront, was to charge the town from the northeast and take the Rebels on the flank. The two movements were to be coordinated and not cease until Independence had been taken.

Over on the Union right the advance company of the 2nd Arkansas Union Cavalry had covered half the distance to the town before the order for the general charge was given. A thin gray skirmish line at the edge of the town kept up a rapid fire as it retired before the onrushing blue cavalrymen. Entering Independence, Colonel Phelps dismounted the 2nd Arkansas and sent it pouring into the streets ready for hand to hand combat.[25] As the 2nd Arkansas Union Cavalry rushed into the town, it slammed into General Cabell's Confederate Arkansans coming to Colonel Slemons' aid. The fight between the two forces became local in nature and was rough and bitter. The Union Arkansans succeeded in capturing 300 of their Confederate neighbors and almost taking General Cabell himself. The general, however, escaped by jumping over a piece of artillery, running through a passage of a double log cabin and jumping the yard fence.[26] Two days hence at Mine Creek General Cabell would not be quite so fortunate.

General McNeil's attack from the east was mounted and the yelling Union cavalrymen came charging into the streets of Independence with flags snapping and sabers waving. Fanning out, they swarmed through the town and raced toward the western limits. Metal twinkled just ahead, and suddenly a small band of

Confederates appeared, running a field gun down the street. The trail dropped and the muzzle swung around toward the charging Yankees and threatened them like the eye of a Cyclops. A spatter of shots popped and two of the gunners fell. Then heavy smoke rolled out of the cannon's muzzle and canister burst with a loud crack. But that was all. In seconds the blue wave poured over the gun and its crew.[27]

From the windows of stores and houses came a small but steady crackle of small-arms fire. Wild yelling rose above the noise and blue horsemen plunged headlong down the street behind their guidon. Here and there an isolated group of gray cavalrymen tried to maintain a running fight, but for the most part the Rebels fled, throwing away equipment as they ran. A section of Confederate artillery in Noah Miller's yard cut loose the traces as the artillerymen dropped their gun and caisson where they stood.[28] The men scrambled astride their horses and pounded off. Mrs. Robert Hill, from the balcony of her house, watched the Yankee charge and the seizure of the abandoned battery in her neighbor's yard.[29]

Generals Sanborn and McNeil having cleared the town, General Pleasonton then sent his First and Fourth Brigades after the retreating Rebels although darkness had fallen. Sanborn and McNeil were left to clean up the town, take care of the dead and wounded, and to bring up the Federal wagon train. The local bank was utilized as a Union hospital and the Jones Hotel as a Confederate hospital.[30] In the former, forty wounded Kansans from General Blunt's command were found. They had been left on the field in the previous evening's fighting.[31]

In the rapidly increasing darkness General Egbert Brown pushed his First Brigade out along the Independence-Westport road down which a portion of the Rebel rear guard was retiring. Coming upon them in the darkness, General Brown attacked and drove the Confederates some two miles down the road. General Brown then pulled back to Independence, having exhausted his ammunition, and requested Colonel Edward F. Winslow to take the advance with the Fourth Brigade.[32]

Colonel Winslow, a veteran combat officer and a natural born horse soldier, was as energetic and hard-hitting as his commanding officer, General Pleasonton. Out the Byram ford road galloped the Fourth Brigade. They had not gone far when they ran into enemy pickets. It was quite dark now, but Colonel Winslow quickly dismounted the 3rd Iowa Cavalry and deployed it across the road. He held the 4th Iowa Cavalry and the 7th Indiana Cavalry mounted and in column of fours in the road behind the 3rd Iowa. A detachment of the 10th Missouri Union Cavalry under its commander, Lieutenant Colonel Frederick W. Benteen, was sent to the left to find the enemy's right, and by firing and yelling to give the signal for the attack. It did not take the veteran Benteen long to accomplish his objective and upon signal the 3rd Iowa Cavalry rushed forward. The blue horsemen found the Confederate advance line partly concealed in a strip of timber along a small stream. The 3rd Iowa Cavalry, despite the darkness, soon drove the line back upon its supports and then, still backed by the 4th Iowa and the 7th Indiana, quickly compelled the whole Rebel force to retire.[33]

Not content with his initial success, Colonel Winslow regrouped his command and pressed steadily forward down the Byram ford road. By ten-thirty o'clock he had driven the Confederate cavalry to within three miles of the Byram ford crossing of the Big Blue river. Halting his command in the road, he ordered the Fourth Brigade to rest on its arms until all units could come up in the darkness. The 4th Iowa Cavalry, under Major Abial Pierce, then moved to the front of the brigade and remained mounted while awaiting orders to attack. As they waited the cavalrymen came under fire from the Rebels farther down the road and lost to sight in the impenetrable darkness. These Confederates were the 8th Missouri Confederate Cavalry, Colonel William L. Jeffers commanding, and had been acting as the rear guard for General John B. Clark's Brigade of Marmaduke's division. They had taken rather severe losses in the darkness as Colonel Winslow struck them time and again in their flight along the Byram ford road and they were mad.[34] Now in a more favorable position, they were ready to deal out punishment to Colonel Winslow's Brigade if another attack should come. But it didn't. Before Colonel Winslow could move his cavalry into action again, he received orders from General Pleasonton to wait for the moon to rise.[35]

The Fourth Brigade welcomed the order. After throwing out pickets, the weary troopers were soon in bivouac along the road. Determining that Colonel Winslow had ceased his advance, General Marmaduke withdrew the remainder of his division across Byram's ford and occupied the positions from which Colonel Jennison had been outflanked that afternoon. The exhausted grayclads threw themselves upon the ground and despite their hunger and the increasing cold were soon asleep.[36]

7. *"I Am Preparing to Renew the Attack"*

It was almost midnight when General Curtis rose from his desk at the Gillis House in Kansas City and went to meet his staff in an adjoining room of the hotel. A decisive plan of action for tomorrow's fighting had to be devised. Much of his optimism of Friday night had vanished, but not his determination to halt General Price and the Army of Missouri.

Soon after General Shelby had forced the crossing of the Big Blue river at Byram's ford, General Curtis had moved his headquarters to Kansas City. There he had received reports from his scattered units and there he had learned at last of General Pleasonton's attack on Independence. Quietly but skillfully, General Curtis directed the pivoting of his army as he changed the direction of his front.

Later that Saturday afternoon he had taken time to pay his last respects to the gallant major of the 2nd Colorado Cavalry. Major J. Nelson Smith, killed on the Little Blue, was buried just before sundown in a tiny cemetery near the McGee house north of Westport.[1] Because of the fluid military situation General Curtis did not remain for all of the ceremonies but returned in a very short time to his headquarters in the Gillis House.[2]

In all probability Major Smith's funeral must have reopened a deep wound in General Curtis' heart for upon returning to Kansas City his first act was to write a note to Mrs. Curtis:

Mrs. Curtis:

It is certain that among the rebels killed yesterday the notorious Todd, one of the murderers of our son, was one among
many who were killed. Their loss was much heavier than
mine. They are retreating northwest, but fighting us hard.

S. R. CURTIS,
Major-General[3]

General Curtis' son, Major Henry Z. Curtis, had been killed
in October, 1863, near Baxter Springs, Kansas, when Quantrill
and 250 of his guerrillas attacked General Blunt who with one
hundred men was on the way to Fort Smith. Major Curtis had
been General Blunt's adjutant at the time.[4]

After writing his wife, General Curtis began the task of
drawing together his widely scattered Army of the Border. Soon
after dark he had heard from all his brigade commanders as
well as from General Pleasonton. It was then that he wired
General Halleck in Washington, apprising him of the day's events
and assuring him that "I am preparing to renew the attack and
pursue it at daylight with all my available cavalry."[5] General
Curtis's mind was made up and he needed only to perfect his
plan of attack. For that purpose he had called for a meeting of
his staff.

It is not known what General Samuel Curtis really thought
about his situation that Saturday night. But as a professional
soldier he must have recognized his position to be most dangerous. Two of his strongest brigades, Colonel Jennison's First and
Colonel Moonlight's Second, were detached from the main body
of the Army of the Border, and, in turn, each of those brigades
was separated from the other. To make the situation even more
precarious, the main body, composed primarily of militia whose
performance had been most erratic that day, was pinned in the
apex of a triangle formed by the Missouri and Kansas rivers
which were neither bridged nor fordable. There was every
chance of General Curtis being annihilated the next morning
except for the fact that Generals Pleasonton and A. J. Smith

were now at hand. However, that afternoon, after taking Independence, General Pleasonton had sent a dispatch to General Rosecrans urging him to send A. J. Smith's infantry to Independence.[6] General Rosecrans reluctantly complied but in doing so pulled the infantry out of position to block the Army of Missouri if it should suddenly turn or be pushed south.[7]

If General Curtis' position was dangerous, General Sterling Price's was even more so. The Confederate commander was confronting two Union forces on two fronts. The divisions of Generals Shelby and Fagan, minus General W. L. Cabell's Brigade, were strung out above the south bank of Brush Creek from the state line eastward to where the creek flows into the Big Blue river. General Marmaduke's division was concentrated along the west bank of the Big Blue opposite Byram's ford. However, the immense wagon train of the Confederate Army of Missouri was still east of the Big Blue river moving southwestward toward Little Santa Fe and the military road to Fort Scott. The 600 wagons, heavily laden with the "fruits" of the expedition, and accompanied by a herd of 3,000 cattle, were guarded only by General Cabell's Brigade and a rag-tag brigade of unarmed recruits under Colonel Charles H. Tyler.[8] If General Price chose to engage the Army of the Border along Brush Creek the next morning, it would be possible for General Pleasonton's cavalry to swing southward, cut off the Confederate line of retreat, capture the wagon train, or both. If General Marmaduke was successful in holding Byram's ford then it was still possible for General A. J. Smith's veteran infantry, now nearing Chapel Hill, to swing in behind the Confederate army and destroy the train. In either case General Price and the Army of Missouri would face annihilation.

But General Sterling Price that Saturday night was determined above all else to save the wagon train. He chose to attack the Union Army of the Border at dawn with Fagan's and Shelby's divisions while General Marmaduke kept General Pleasonton from crossing the Big Blue.[9] Fortunately for the Confederate

commander, General Rosecrans had issued the ill-fated order re-
calling General A. J. Smith from Chapel Hill.

From his headquarters in the Boston Adams house, a mile
and one-half south and west of Byram's ford, General Price
wrote the order for General Cabell to put the wagon train
and beef herd in motion along the Hickman Mills road until
he could take the wagon road leading southwest to the military
road at Little Santa Fe.[10]*Orders were sent to Generals Shelby
and Fagan to attack at dawn and General Marmaduke was instructed to hold Byram's ford. With his plans readied, old Pap
sought his bed for the few hours that remained before daybreak.

Midnight had passed and General William S. Rosecrans was
still in his headquarters at Lexington, Missouri, writing a final
dispatch to General Pleasonton. Old Rosy dated it "October 23,
1864—1 a. m." It was brief, telling the dapper cavalry commander that General Smith had been ordered to march to Independence by the shortest route and for Pleasonton to delay
a general engagement until Smith and the infantry could
come up.[11]

Apparently General Pleasonton never received this dispatch
for in his communications of October 23 Pleasonton writes as
though he expected General Smith to arrive momentarily at
Pleasant Hill.[12] Shortly after penning the message to Pleasonton, the troubled Rosecrans left Lexington, accompanied by the
1st Iowa Cavalry, and galloped off into the darkness toward
Independence.[13]

That same midnight saw General Alfred Pleasonton send
General John McNeil and the Second Brigade south on the
Independence road with instructions to proceed to Little Santa
Fe by daylight.[14] The enterprising Pleasonton was not intending
to depend entirely upon A. J. Smith and the infantry to get in
behind the Confederate army. After General McNeil began his
movement, Pleasonton ordered General Egbert Brown to take
the First Brigade out along the Byram ford road, relieve Colonel
Winslow's Fourth Brigade, which had gone into bivouac three

miles east of the ford, and attack the enemy at daybreak.[15] The Third and Fourth Brigades would support.

It was two o'clock in the morning when General Pleasonton completed his arrangements for the attack. He was still ignorant of General Curtis' plans for the new day and it must have been with an uneasy mind that he lay down by the side of the road for a brief rest. So much could be accomplished during the Sunday that would soon dawn. Yet, so many things could go wrong.

About the time General Pleasonton completed his plans, General Sam Curtis' conference with his staff at the Gillis House in Kansas City was breaking up. The decision had been made to stand and fight at Westport.[16] By 3 a. m. orders were coming out of General Curtis' headquarters and the Federal concentration along Brush Creek had commenced.

Rations and ammunition were rushed from Kansas City to Westport and hastily distributed among the divisions of Generals Blunt and Deitzler. Colonel Jennison was ordered to move his First Brigade from its camps around the A. B. H. McGee farm just north of Westport to a position along Brush Creek. Colonel Moonlight at the Shawnee Mission was to deploy his Second Brigade in line of battle along the state line south of Brush Creek. Colonel Ford with the Fourth Brigade was moved from Westport to Brush Creek, taking a position on the left of Jennison. Colonel Blair and his Third Brigade moved south out of Westport in support of the First and Fourth Brigades. General Deitzler was assigned the task of bringing all militia units out of the entrenchments around Kansas City and concentrating them at Westport. The Kansas City Home Guards were to remain in Camp Union within the city and in the earthworks surrounding the city until they received further orders. Then word went out to General Blunt to attack at daybreak and a verbal message was sent to General Pleasonton informing him of General Curtis' intent.[17]

The die was cast. All available troops in the Federal Army of the Border were to be engaged; none were to be held back. Here in front of this already historic frontier outpost of Westport, the fate of this borderland would be decided, once and for all time.

Dawn came with an agonizing slowness. First daylight seemed to rise out of the earth and to filter eastward across the tops of the timber along Brush Creek. Smoke lifted in tendrils from a hundred encampments and stood in lean columns in the cold air. The early morning had a taut, stealthy chill to it; the water in the creek bore a thin crust of ice.

KEY TO SYMBOLS
▨ CONFEDERATE
▬ UNION

⬚ BATTERY
▦ TOWNS

ACTION BEFORE WESTPORT
ABOUT 11 A.M. OCT. 23rd 1864

TO KANSAS CITY

WESTPORT

ROAD TO INDEPENDENCE

N
W — E
S

SHAWNEETOWN

11th KANSAS CAVALRY

19th KANSAS MILITIA
10th KANSAS MILITIA
BARKER'S BATTERY
6th KANSAS MILITIA
15th KANSAS CAVALRY
9th WIS. BATTERY

COLORADO BATTERY
16th KANSAS CAVALRY

4th KANSAS MILITIA
2nd COLORADO CAVALRY

BRUSH CREEK

CURTIS

CO. G
11th KANSAS CAVALRY

SHAWNEE MISSION

5 KANS.
CAVALRY

BENT'S HOUSE

11th MO. CAVALRY
JACKMAN'S MO. CAVALRY
6th MO. CAVALRY
5th MO. CAVALRY

COLLIN'S BATTERY

BLOCHER'S
ARKANSAS
BATTERY

SHELBY and FAGAN

SLAYBACK'S
MO. CAVALRY
SIMPSON'S HOUSE

HUNTER'S
CAVALRY MO.

ELLIOT'S MO. CAVALRY
WILLIAMS' MO. CAVALRY

McCRAY'S MO. CAVALRY
47th ARKANSAS CAVALRY

HARRISONVILLE ROAD

MARMADUKE

PLEASONTON

BIG BLUE RIVER

12th KANSAS CAVALRY

STATE LINE ROAD

DOBBIN'S BRIGADE

WORNALL'S LANE

WORNALL HOME

SLEMMONS' BRIGADE

45th ARKANSAS CAVALRY

ADAMS HOUSE

BYRAM'S FORD

SHELBY'S   LAST LINE OF DEFENSE

HINKLE'S GROVE

FOREST HILL CEMETERY

LITTLE SANTA FE'

CONFEDERATE WAGON TRAIN MOVED ALONG

CABELL'S BRIGADE
THIS V ROAD

HICKMAN MILLS

McNEIL'S BRIGADE

8. Sunday, October 23, 1864

By DAYLIGHT General James Blunt had completed the disposition of his division along the north bank of Brush Creek. The heavy timber which bordered the shallow stream at an average depth from north to south of two miles had made his work in the darkness doubly hard.[1] At the extreme left of the Union line he had placed the 2nd Colorado Cavalry, now commanded by Major J. H. Pritchard. On the right of the Coloradoans was the 16th Kansas Cavalry whose right flank rested on Wornall's lane, a narrow country road which crossed the creek and meandered southward through the timber and over the heights above the stream. Planted in the middle of this road was Captain W. D. McLain's Independent Colorado Battery, its six rifled field pieces ready to race up the lane in support of the Union line. These units comprised Colonel James H. Ford's Fourth Brigade and numbered approximately nine hundred men.[2]

To the west of Wornall's lane was Colonel Jennison's First Brigade with an additional six hundred men.[3] From the country lane to the state line the regiments deployed were the 3rd Wisconsin Cavalry and the 15th Kansas Cavalry. The brigade's battery of five howitzers under Lieutenant H. L. Barker was in position on a rise of ground behind the brigade.

Colonel Moonlight's Second Brigade was strung out along the Westport-Shawnee Mission road at right angle to the First

Brigade. The 11th Kansas Cavalry was in line perpendicular to the 15th Kansas Cavalry and the 5th Kansas Cavalry (companies L and M) were on the right of the 15th Kansas and also facing east. The four howitzers manned by Company E of the 11th Kansas Cavalry were in support of their regiment.[4]

With the 1,500 veterans of the First and Fourth Brigades, General Blunt intended to launch his initial attack. As Colonels Jennison and Ford advanced, Colonel Moonlight would be in position as needed to come either upon the Rebel left flank or to swing in behind the two attacking brigades with additional support. By this movement General Blunt sought to gain time for the Kansas Militia to come up from Kansas City and Westport and deploy. Only with sufficient reserves could General Blunt ever hope to destroy Shelby and Fagan.[5]

The day dawned clear and cold but with a morning mist that hugged the ground. With the rising of the sun, General Blunt ordered the advance. Carefully the First and Fourth Brigades crossed the ice-coated creek and pushed up through the timber and over the heights south of the stream. With them moved the artillery, following the lane.

The Yankees emerged from the timber onto a softly rolling plateau criss-crossed with neat stone fences and well-tended fields. A skirmish line was thrown out in a cornfield just south of the Bent house and to the west of Wornall's lane.[6] Cautiously the blue line crept forward, every soldier's eyes straining to penetrate the mist ahead and ears tuned to catch the slightest movement from the timber that swept like a crescent along the state line on their immediate right.

One mile to the south, beyond the Wornall house, the Confederate cavalry was already in motion, riding to meet the blue skirmish line. Just before daylight Generals Shelby and Fagan had received their orders to attack General Curtis and hold him before Westport thus keeping the road open for the Confederate wagon train and beef herd to march southward.[7] In accordance with these orders the Confederate battle line was formed. General Shelby's division took the advance with General Jeff Thompson's Iron Brigade in the center and units of Colonel Jackman's Brigade on both flanks. In support of the line were two of General Fagan's brigades—Colonel Archibald S. Dobbin's and Colonel W. F. Slemons'.[8] Colonel T. H. McCray's Brigade of Fagan's division was strung out south of Brush Creek near the Harrisonville road.

Off in the mist that masked the front a single shot cracked out and was answered by a broken ripple of fire as the gray skirmish line started shooting through the haze. Shapes began to show ahead and the gun crews with the Yankee batteries in Wornall's lane sprang to their positions. The shapes came on, broke into a sharp trot. These were the blue skirmishers falling back.

Hastily the Yankee cavalrymen dismounted, sent their horses to the rear, and advanced to meet their skirmishers. Then the mist in front was suddenly shattered with a series of dull flashes. The bluecoats flung themselves on the ground and resumed their firing.[9]

Out in the lane Captain McLain raised his hand, dropped it. The gunners of the Independent Colorado Battery snapped the lanyards and fire crashed out, smothering the thin, sharp spatter of the rifles. Rammer staffs whirled, cannoneers covered the vents with leather-shielded thumbs, the pieces were run back into place from their recoil. "One of the first shots knocked off the head of a man in Slayback's Battalion, as smooth as a guillotine could have cut it," wrote General M. Jeff Thompson.[10]

The cannon and rifles made a continuous din that rose in volume to a steady, rattling crescendo as more and more Yankee artillery went into action. Men came running up from the rear, bringing extra ammunition from the limbers, and jumped to their posts at the pieces. Off to the right the 3rd Wisconsin Cavalry and the 15th Kansas Cavalry were firing steadily, blasting into the mist that drifted to show long lines of gray figures coming on at a steady lope. The mist dropped again, lifted, dropped. The gray lines had slowed down. Over on the left the attackers had halted entirely, thrown themselves to the ground and opened a careful fire on the 2nd Colorado Cavalry and 16th Kansas Cavalry.[11]

An hour went by and the firing increased; so did the pressure exerted by Generals Shelby and Fagan. Then slowly, from fence to fence, the Federal line was pushed back to the timber along the heights above the creek. Regaining their horses, the First and Fourth Brigades retreated to the north bank of Brush Creek and the Second Brigade to Shawnee Mission.[12]

General Shelby did not press his advantage. Ammunition had run low and the gray cavalrymen had to wait for their supply to be replenished. "The men were now thoroughly exasperated," wrote General M. Jeff Thompson, "and had we not had to wait for more ammunition, I believe that I could have taken Westport with that portion of the Brigade then with me."[13]

Within an hour a supply of ammunition was obtained but the Confederate advantage had been lost. Shelby and Fagan remained on the heights south of Brush Creek and awaited General Curtis' next move. It was not long in coming.

General Curtis arrived in Westport and set up his headquarters in the Harris House at about the same time General Blunt began to fall back across Brush Creek.[14] From the roof of the hotel, Curtis' staff officers had witnessed the repulse of General Blunt's division. They immediately informed General Curtis on his arrival of the precarious situation of the Army of the Border. The General hurried to the rooftop where he found General Blunt surveying with his field glass the Rebel forces deployed in endless lines beyond the timber of Brush Creek.[15]

The view, instead of adding to General Curtis' depression, seemed to revive the victor of Pea Ridge, and for the next two hours Union headquarters bustled with frantic activity. Orders were given to General Blunt to engage all of his artillery but not to advance his lines until his brigades had been reinforced by the Kansas Militia still moving southward out of Kansas City and Westport.[16]

General Blunt hurried to join his division sprawled along the north bank of Brush Creek and to position his artillery. The blue cavalrymen lay there for the next hour among the trees, waiting in the warming sun that filtered down through the blackjacks. The spatter of skirmish fire ran along the lines, swelled, abated, and then swelled again as artillery joined in far over to the right. Then the batteries all along the ridge to their rear opened fire on the wooded crest to their front. The projectiles whirred overhead and burst in the trees with a muffled sound, and sometimes they could see dirt and smoke shower upward, but more often they could see nothing at all.[17]

A few minutes after the Yankee guns opened the Confederate artillery began to reply, and now the blue troopers could see the pale flame leap from the imperfectly concealed Rebel batteries on the crest as a salvo started on its way. Behind them and to their left, the shells began to burst, spewing dirty smoke and cracking loudly, for all the world like giant firecrackers.

Since sun-up Colonel Charles W. Blair had been striving feverishly to get his Third Brigade into battle position. This brigade, consisting of the 4th, 5th, 6th, 10th, and 19th regiments of Kansas State Militia, with the 9th Wisconsin Battery and a section of artillery belonging to the Colored Battery under Lieutenant Miner, moved into line like seasoned veterans. The artillery fire and General Blunt's initial assault seemed only to increase the brigade's appetite for action.[18] Part of the brigade joined the left of the Fourth Brigade and the remainder the right of the Second Brigade in time for the first attack. A battalion of the 12th Kansas State Militia, arriving from Westport, was immediately absorbed in Colonel Moonlight's Second Brigade.[19]

General Curtis had now joined General Blunt along Brush Creek. Although militiamen were still pouring southward toward the front, Sam Curtis felt he could wait no longer. Word went out that the general himself would lead the next attack.

Sunday, October 23, 1864

Riding to the right of the line Curtis galloped to join Colonel Blair, who with part of his brigade and the 9th Wisconsin Battery was preparing to move forward.[20]

Restlessly the militiamen waited for orders to advance. All down the line men were checking the loads in their rifles, tightening their belts, pulling their hats down still farther over their eyes, as if the hat brim were some sort of shield that would protect them from the withering fire that was sure to appear the moment they started moving over the timbered heights.

It was almost eleven o'clock and before General Curtis could reach a position to lead the attack Colonel Blair on the extreme right of the line went into action. Believing he was about to be flanked, the enterprising commander of the Third Brigade splashed across the creek with the 10th, 5th and 6th Kansas State Militia and moved into the dense timber.[21] This movement he initiated without orders but sent a messenger to find General Curtis and inform the commanding general of what had been done. Upon receipt of the message Curtis sent the 19th Kansas State Militia in support of Blair with orders to swing around on Blair's right. Colonel Blair's Third Brigade now held the right of the Union line along Brush Creek since General Blunt had ordered Colonel Moonlight to take the Second Brigade and pass around the enemy, keeping between the Confederates and Kansas.[22]

General Curtis immediately ordered the remainder of his line forward. Taking the 9th Wisconsin Battery and his escort, which consisted of Company G of the 11th Kansas Cavalry and Lieutenant Edward Gill's two mountain howitzers, Curtis attempted to lead them up the heights. At first the advance made progress but before the blue line could reach the crest, the dashing General Shelby had reinforced his line and beaten the attackers back. Once more the Army of the Border retreated to Brush Creek. There General Curtis regrouped his forces and advanced up the heights again.

It was then that George Thoman, a farmer living just south

of Westport, came up to General Curtis and offered to show him a defile that led to the plain south of the heights. The defile proved to be a narrow gulch cut by Swan Creek which flowed from the southwest into Brush Creek.[23]

George Thoman was more than eager to aid the Army of the Border. Some soldiers had stolen his gray mare, along with some hams and tableware, the night before and he was certain the thieves had been Confederates. With his burly beard quivering and in his broken German accent he had pleaded with them not to take the mare as she was about to foal and would be of little use to them. Not understanding him or not caring, the intruders failed to heed his pleas and took the animal. Concerned for the mare, the farmer had gone to look for her that Sunday morning and had wandered into the Union lines.[24]

Refusing General Curtis' offer of a ride, George Thoman led the general and his escort with the 9th Wisconsin Battery up the gulch to a position just west and south of the Bent farmhouse. They were now on the left and rear of General Shelby's line. Quickly the battery unlimbered and went into action. The movement caught the Confederates totally unaware. The guns bellowed and roared as they started firing down the Rebel lines. For a few minutes Shelby's line wavered, fell back from the crest and across the little south valley. There it held as Captain Richard A. Collins of the Iron Brigade wheeled his battery into position to engage the 9th Wisconsin Battery. Captain Collins' four Parrott guns erupted with a violence that brought cheers from the Rebel line. The Wisconsin Battery increased its fire, aided now by Lieutenant Gill's two mountain howitzers.[25]

While General Curtis was negotiating the Swan Creek defile, General James Blunt had been pressing up the heights of Brush Creek with the First and Fourth Brigades. The going had been extremely difficult and was not meeting with any great degree of success until the 9th Wisconsin Battery went into action on the Rebel left and rear. Then with a terrible shout the Army of the Border poured up and over the heights of Brush Creek.

Sunday, October 23, 1864

Immediately occupying the stone fences from which the Confederates had fled when outflanked by General Curtis, General Blunt's forward movement halted while the Union artillery was brought up the heights and positioned. Captain E. D. McLain's Colorado Battery occupied the crest on the west side of Wornall's lane. Its six rifled field pieces joined the chorus of roaring guns that swelled across the little valley. Up came Lieutenant Barker's five twelve-pounders, Lieutenant D. C. Knowles' Battery of the 2nd Kansas State Artillery, and additional pieces from the militia units, all of which had now arrived on the field.[26]

The Union line left the shelter of the stone walls and inched forward across the valley as the volume of artillery fire increased. Stubbornly the grayclads fought back in sharp and bitter thrusts against the advancing blue line. Then, without warning, pressure on General Shelby's line slackened, died away altogether as the bluecoats fell back to the stone walls. It would not be for long, however. Already the blue ranks were massing across the little valley again and soon a bugle shrilled and the ranks spilled down into the little valley from the crest and came at the gray line once more.

Things had not gone too badly for Generals Shelby and Fagan in this last assault. The Yankee lunge against the Confederate center and right had been shattered. But over that wrecked attack other blueclads had poured yelling. Twice the Confederate center had bulged back to where Collins' battered guns were still dueling with the 9th Wisconsin Battery, and lapped around the flanks. But each time it had sprung back, once through a bare-toothed slamming charge of Colonel Slayback's Missourians and once by a stinging flank movement by Colonel Gordon and his 5th Missouri Confederate Cavalry.[27]

The artillery fire never slackened. For an hour now the gunfire from more than forty cannon had rolled and swelled from the farmland and the woods south of Brush Creek.[28] Sometimes it reached a high, obscene roar that precluded speech; sometimes it dropped to a low grumbling. Rags of gray battle smoke were caught on the distant trees, and the sun shone with merciless revelation on the festering wounded and the battered gray and blue regiments sprawled behind the irregular stone walls. So hot was Collins' fire as he dueled with the 9th Wisconsin Battery that he burst one of his Parrotts.[29]

Blocher's Arkansas Confederate Battery was wheeled into position directly across Wornall's lane from the Ben Simpson house which was nestled in a cluster of tall pines east of the road. The gunners were ramming home a charge when the terrain in front of the house erupted without warning. A wild scream high in air was followed by a splintering of boards and glass, a trembling of the walls as a Yankee shot crashed into the building. Then another and another.

Lumps of plaster pattered down through the pines and the air was riddled with splinters. The sky above ripped and crashed. Shot thudded into the ground in a whirl of clods, skidded, bounced, crashed into the house, against trees, or vanished into the unseen rear. The volume of Yankee fire increased. It came from McLain's Independent Colorado Battery whose position still was at the edge of the timber along the crest south of Brush Creek.[30]

The whole blue line edged forward and by noon had succeeded in occupying the lane just south of the Bent house. Shelby's two brigades with Dobbin's Brigade of Fagan's division had fallen back to a row of stone walls just north of the Wornall house. General Fagan, with Slemons' and McCray's Brigades had swung eastward toward the Harrisonville road to meet the threat that seemed to be developing in that direction, for the sound of General Pleasonton's guns at Byram's ford was definitely increasing.[31]

As the lines advanced and retreated, so likewise did the artillery. More than thirty Federal cannon were now in action and their fire had been devastating. Collins' Confederate Battery had been reduced to one gun, the remainder having been wrecked by Union artillery fire.[32] McLain's Colorado Battery of rifled field pieces was causing particular damage to General Shelby's

Major General James G. Blunt commanded the First Provisional Cavalry Division of the Union Army of the Border. The brigades in this division were composed primarily of Kansas regiments and militia as well as the 2nd Colorado Cavalry. (Kansas State Historical Society, Topeka)

Colonel Thomas Moonlight commanded the Second Brigade of Blunt's division at the Battle of Westport. (State Historical Society, Topeka)

Senator James Henry Lane, the fiery Kansas free-soil politician, served as an aide to General Blunt in 1864. (Kansas State Historical Society, Topeka)

Much controversy and romantic notion surround the almost mythical but minor roles played by Hickok and Cody at the Battle of Westport. (Kansas State Historical Society, Topeka)

Major General James G. Blunt and staff. (Kansas State Historical Society, Topeka)

Major General Samuel R. Curtis, commander of the Army of the Border in Missouri in 1864. Curtis' Department of Kansas would suffer a prolonged Indian War because of his preoccupation with Price's Confederates. (State Historical Society of Missouri, Columbia)

"Banished" to the Trans-Mississippi front by his superiors, Major General Alfred S. Pleasonton commanded the Provisional Cavalry Division of Rosecrans' Army of the Department of Missouri. (State Historical Society of Missouri, Columbia)

Major General William Starke Rosecrans, Pleasonton's commander, likewise had been transferred west in 1864. (State Historical Society of Missouri, Columbia)

Major General Sterling Price. Noted for his military actions at Taos Pueblo during the Mexican War and at Lexington and Westport during the Civil War, "Old Pap" was a better politician than military commander. (State Historical Society of Missouri, Columbia)

A Yale and Harvard scholar, Major General John S. Marmaduke was the last major general to be appointed by the Confederacy. The commission came while Marmaduke was in prison following his capture at the Battle of Mine Creek. (State Historical Society of Missouri, Columbia)

Arguably the best Confederate commander in Missouri during 1864, Brigadier General Joseph O. Shelby would go to Mexico after the war rather than surrender. (State Historical Society of Missouri, Columbia)

Captain George Todd. Sterling Price's denunciation of the border guerrilla chieftains like Todd deprived the Confederates of one of their most effective weapons of terror. (State Historical Society of Missouri, Columbia)

Brigadier General Meriwether Jeff Thompson commanded
Shelby's famous Iron Brigade. (State Historical Society of Missouri, Columbia)

lines as it steadily advanced, always maintaining a position just west of Wornall's lane with one section planted in the road itself. These guns were supported by two squadrons of the 2nd Colorado Cavalry. The battery had just taken position again and was unlimbering when Colonel James H. McGhee with his Confederate Arkansas Cavalry, Dobbin's Brigade, came thundering down the lane toward the guns.

Colonel Jennison, leading the Union advance on the right of the battery, saw the Confederate charge forming and realized that a desperate effort would be required to save the guns. If he could possibly come upon the flank of the charging Arkansans before they reached the battery, he might be able to knock them out of position. Looking about him for help, Colonel Jennison seized upon Company E of the 15th Kansas Cavalry. The company's captain, Curtis Johnson, had also seen the danger and hastily rallied his horsemen to follow the colonel.[33]

There was momentary confusion at the head of the forming column but it quickly dissolved as the blue horsemen grasped the situation. A shout from the colonel and then they were racing down the slope toward the flank of the charging Rebels. One hundred yards and the ground rose and the fearful din ahead rose with it. Colonel Jennison vaulted a stone wall; his troopers following him cleared the same wall and drove ahead through a cornfield toward Wornall's lane. Hot noises keened through the air and the dry cornstalks rustled to the rap-rap of spent bullets. A new sound arose, thin and knife-like. It came from the charging gray column, a high, human yipping, "Yi-yi-yi-yi!" The Rebel yell, and the shock of it struck each blue horseman like a clenched fist. The keening noise grew thicker, closer, as the Yankee column raced nearer. Then came a dull crash and a clatter that rose above the shrieking of animals and the shouts of men as the blue and gray columns collided at an angle. The wild melee that followed was a desperate hand-to-hand contest, each soldier fighting his own personal war.[34]

Captain Curtis Johnson singled out the Arkansans' leader,

Colonel McGhee, for personal combat. As if by common consent, each drew his revolver and riding headlong toward his opponent, each fired at the same moment. Captain Johnson reeled in the saddle as the ball tore through his arm. Colonel McGhee pitched from his horse, a bullet in his heart. Jennison's little troop fought desperately and then began to waver as the Confederates' superior numbers began to tell. It was then that the two squadrons of the 2nd Colorado Cavalry, supporting Mc-Lain's Battery, charged in upon the Arkansans who broke and fled leaving twenty-five dead and wounded on the field and a hundred prisoners in Colonel Jennison's hands.[35]

Once more the Union line commenced its forward movement. First it was the Third Brigade on the extreme right that began demonstrations against Shelby's line, then it was the center under Colonel Jennison that increased its pressure. All the while the Colorado and Wisconsin batteries kept pouring in their heavy charges.

At about this time General Shelby received word that General Marmaduke had fallen back from Byram's ford. Immediately withdrawing Colonel Jackman's Brigade from the line, he sent it back to find the wagon train. Colonel Jackman never found it. Before he had gone very far to the rear, he met couriers from General Fagan asking for help at the gallop for the whole prairie east of the Harrisonville road "was dark with Federals."[36] General Pleasonton had forced a crossing of the Big Blue river and the whole right flank and rear of the Confederate army was exposed.

With the departure of Colonel Jackman's Brigade, General Shelby was left with only the Iron Brigade to hold Curtis' Army of the Border. It was almost one o'clock now and the blue line was steadily moving closer.

General Sam Curtis, hearing the sound of battle on the Rebel flank and rear, ordered a general charge. Colonel Jennison hastily formed his First Brigade across Wornall's lane and with additional help from the 2nd Colorado Cavalry advanced down

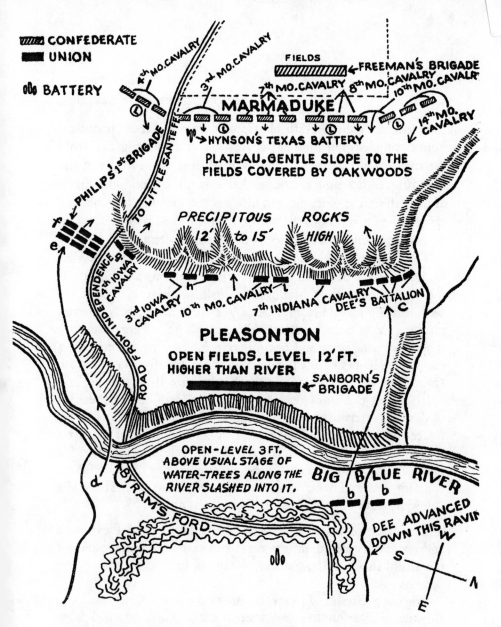

CONFEDERATE
UNION
BATTERY

× MO.CAVALRY

3rd MO.CAVALRY

FIELDS ← FREEMAN'S BRIGADE
7th MO.CAVLRY   8th MO.CAVALRY   10th MO.CAVALR
MARMADUKE   14th MO.
→ HYNSON'S TEXAS BATTERY   CAVALRY
PLATEAU. GENTLE SLOPE TO THE
FIELDS COVERED BY OAKWOODS

PHILIP'S 1st BRIGADE

TO LITTLE SANTEFE

f
e

PRECIPITOUS   ROCKS
12' to 15'   HIGH

ROAD FROM INDEPENDENCE

4th IOWA CAVALRY
g
3rd IOWA   h
CAVALRY   10th MO. CAVALRY   i   7th INDIANA CAVALRY
DEE'S BATTALION
C

PLEASONTON
OPEN FIELDS. LEVEL 12'FT.
HIGHER THAN RIVER
SANBORN'S
← BRIGADE

OPEN-LEVEL 3 FT.
ABOVE USUAL STAGE OF
WATER-TREES ALONG THE   BIG BLUE RIVER
RIVER SLASHED INTO IT.

d
BYRAM'S FORD   b   b
DEE ADVANCED
DOWN THIS RAVIN
W
S
E   N

BYRAM'S FORD 11A.M. OCT. 23rd 1864

a. BATTERY PLANTED BY ∼
PLEASONTON
b DEE'S 1st ADVANCED
POSITION
c DEE'S 2nd POSITION
d PHILIP S' 1st POSITION
e PHILIP S' 2nd POSITION

g 4th IOWA CAVALRY (h) 3rd
(h) IOWA CAVALRY (i) 10th
MISSOURI CAVALRY (j) 7th
INDIANA CAVALRY

(f) PHILIP S 1st BRIGADE
(L) MAIN LINE OF REBELS

the road at a gallop. With clouds of dust rising from pounding hoofs, the charging blue cavalrymen took a flanking fire from the roadside as they passed the Wornall house and then met the Iron Brigade head on a little farther down the road. The shock of the collision echoed, merged into a screaming, hacking, blazing tangle of men and horses, fighting hand to hand with sabers and revolvers, many of the troopers unhorsed in combat.[37]

The Iron Brigade began to fray out at the sides, wavered. Men broke in quick panic, threw away their weapons and accoutrements as though they found safety in disassociating themselves with the fighting. General Shelby rode among the fugitives, pleading with them to stand. General M. Jeff Thompson was everywhere, fighting and encouraging his rapidly disintegrating command. Knots of men staggered about blindly, faced to the front, then to the rear, while the Yankee fire from the east and north struck them down. A ripping salvo from one of Pleasonton's newly-arrived batteries, now unlimbered in Hinkle's Grove, poured in upon the Rebel flank and the remnants of the Iron Brigade fled to the rear. It was a pell-mell gallop, every man for himself. They galloped until they came to a string of stone fences running east and west as far as the eye could see. There the Confederates rallied and turned "like lions at bay."[38]

The chain of events which had brought General Pleasonton and his cavalrymen upon the right and rear of General Shelby's command that autumn Sunday afternoon had been devious and bloody.

Brigadier General Egbert B. Brown, commanding the First Brigade of Pleasonton's provisional calvary division, had been instructed to move his brigade forward and attack the enemy at Byram's ford at daybreak, coordinating his assault with that of General Curtis along Brush Creek. To execute this order it was necessary for Brown's Brigade to relieve Colonel Winslow's Fourth Brigade which was in advance along the Byram ford road. However, General Brown was tardy in starting his columns that morning and it was almost two hours after daylight before he had passed Winslow's Brigade and assumed the advance.[39]

General Pleasonton, who had spent the night by the side of the road in the rear of his division, rose at daybreak and soon thereafter became alarmed at hearing no sound of an attack at the ford. Time passed and still no thunder of artillery or clatter of small arms fire stirred the quiet of that bright blue Sunday morning. The commanding general waited no longer. Mounting his horse, he galloped down the road toward the ford. Racing past the Third and Fourth Brigades, he came upon the rear of the First Brigade strung out along the road and certainly in no condition to attack. The general's temper flared. He placed Colonel James McFerran of the 1st Missouri State Militia Cavalry under arrest and then thundered up to the head of the column. There he found General Brown in consultation with Colonel Winslow but no evidence of any preparation for an attack.[40]

It was more than the West Point trained Pleasonton could endure. He severely reprimanded the hapless General Brown, placed him under arrest and sent him to the rear. Then turning to Colonel John F. Philips, commanding the 7th Missouri State Militia Cavalry, General Pleasonton placed him in command of the First Brigade and ordered an immediate attack on the ford in conjunction with Winslow's Fourth Brigade.[41]

Colonel Winslow immediately took charge of the situation. He noted that the Union cavalry was resting on a hill about one hundred feet above the river and that the road to the ford swung down the face of the hill three hundred yards to the ford. Winslow placed Battery H, 2nd Missouri Light Artillery, consisting of three three-inch Rodman guns, just east of the brow of the hill and near where the road swung downward to the river. These guns under Lieutenant Philip Smiley quickly opened fire on the enemy artillery and the advanced Rebel line resting on the west bank of the Big Blue. Colonel Philips dismounted all of his brigade except the 4th Missouri and taking position to the left of the road pushed forward toward the ford. Simultaneously with Colonel Philips' advance, Captain Edward Dee with the Third Battalion of the 4th Iowa Cavalry led his dismounted troopers to the river by a wooded ravine three hundred yards to the right of the ford.[42]

The First Brigade passed cautiously over the brow of the hill and rushed down the road to the river. The Confederate line on the opposite bank exploded in a sheet of fire that pinned down the Union cavalrymen just short of the ford. The Rebel artillery pounded and screamed at the blue column. Captain Dee was faring better in the ravine. His battalion was able to reach the river and cross before Marmaduke's pickets were aware of it. Securing a foothold on the west bank, the Iowans hugged the ground and pumped their repeating rifles at the astonished Rebels. It was then that Colonel Philips led his Missouri brigade into the stream. Under a galling fire the bluecoats slowly but certainly pushed their way across the ford. The icy water ran breast high and a number of the Missourians were killed and wounded in the river. They proved good targets for General Marmaduke's sharpshooters as they crossed the ford, holding their cartridge boxes and rifles above their heads. Rebel artillery swept the ford, shelling it with devilish accuracy.[43]

Reaching the road on the west side of the ford, the brigade raced up the hollow and poured over the river bank, sending Marmaduke's advance line scampering to the rear. Ahead of the wet and dripping blue cavalrymen was nine hundred yards or more of open field, and beyond that a ledge of rock fifteen to twenty feet high. The advance line of the Rebels had now fallen back on the open plain some two hundred yards from the river. Marmaduke's main line occupied a most formidable position as it rested on top of an oak-crowned hill above the rock ledge. The position was further strengthened by a row of fencing above the rock, as well as two log houses near the crest of the hill on the Rebel left. Here General Marmaduke had stationed the best of his sharpshooters, some of them in the tree-tops. On the right of the main Rebel line Hynson's Texas Battery was so planted as to command the plain and the road which, after leaving the ford, ascended the hill to the south of the rock ledge.[44]

While Colonel Philips and Captain Dee were forcing a crossing, Colonel Winslow and General Pleasonton were frantically bringing up the rest of the division into position to assist. Colonel Winslow led his Fourth Brigade, still mounted, across the stream and fanned out along the bank. Reaching a position so as to plug the gap between Colonel Philips' right and Captain Dee's left, Winslow's troopers swung to the ground, pulling their gasping horses behind them, their feet tripping from weariness. The animals, stinking wet and plastered to the withers with ripe mud, were held just behind the line. Winslow, the senior colonel, now assumed command of the line while General Pleasonton was busy advancing General John B. Sanborn's Brigade to the ford as support.[45]

Colonel Philips mounted his troopers and advanced immediately along the road, pressing toward the rock ledge. He reached the boulders but could proceed no farther for the precipitous rocks could not be scaled by the horses. The cavalry could only advance by the road in column of fours which made the horsemen particularly vulnerable to the Rebel battery at the top of the hill and to Marmaduke's sharpshooters. Twice Colonel Philips sent the 1st Missouri State Militia Cavalry, now under the leadership of Lieutenant Colonel B. F. Lazear, charging up the road in column. Twice the regiment was hurled back by the concentrated Rebel fire which swept the narrow roadway. No such maneuver, however, could ever dislodge the Confederate cavalry from the oak-crowned crest beyond. Only dismounted soldiers, able to clamber over the rocks, could ever assail that hill.[46]

Bringing up his Fourth Brigade, Colonel Winslow now formed a dismounted line out on the meadow in front of the rock ledge. Colonel Philips' First Brigade remained on the left of the road, the 7th Missouri State Militia Cavalry, Lieutenant Colonel T. T. Crittenden commanding, adjacent to the road. Major George

W. Kelly's 4th Missouri State Militia Cavalry was on the left of the 7th and the 1st Missouri on the left of the 4th. To the immediate right of the road was the 4th Iowa Cavalry, the 3rd Iowa Cavalry, and the 10th Missouri Cavalry in the order named. In support of this end of the line was the 7th Indiana Cavalry and Dee's Battalion.

It was almost eleven o'clock and for the next hour the fighting in the meadow and along the rock ledge grew in intensity until all units of the First and Fourth Brigades were engaged. From base to crest, the hill beyond the rock ledge erupted as smoke and flame from the Confederate guns stabbed through the Union shell bursts. Down on the meadow General Pleasonton's attack came on. A few blue dots showed motionless on the ground. Here and there a flag went down, was caught up again. Suddenly the whole Yankee line broke into double time and a faint wisp of yelling drifted upward through the din. The line reached the rocks, attempted to go over them but failed and fell back again on the meadow. That night, writing about this attack, Colonel Philips was to scrawl hastily in his diary: "Fought desperately. Under a most frightful fire for one hour. Wounded passing by me. Capt. Blair of 4th killed and Lt. Christian mortally wounded. Capt. Vansickle and Hamilton of 4th severely wounded. Lt. Dale mortally wounded. Lt. Brison and Barclay wounded. Brown struck on pistol handle. Col. Crittenden knocked down with spent ball."[47]

Again both brigades charged. They crossed a cart path at the base of the rock ledge and then plunged in among the boulders. Yells broke out on all sides. There was blue everywhere now among the rocks and a hurrying drift of gray skirmishers ran back up the hill, all order lost in the wild scramble toward the crest where the main Rebel line was waiting to receive them before it burst into heavy fire.

Hynson's Texas Battery thundered louder and shells flowered among the advancing Yankees. Then from the rock ledge on the immediate right of the road a single blue figure broke. Another followed, ten, a dozen, a hundred. They ran and scrambled and scurried, ducking for cover, reappearing, driving on up the hill. This first wild wave was the 4th Iowa Cavalry swarming up a brush-choked ravine paralleling the road above the rocks.[48] Others followed and then fanned out to join other lines that broke above the ledge and formed.

Up and up both Union brigades pressed toward the ridge and the plateau beyond. The firing increased in tempo. Colonel Winslow was hit and command of the brigade and the assault devolved upon the able Lieutenant Colonel Frederick W. Benteen of the 10th Missouri Cavalry. The Federal line rocked back, steadied, and then moved forward again toward the crest, scant yards away. Suddenly there were no more lines. The dismounted Yankee regiments had vanished among the gray lines. A ragged surf of gray broke from the melee, formed in tight desperate knots that were engulfed, shattered, and swept away. General Marmaduke's division was in retreat.[49]

Behind the charging Yankee line bodies were strewn like jetsam left by a careless tide. They lay as they had fallen, with their arms, blue and gray clumps huddled in the road, crumpled among the rocks, sprawled in the thickets of the ravine. Men's limbs were as lifeless as the rifles, useless debris left by the receding waves of the Yankee assaults. On the meadow and the hill, General Pleasonton had suffered two hundred casualties.[50]

The victorious blue cavalrymen plunged into the belt of woods which lined the crest of the hill and followed closely upon the retreating Confederates. Far from being completely scattered and demoralized, General Marmaduke's men offered resistance but were steadily shoved back through the timber to the prairie beyond. Out in the open the grayclads ceased their resistance and fled westward across the prairie as Battery H of the 2nd Missouri Union Light Artillery rolled up with its Rodman guns and opened on the gray horsemen. It was then that General Pleasonton came riding in among the artillerymen, wild with excitement and shouting, "Rebels, Rebels, Fire, Fire, You damned Asses!"[51]

With the arrival of General Pleasonton had come General John B. Sanborn and the Third Brigade. While the First and Fourth Brigades stopped to re-form and mount, Sanborn led the Third Brigade in pursuit of the Rebels, pushing them back to the Harrisonville road. There General Marmaduke and his cavalrymen, reeling and on the ragged edge of panic, encountered General Fagan moving toward them with a section of Blocker's Arkansas Battery. Fagan let Marmaduke pass through the lines and then opened on General Sanborn with the artillery. The pursuing Yankees were halted long enough to allow Colonel Jackman to join Fagan. Desperately striving to prevent a junction of Sanborn and Curtis until General Shelby could extricate himself, Jackman and Fagan charged the Yankee line. It was a mad, frantic charge that succeeded in shaking the right of General Sanborn's Brigade and driving it back in great confusion. Pressing their advantage, the Confederate cavalry sent Sanborn staggering back across the Mockabee farm in savage hand to hand combat. The Yankee brigade was close to panic now and was beginning to break when Colonel Benteen, leading the Fourth Brigade, came slashing in on the Rebel flank with the 10th Missouri Union Cavalry. The Rebels broke and fled.[52]

General Pleasonton came galloping up with the First Brigade and hastily reformed his command for further pursuit. He sent Battery H ahead to Hinkle's Grove where the gunners found themselves upon General Shelby's right flank. They opened up with a searing fire on the Iron Brigade just as General Curtis launched his general charge. The combination had sent the Rebels reeling back to a long line of stone fences. There General Shelby made his last stand. In a deadly, obstinate fight the remnants of Shelby's division resisted the now combined advance of Curtis and Pleasonton. At the wall the valiant gray troopers bought time—time for General Marmaduke and General Fagan to escape to the south—time for the wagon train and the beef herd to push farther down the state line. Only then did they begin to fall back upon the retreating Confederate army.[53]

General Shelby had saved General Sterling Price's Army of Missouri from complete disaster. He had done "great and splendid service." Years later General Shelby's adjutant was to write, "We shall never forget the impression made upon our mind when we saw General Shelby coming out of the fight at Westport without a hat on his head, his sandy locks streaming on the wind, his six-shooter in his hand, and his gallant division, after three days of hard fighting, overpowered and cut to pieces, but still not whipped, gathering around their beloved chieftain and ready to turn at a moment's notice on the rapidly advancing enemy."[54] That Sunday night Dr. J. H. Baker, Shelby's surgeon, was to write in his diary, "If our safety can be attributed to any one man, Jo Shelby wears the laurel."[55]

Generals Pleasonton and Blunt joined forces along the state line road, offered each other congratulations, and pushed on to Indian Creek where they halted at a farmhouse to meet General Curtis and the staff of the Army of the Border. The pursuit was continued by Colonel Jennison's Brigade and a battalion of the 2nd Colorado Cavalry who kept doggedly after the fleeing Rebels until sundown.[56] By then the Confederate army had recrossed the Big Blue river four miles beyond Little Santa Fe and was moving southward toward the middle fork of the Grand river.[57]

General John McNeil with the Second Brigade of General Pleasonton's provisional cavalry division was also having his troubles that momentous autumn Sunday before Westport. However, McNeil's difficulties were to prove too much for him to handle.

Having been ordered Saturday night by General Pleasonton to proceed from Independence to Little Santa Fe so as to reach that point by daylight, General McNeil had begun his march shortly after midnight. By four o'clock Sunday morning he had reached a point on the Independence-Little Santa Fe road opposite Byram's ford. Noticing a large encampment on the west side of the Big Blue river, he had detached a part of the 2nd Missouri Union Cavalry and sent the detail to the ford to investigate. After ascertaining the camp was Confederate, General McNeil continued his march toward Hickman Mills and Little Santa Fe, his curiosity apparently satisfied. He halted again just before daybreak to feed his horses. The animals had had no forage for two days and nearly two nights. As a result of these delays, daylight found General John McNeil and the Second Brigade far from Little Santa Fe.[58]

Soon after daybreak, McNeil became aware of heavy firing at Byram's ford and in the direction of Westport. This seemed to shake him from his lethargy and he pressed on toward Hickman Mills at an increased pace. He had marched about four miles when he found himself on the left and rear of General Sterling Price's wagon train. Because he could no longer hear the firing at the ford and Westport, he believed, for some strange reason, that he alone now faced "the entire force of the enemy."[59]

Brigadier General William L. Cabell with his brigade of Fagan's division and Colonel Charles H. Tyler's Brigade of Shelby's were doing a fairly efficient job of moving General Price's wagon train and beef herd southward. Colonel Tyler's Brigade, which consisted primarily of several thousand unarmed recruits, was strung out ahead and along the sides of the train. General Cabell's Brigade, the only Confederate troops capable of offering any serious resistance to McNeil, was in the rear of the train and column.[60] During the night the movement of the wagons and herd had been particularly difficult. The road went up one hill and down another and in the darkness the files stretched and came together again, accordion fashion, until the officers swore at the continual halts, succeeded by bone-jarring trots to keep up as the leading units stretched their pace on the downhill stretches. The unarmed recruits, most of them dismounted, had been hard to control in the darkness. But with the passing of night the train had picked up speed and for several hours had made rapid progress. The herd was in Little Santa Fe and the leading wagons were in Hickman Mills and pressing toward the crossing of the Big Blue river when the Yankees came upon General Cabell, guarding the rear of the train.[61]

General Cabell quickly thrust his brigade between the train and General McNeil's advancing columns. Throwing out a heavy line of skirmishers, the Arkansans were able to drive McNeil back about a mile. The confused McNeil, still astonished at the large body of Confederate cavalry guarding the huge number of wagons, finally formed his brigade in battle line, advanced his skirmishers and began to push forward again toward the wagon train. The 7th Kansas Cavalry and the 2nd Missouri Union Cavalry moved out toward the center of General Cabell's line under cover of Battery L of the 2nd Missouri Light Artillery. The battery's three three-inch Rodman guns under the command of Captain W. C. F. Montgomery were lending excellent support to the advancing Yankee cavalry until General Cabell brought up Captain W. M. Hughey's Arkansas Battery and caught Montgomery in a well-directed cross-fire. General McNeil was then forced to sound the recall and fell back four hundred yards to a new position.[62] There for the remainder of the morning General McNeil contented himself with skirmishing and cannonading with the enemy.

In the meantime General Sterling Price, who was near Westport in the rear of Shelby's line, received word from General Cabell that the wagon train was threatened. The Confederate commander immediately informed Generals Fagan and Shelby and instructed them to fall back to the train as soon as they could do so with safety.[63] That time, of course, never arrived for shortly thereafter General Shelby received the word that General Marmaduke was being forced back from Byram's ford.

After informing his subordinates of the situation of the wagon train, General Price with his escort rode south to the aid of

General Cabell and Colonel Tyler. Arriving on the scene, the commanding general hurried the wagons across the Big Blue river and on to Little Santa Fe. The unarmed recruits were formed in an extended battle line alongside the train to give the appearance of heavy support troops. General Cabell's Brigade continued to form the first line of defense east of the river crossing.[64] The ruse worked. General McNeil who had pushed the 17th Illinois Cavalry toward the enemy line hastily recalled it upon seeing the Rebel battle lines. The colonel of the 17th Illinois, John L. Beveridge, had worked his way through the thick brush, across the steep and rocky banks of the river, and had come undiscovered upon General Cabell's flank when the order to retreat came.[65] The timid McNeil had been easily bluffed.

In the afternoon, despite the fact that fleeing units from General Marmaduke's command defeated at Byram's ford were joining the wagon train, General McNeil began another cautious advance. This time General Cabell stopped it by ordering his men to set fire to the dry prairie grass. The grass was unusually tall and the wind high, blowing directly toward the advancing Yankees. A cracking line of fire bore down on McNeil's Brigade and behind the flames came the gray skirmishers sending a shower of minie balls through the leaping flames. It was more than the bluecoats could stomach. For the remainder of the day they kept their distance as the Confederate wagon train reached Little Santa Fe and turned south toward safety on the military road.[66]

Thus the first of two opportunities for total Union victory at Westport was lost. Because of his dilatory march toward Little Santa Fe and his unwillingness to attack General Cabell in force, General John McNeil was not in position to intercept the Confederate retreat from Westport. Had he moved promptly, as instructed by General Pleasonton, General McNeil would have come upon the wagon train in darkness when he could have by-passed it and reached Little Santa Fe ahead of the clumsy vehicles. There he would have been in position to attack the train from the front, throwing it back upon itself and creating great havoc. In all probability such an attack would have caused an earlier withdrawal of General Price's forces before Westport and at Byram's ford, thereby allowing the combined troops of Curtis and Pleasonton to push the Army of Missouri back upon the wrecked wagon train. For McNeil's failure to carry out orders, General Pleasonton later preferred charges against the unfortunate general. McNeil was court-martialed and suspended from rank and pay for three months.[67]

The second opportunity for total Union victory at Westport had been lost at eight o'clock on Saturday night, October 22, when General Pleasonton had urged General Rosecrans to order General A. J. Smith to Independence. This was a faulty judgment on the part of General Pleasonton and was due primarily to a lack of communication between Pleasonton's provisional cavalry division and Curtis' Army of the Border. General Pleasonton had been fighting hard with Marmaduke and Fagan all day Saturday and the only definite news he had of the Army of the Border that Saturday night was that it had been defeated along the Big Blue river and had fallen back to Westport and Kansas City. Therefore, assuming that General Price would attack again Sunday morning, General Pleasonton urged the recall of A. J. Smith's infantry to Independence where it would be in position to assist Curtis and Pleasonton.

The irascible General Rosecrans reluctantly agreed to Pleasonton's request and issued the order. General Pleasonton, who was on the ground, should have been better able to judge the situation than General Rosecrans who had not left St. Louis until October 13 and was still in Lexington that Saturday night. Because of this mistaken judgment General Smith broke off his march to Hickman Mills, marched back to Independence and then to Byram's ford where he arrived Sunday evening after the battle was over. Had the order not been issued and the infantrymen allowed to continue their line of march, General Smith and his veterans would have been squarely across the Confederate line of retreat Sunday afternoon.[68]

The comparative losses for the three days of fighting comprising the action before Westport (October 21, 22, and 23) have never been accurately determined. This has been due in part to the absence of reports from Fagan, Marmaduke, and Cabell, the latter two captured at Mine Creek, to the irregular filing of reports by brigade and regimental surgeons, to inaccurate and incomplete militia returns, but, above all, to the nature of the fighting itself. The action before Westport was cavalry action and the fight was a running fight that spread out over many miles of western Missouri. In fact, the action at Lexington on October 19 through the action before Westport on October 23 constituted one continuing operation with no time left for burying the dead or counting the casualties.

The situation was best expressed by General Pleasonton's surgeon-in-chief, Ferdinand V. Drayton of the 2nd New Jersey Cavalry. In his official report of the action before Westport, Surgeon Drayton wrote: "On account of the length and rapidity of the march and the extent of country that the engagements extended over it was with great difficulty that the wounded could be collected or the dead buried; in fact, at no time, to my knowledge, was a proper burying party detailed, so that I was obliged to use hospital attendants and stragglers for that purpose, and with the aid of citizens I hope that most, if not all, of our killed were interred."[69]

General Curtis, in his official report to General Halleck, made the statement, "The victory of Westport was most decisive. We did not stop to count our losses or bury our dead in any of the conflicts."[70] General Price in his official report never mentions his casualties except to say, "I do not think I lost 1,000 prisoners, including the wounded left in their hands."[71]

That very little was done to bury the dead and tend the wounded there can be no doubt. Those who visited the battlefield immediately after the armies had passed on testify to that.

Sunday, October 23, 1864

Lieutenant H. Warren Phelps, one of Smith's infantrymen, who marched over the Byram ford field early Monday morning wrote in his diary under entry of October 24, "There was no one that I talked with that could tell much about the battle. I think that the few people who resided near got away into the woods. We searched through the woods and found the bodies of men who were wounded and carried them out to the place of burial, or to a frame house which was used as a hospital. I came upon the bodies of twenty-four Union cavalry men with overcoats on, lying in a row on a rise of ground to the right of the road. They had been carried there. Their hats were placed over their faces."[12]

Private Henry Klinge, Company C, 49th Illinois Infantry, on visiting the same field, scratched in his diary, "At 6 o'clock we went into camp. During the day we stayed there quietly. Our cavalry had fought hard with Price. There lay over 50 dead and wounded of the rebels and of ours also about 50."[13]

The Kansas City Western Journal of Commerce in its issue of October 25, 1864, printed the following description of the battlefield adjoining Wornall's lane: "The battlefield exhibited evidences of the fiercest contest. The enemy had fled in such haste that he had been forced to leave his dead and many of his severely wounded. In the field next to the lane, on this side of Wernel's (sic) house, there were seven dead rebels lying side by side and near them an officer, said to be Colonel McGee (sic); around the latter the rebels had built a little pen of rails. A little further on were the remains of a rebel cannon, broken to pieces by a shot from one of our guns. Striking the open prairie beyond Wernel's (sic), the evidences of the fight were visible all about—dead horses, saddles, blankets, broken guns and dead rebels."

General Shelby's adjutant claimed that the October 23 action "cost Shelby somewhat over eight hundred men."[14] General Curtis reported his casualties for the same day "was probably 500."[15] Colonel Jackman records a loss in his brigade of 25 killed and 80 wounded in his fighting on October 22 and 23.[76]

From the meager and incomplete casualty lists that are on record 240 cavalrymen are recorded killed, 868 wounded, and 437 captured or missing in the action on October 21, 22, and 23.[77] These, of course, embody only a small fraction inasmuch as the majority of units involved in the action did not report their casualties. 1,500 killed or severely wounded on both sides in the action of October 23 would be a conservative figure and for the three days of action, October 21, 22, 23, 3,500 would be as near a correct estimate as is possible.

The task of gathering up the wounded fell to Surgeon-in-chief Ferdinand V. Drayton of General Pleasonton's force and Major Samuel B. Davis, Division Medical Director of the Army of the Border. Their job was monumental but they performed with a quiet efficiency that soon brought order out of the chaos. Organizing the regimental surgeons into an ambulance corps, they covered the battlefields from the Little Blue to Little Santa Fe. Field hospitals were established in houses near the various fields of action. There the wounded that could be moved were quickly transported. The severely wounded were left on the field and tended there until they died or recovered sufficiently to be moved.[78] The Wornall home on Wornall's lane became such a field hospital, used primarily for housing the Rebel wounded.[79]

From the field hospitals the wounded were sent to the general hospitals set up in Westport, Kansas City and Independence.[80] The river steamer, *Tom Morgan*, proceeded to Kansas City and Independence, picked up 86 wounded Kansas State militiamen and transported them to the Federal hospital in Fort Leavenworth.[81] Arriving at Little Santa Fe in the wake of the victorious Union army, Surgeon Drayton sent back from the supply train three days provisions to the field and general hospitals. That was all that could be done for the wounded. The dead became the problem of the local citizenry.[82] The army must press on after the retreating Rebels.

III. THE RETREAT FROM WESTPORT

1. "A Vigorous Pursuit Was Necessary"

"THE ENEMY having been fairly defeated at Westport after over three days of fighting, a vigorous pursuit was necessary to prevent his taking our military posts which are located near the State line at various points between the Missouri and the Arkansas, a distance of about 300 miles," so wrote General Sam Curtis in his official report of the action before Westport.[1] Although Curtis recognized the necessity of pressing his advantage, the Federal pursuit of the Army of Missouri was far from being "vigorous." The Union forces had become as thoroughly disorganized in victory as the Confederates had become in defeat.

At about 2:30 on Sunday afternoon, October 23, in a farmhouse on the banks of Indian Creek the various Federal commanders came together for the first time—Curtis, Pleasonton, Blunt, Deitzler, Sanborn, their staffs, and the Honorable Thomas Carney of Kansas. Over a hasty meal they held a consultation.[2]

The conference was lively. General Curtis pressed for immediate pursuit by all forces available. General Pleasonton said his cavalrymen were tired, as well as their horses—after all they had chased the Rebels across the state of Missouri. General Deitzler, still commanding the state militia of Kansas, argued that he had to get his men home for the coming election. Governor Carney supported Deitzler's position. He needed their votes. Back and forth the arguments surged.[3] At last an agreement was reached. The pursuit column would consist of General Pleasonton's provisional cavalry division and General Blunt's division of the Army of the Border. This, of course, was to be subject to the approval of General Rosecrans who had finally arrived at Independence.

Before leaving the farmhouse, General Curtis issued a field order revoking martial law north of the Kansas river.[4] He then released all of the Kansas militiamen except those living south of Aubry and sent them to Kansas City under the supervision of General Deitzler and Governor Carney. There the citizen-soldiers were to be mustered out and marched home.[5]

The newly formed pursuit column reached Little Santa Fe by dark and went into bivouac. Colonel Moonlight with his Second Brigade, still protecting the state line, remained apart from the main body and spent the night in Aubry.[6]

The next morning the pursuit of the retreating Rebels was resumed—twelve hours after the Confederates had fled the battlefield. But General Price had not taken advantage of the time which had been allowed him. The three successive marches made by the retreating Confederate army after the battle of Westport were only of twenty-four, thirty-three, and twenty-eight miles.[7] This is not the mileage of which a cavalry column is capable in the face of disaster.

The reason for the short marches is quite evident. General Sterling Price did not want to give up any part of his enormous wagon train, which included numerous loads not to be accounted for on the basis of military necessity.[8] Many of the fleeing Rebel soldiers came to hate the plunder which they had so gleefully gathered during the halcyon days of the expedition. Now it had become an oppressive burden, threatening to destroy them completely.

"Battered and bruised, and with its ranks decimated, the army emerged from the trap in which it had been caught with a feeling of personal hostility on the part of the men to the enormous and useless wagon train which had been the principal cause of their discomfiture and losses, but with the idea that now they had started southward in retreat and had the enemy behind them, the column would be stripped of all superfluities and incumbrances and would move forty or fifty miles a day. With them retreat meant hard, rapid marching . . . They were, therefore, surprised and disgusted when it became evident there was to be no decrease in the number of wagons that incumbered the march and which they had to guard at the hazard of their lives, and that the column was moving leisurely and at a speed that would not have been rapid for infantry."[9] Crossing the state line into Kansas, the Rebel raiders retreated from Westport in parallel columns with their wagons and artillery between—compact and disciplined with despair.[10]

The Confederate Army of Missouri, in a tangle of cavalrymen, horses, cattle, refugees, and wagons and with regiments hopelessly intermixed, spent the night of October 23 in an irregular line extending from the middle fork of the Grand river to a point eight miles south of Little Santa Fe.[11] "On the morning of the 24th we lost several hours in getting the train untangled and forming the Brigades, for in the confusion of the night before, men and wagons—artillery and refugees were so mixed that it was nearly impossible to unravel them," wrote General M. Jeff Thompson.[12]

The countryside was bleak and desolate and wet from a rain that began to fall late on the 24th. The farms were deserted and the blind windows of the houses gazed on the defeated Rebel army like the eyes of someone long dead. There had been a drought in this borderland during the summer, and the remnants of crops that still survived revealed that the growth had been stunted and parched. Several times the weary soldiers passed the blackened chimneys of burned houses, mementos of guerrilla raids.[13] Some of the men remembered the gleaming white houses and lush crops of 1861 when they had come marching up this way from the south, flushed with victory at Wilson's Creek.[14] Now they saw only the peeling paint, the blackened chimneys, and the damp wind that blew was freighted with the pungent smell of old wood ashes.

Once the Federal pursuit was begun it was pushed rather vigorously by General Curtis who had assumed command more or less by cooperative arrangement. General Blunt took command of the Kansas troops and General Pleasonton of the Missourians, the latter still issuing orders, however, independently of General Curtis. By 10 o'clock the morning of the 24th the Yankee columns were in full pursuit and continued southward until 2:30 the following morning.[15] Their rest was brief. In the black wetness of the night they again got orders to fall in by regiments. Officers moved here and there in the downpour with the cold rain rolling off their india-rubber capes, attempting to bring some order into the forming columns. Slowly they moved out along the road, sliding in the mud, too tired to curse, too hungry to care much what happened.[16]

With the coming of daylight, October 25, General Pleasonton made contact with Confederate pickets on the banks of the Marais-des-Cygnes river.[17] Driving the pickets before them, the Union cavalrymen soon ran into the Confederate rear-guard under General John S. Marmaduke. The still demoralized Rebel army was strung out for several miles over the open prairie between the Marais-des-Cygnes and Mine Creek.

Cautiously General Pleasonton pressed forward. As the timber of Mine Creek came in sight he saw Marmaduke being joined by General Fagan's division and the Rebels deploying in line of battle. Beyond the creek to the south the wagon train extended for several miles, guarded by General Jo Shelby's division. This open prairie, falling away to the timber-shrouded creek, afforded an excellent field for cavalry action. Here the battle must be fought.[18]

Already Union artillery was playing havoc with the ford where Confederate wagons were still crossing Mine Creek. The Rebel artillery on the left of the line was having a certain measure of success with Pleasonton's First Brigade, still under Colonel

John F. Philips' command. Lieutenant Colonel Frederick Benteen with the Fourth Brigade was hurried into line. The two brigades charged upon the Rebels before the bewildered Confederates could mount an attack of their own. Before they quite realized it, Benteen and Philips were thundering in upon the center and left of their position.[19]

The oncoming Federals struck with the crash of artillery and a rip tide of wielded sabers and cracking rifles. The melee became a whirling chaos, men fighting on horse and on foot, slashing and shooting, all semblance of military lines lost in the turmoil. Rebel soldiers plunged through the Mine Creek tree belt, falling over one another in their fear, and hurtled into the churning water where wagons from the illfated train were backed up against the steep bank in terrorizing confusion.[20] Flames ate at ripped canvas and exploding ammunition boxes tore at the smoky heavens. It was more than many of the graybacks could endure. Colonel T. R. Freeman's Brigade of Marmaduke's division quit the field in a body and without firing a shot. Their hasty departure opened a sinister gap in the Confederate lines. Through it poured the blue cavalrymen. In seconds they had engulfed all of the Rebel artillery and turned it upon the hard-pressed Confederates. Minuntes later Generals Marmaduke and Cabell with some five hundred of their men were surrounded and captured. Sheer panic swept over the staggering Rebels.[21]

The sounds of combat reached the ears of General Sterling Price riding in the advance column, now some two miles south of Mine Creek. Descending from the ambulance in which he had been traveling, the Confederate commander mounted his horse and raced toward the creek, but not before he had sent word to General Shelby to come to the rescue. Within a matter of minutes Price had "met the divisions of Major-Generals Fagan and Marmaduke retreating in utter and indescribable confusion, many of them having thrown away their arms. They were deaf to all entreaties or commands, and in vain were all efforts to rally them."[22]

Just prior to the collapse of Fagan and Marmaduke on Mine Creek, General Shelby had been ordered to make a side trip to Fort Scott and determine if that Union installation could be captured and destroyed. He was well on his way to his destination when General Price's appeal for help reached him.[23] Although the disaster at the creek had reached its climax about ten o'clock that morning, it was well into the afternoon before General Shelby with his old Iron Brigade and one additional regiment could attain an effective position.[24]

In a headlong twelve-mile gallop through panic-stricken fugitives, General Shelby and his men finally formed on a low ridge about a mile south of the Little Osage river. "I soon met . . . the advancing Federals," Shelby later wrote in his official report, "flushed with success and clamorous for more victims. I knew from the beginning that I could do nothing but resist their advance, delay them as much as possible, and depend on energy and night for the rest."[25] Delay them he did and here, as at Westport, with the able assistance of M. Jeff Thompson, he employed the Iron Brigade in a masterful exhibition of cavalry delaying tactics.[26] The fighting was constant and severe, often hand to hand. But the Federals never once relinquished the pressure. General John McNeil's Brigade had relieved that of Colonel Philips' and together with Benteen, McNeil pushed relentlessly forward.[27]

For an hour Generals Shelby and Thompson were able to maintain their poisition there on the ridge above the Little Osage. But gradually the blue cavalrymen began to envelop the Confederate flanks. Calling upon Colonel Sidney Jackman to cover his retirement, Shelby prepared to fall back upon the wagon train, by now nearing the crossing of the Marmaton river. Jackman charged the victorious Yankees as General Shelby retired at a mad gallop to a position just north of the Marmaton. Here he took up line of battle again and was successful in holding off McNeil and Benteen until darkness had fallen. "We marched until 12 o'clock that night," wrote Private James H. Campbell of the 14 Missouri Confederate Cavalry, "but left there before daylight in the morning as it was cloudy and raining and Price corralled his wagons and set them on fire to destroy them. The terrific noise of the bursting ammunition and the burning of the wagons abandoned by us in the dark, rainy morning was a sight never to be forgotten by anyone that saw it. After we abandoned the wagons we would see flashes of powder go up in the air like lightning and the constant bursting of the shells was terrific."[28] General Price burned almost one-third of his wagon train that morning and the Army of Missouri was able to march fifty-six miles before the day ended.[29]

It was at the point of action along the Marmaton river that the pursuing Federals were in position to destroy completely Price's army. But like so many other times during the course of the Confederate expedition, a set of circumstances combined to save the fleeing Rebel army and thwart the plans of frustrated Sam Curtis. The engagement of Generals McNeil and Benteen with Jo Shelby had been vigorous and intense and by the time the fighting reached the timber along the Marmaton many of the Yankee cavalrymen and their horses were near exhaustion. Now was the time for General Curtis to send in the remnants of Blunt's and Pleasonton's commands. Eagerly McNeil and Benteen waited the expected help. It never came.[30]

General Pleasonton, convinced that Fort Scott was no longer in danger and that the pursuit had gone far enough, took his remaining two brigades, Philips' and Sanborn's, and headed for Fort Scott. "I was compelled to go to the fort for forage," he later alibied. Besides "my horses were too much exhausted to go into action."[31] So were McNeil's and Benteen's.

General Blunt, observing Pleasonton moving toward the fort, presumed this to be on orders from General Curtis and immediately directed his division there also.[32] Wagons coming from the fort laden with provisions for the brigades of McNeil and Benteen turned about with General Pleasonton, leaving the two unhappy brigades unfed. Crusty Sam Curtis, seeing his army leave the battlefield, hurried to overtake Pleasonton.[33] Curtis demanded an explanation. The argument that ensued was heated. It continued all the way into the fort.

There should have been no argument. By right of rank and seniority, General Curtis was in command of the pursuit.[34] His orders should have been obeyed. But again, a series of circumstances had placed him in an untenable position. With the departure of the Kansas Militia after the battles of Westport and Mine Creek, General Curtis' Army of the Border was again reduced to its original 4,000 cavalrymen—now minus substantial casualties. This placed him in the embarrassing position of having to conduct a pursuit with a majority of his soldiers being drawn from another Federal department—The Department of the Missouri. These troops were under the command of Alfred Pleasonton, also a Major General. Pleasonton, in turn, then found himself having to serve not only General Curtis, but his own departmental commander, Major General Rosecrans, who outranked Curtis! It is no wonder that Sam Curtis found his command of the pursuit to be a rather nebulous matter and that arguments ensued.[35]

From evidence now available it is quite certain that General Pleasonton quit the fight along the Marmaton river, not entirely because he needed forage and rest, but because he wanted to contact General Rosecrans.[36] On reaching the fort Pleasonton sent a message, without General Curtis' knowledge, to the Missouri departmental commander recommending that the pursuit be terminated as far as Missouri troops were concerned. General Rosecrans was inclined to agree with Pleasonton but hesitated to comply as long as General Curtis was so determined on a vigorous pursuit.[37]

After dispatching his message to Rosecrans, General Pleasonton notified Curtis that because of poor health he personally would not be able to continue the chase.[38] This suited General Curtis exactly. Now he would be able to exercise closer command of Pleasonton's four brigades with Pleasonton out of the way—so Curtis must have thought. Time would prove him wrong.

The Federals followed the enemy's trail all day and most of the night of October 27-28, halting at 3 a.m. at the ruins of Carthage, Missouri. Here the blue cavalrymen halted for three hours for resting and breakfasting.[39] Again the pursuit was resumed with General Blunt in the lead. About two o'clock in the afternoon of October 28, just south of the small village of Newtonia, Missouri, they caught up with the Confederate army.[40]

Making contact with only two of his brigades, the rest of the Yankee column having stopped some miles back to feed men and animals, General Blunt did not hesitate. Trusting the others would soon come to his aid, he pushed forward and engaged the enemy. Again it was General Shelby who deployed to meet the pursuers, but this time the superiority of numbers was with the Confederates.[41]

General Blunt made effective use of McLain's Colorado Battery and Patterson's mountain howitzers. He sent the 16th Kansas Cavalry and the 2nd Colorado Cavalry headlong against the Rebel lines. Shelby never wavered. Blunt flung the remainder of his force into the battle, personally supervising each movement. The engagement grew in severity. The fighting was close-in and efficient.[42]

For a while the superiority of fire-power in the Yankee breechloaders overcame the disparity of numbers. The howitzers poured canister into the heavy flanking column which General Shelby sent around the Union right. The movement was checked, but as the afternoon wore on and the fighting became more intense the Rebel numbers began to tell. General Blunt became aware of the enemy's attempt to flank the other end of his line. Through a cornfield on the Union left gray cavalrymen were advancing. Powerless to meet them, Blunt prepared to pull back just as General John B. Sanborn arrived with his brigade.[43] Instantly grasping the situation, Sanborn galloped to the edge of the cornfield, dismounted his men and drove forward through the dry cornstalks. The battle was over in a matter of minutes. It was dusk and in the fading light General Shelby withdrew.[44]

General Sam Curtis' optimism was boundless. Now there was no doubt at all in the general's mind but that the Confederate invaders would be destroyed completely.[45] It was simply a matter of logistics. General Curtis had arranged before leaving Fort Scott to have his forces supplied daily by wagon train from the fort. General Price's army on the other hand was entering a region which had been desolated by contending armies for almost four years. The region was virtually barren of food and supplies. All Curtis had to do was to hang on, press General Price constantly, and give the Rebels no time to forage or to rest. Nature would then take care of the situation.

But again the Federal command system intervened. On the following morning, October 29, just as he sent the pursuing column after the now demoralized Confederates, General Curtis received a dispatch from General Pleasonton.[46] The message was brief and to the point. General Rosecrans ordered all troops belonging to the Department of the Missouri to return to their home stations. McNeil, Benteen, Philips, and Sanborn promptly obeyed, withdrawing their brigades from the pursuit. General Curtis was left with the three brigades of General Blunt's division, probably about 2,500 men.[47]

Shocked and disappointed, General Curtis recognized the impossibility of continuing after the Army of Missouri with this reduced force. There was nothing to do but to give up the chase and return north. But as he retraced his route to Newtonia, General Curtis found his disappointment giving way to anger. He stopped in Newtonia long enough to wire General Henry W. Halleck in Washington. In the telegram Curtis laid the blame for the failure of the pursuit upon General Rosecrans.[48]

That night General Curtis made camp at Neosho and there at midnight he received a telegram from General Halleck: "Lieutenant-General Grant desires that Price be pursued to the Arkansas River . . ."⁴⁹ The was enough for General Curtis. This order certainly overruled the order of General Rosecrans. Calling for couriers, General Curtis sent them racing to Benteen, Philips, Sanborn, and McNeil with orders to assemble at Cassville. Then he wired General Rosecrans, informing the Missouri commander of what he had done and needling him for never having arrived "to assume the responsibilities of the movement against Price."⁵⁰

But if General Curtis expected his orders to be obeyed promptly by the missing brigade commanders, he was doomed to disappointment. Colonel Benteen was the first one found by a courier but it was not until November 1 that he rejoined General Curtis south of Newtonia, and then only after long arguments concerning the condition of his animals. Colonel Philips was not reached until November 2 in Warrensburg. The distance involved precluded his return in sufficient time to be of help. Couriers found General McNeil near Springfield. He too was reluctant to return. He did make an attempt to reach Cassville but when there he wired General Rosecrans that he could not maintain his cavalry because the land was destitute of forage. General Rosecrans gave him permission to turn back. McNeil promptly started for Rolla, arriving there November 15. General Sanborn received his order to rejoin General Curtis on October 30 at Springfield. He only complied with the order after complaining to General Rosecrans that he did not think "General Curtis's order legitimate under the circumstances."⁵¹ He got as far as Cassville and there he remained.

After being joined by Colonel Benteen, General Curtis again resumed the chase. But the damage had been done on October 29 when the Missouri cavalry had been withdrawn by Rosecrans. Further pursuit was useless. General Curtis did secure the safety of Fayetteville, Arkansas, on November 4, when he chased off a detachment of Price's troops who were aiding a band of Confederate partisans in an attack on the Federal garrison there. The delay, however, enabled General Price and the remnants of the

Army of Missouri to make good their escape. The Confederates crossed the Arkansas river on November 7, about thirty miles west of Fort Smith. General Curtis, having fulfilled General Halleck's instructions, then issued orders to the several elements of his command to return to their home stations.

The chase was over but not the retreat. Just prior to his crossing of the Arkansas, General Price had sent the brigades of Freeman, McCray, and Dobbin to those sections of Arkansas "where they had raised their commands in order to collect the absentees together and bring them within our lines during the month of December."[52] After crossing the river, the Confederate commander furloughed Cabell's and Slemons' Brigades, and with a greatly reduced force made his way into Indian Territory. During the march through the Choctaw Nation and finally into Texas, the troops suffered greatly. Morale reached its lowest point. Hunger, cold, and even starvation were constant companions. Smallpox attacked the force and caused many deaths. One soldier wrote to his brother, "Men are greatly demoralized, and we present a pitiable, forlorn aspect. G..d d... Old Price, is the almost constant ejaculation from men exhausted in both body and spirit."[53] Another complained to his diary, "This raid reminds me of the children of Israel marching through the Wilderness. But alas! We have no Moses to lead us . . . What is to be the result of this campaign no one can see. A feeling of despondency pervades the army. Low spirits and debility are playing havoc with our men. Many can scarcely go."[54]

But go they did. By November 23 they reached Bonham, Texas. Then turning east they staggered into Laynesport, Arkansas, on December 2, 1864. The long retreat from Westport was over. The final Confederate invasion of Missouri was history. Peace, at long last, had come to the Kansas-Missouri border.

After being driven west from Bryam's Ford, Marmaduke's division made a second stand on high ground next to this log house. (Photo courtesy of Gil Bergman)

On October 23, 1864, Curtis observed the action along Brush Creek from the roof of his headquarters at the Harris Hotel in Westport, seen here in the 1890s. (Photo courtesy of Gil Bergman)

The Confederate Monument at Forest Hill Cemetery, Kansas City, Missouri, was dedicated on Memorial Day, May 30, 1902. (Photo by Gil Bergman)

One of the Monnett Battle of Westport Fund markers. (Photo by Gil Bergman)

Two historic Westport landmarks that were present at the time of the battle: Jim Bridger's store *(left)* and Albert Gallatin Boone's store *(right)*. (Photo by Gil Bergman)

Today a ten-pound Parrott gun, located south of Brush Creek at Loose Park (Kansas City, Missouri), stands defiant as Shelby's Iron Brigade did during the fighting there on October 23, 1864. (Photo by Gil Bergman)

The Gage Monument at Topeka Cemetery, Topeka, Kansas, was dedicated May 30, 1895, to honor members of the 2nd Kansas State Militia killed October 22, 1864, at the Mockabee Farm during the Battle of the Big Blue. (Photo by Gil Bergman)

Traces of the historic Independence-Westport Road are still visible on both sides of the Big Blue River at Byram's Ford. (Photo by Gil Bergman)

Appendix

ORGANIZATION OF THE ARMY OF MISSOURI
MAJOR GENERAL STERLING PRICE COMMANDING
MAJOR WILLIAM W. DUNLAP, CHIEF OF ARTILLERY

FAGAN'S DIVISION
Major General James F. Fagan

Cabell's Brigade—Brigadier General William L. Cabell
Gordon's Arkansas Cavalry, Colonel Anderson Gordon
Gunter's Arkansas Cavalry Battalion, Lieutenant Colonel Thomas M.
Gunter
Harrell's Arkansas Cavalry Battalion, Lieutenant Colonel John M.
Harrell
Hill's Arkansas Cavalry, Major J. L. Adams
Monroe's Arkansas Cavalry, Colonel James C. Monroe
Morgan's Arkansas Cavalry, Colonel Thomas J. Morgan
Witherspoon's Arkansas Cavalry Battalion, Major J. L. Witherspoon
Hughey's Arkansas Battery (2 guns), Captain William M. Hughey

Dobbin's Brigade—Colonel Archibald S. Dobbin
Dobbin's Arkansas Cavalry, Colonel Archibald S. Dobbin
McGhee's Arkansas Cavalry, Colonel James H. McGhee (wounded
October 23); Lieutenant Colonel Jesse S. Grider
Witt's Arkansas Cavalry, Colonel A. R. Witt
Blocher's Arkansas Battery (2 guns), Lieutenant J. V. Zimmerman (plus
two guns captured at Fort Davidson)

Slemons' Brigade—Colonel William F. Slemons
2nd Arkansas Cavalry, Colonel William F. Slemons
Carlton's Arkansas Cavalry, Colonel Charles H. Carlton (wounded
October 22); Lt. Col. R. H. Thompson
Crawford's Arkansas Cavalry, Colonel William A. Crawford

Wright's Arkansas Cavalry, Colonel John C. Wright
Stirman's Arkansas Cavalry Battalion, Lt. Col. Ras Stirman

McCray's Brigade—Colonel Thomas H. McCray
15th Missouri Cavalry, Colonel Timothy Reeves
45th Arkansas Infantry (mounted), Colonel Milton D. Baber (captured
October 22 at Independence)
47th Arkansas Infantry (mounted), Colonel Lee Crandall

Unattached
Anderson's Arkansas Cavalry Battalion, Captain William L. Anderson
Lyle's Arkansas Cavalry, Colonel Oliver P. Lyle
Rogan's Arkansas Cavalry, Colonel James W. Rogan

MARMADUKE'S DIVISION
Major General John S. Marmaduke

Escort: Co. D, 5th Missouri Cavalry
Captain D. R. Stallard

Marmaduke's Brigade—Brigadier General John B. Clark, Jr.
3rd Missouri Cavalry, Colonel Colton Greene (wounded October 21);
Captain Benjamin S. Johnson commanded regiment [Greene's 3rd
Mo. Cav.] on October 23
4th Missouri Cavalry, Colonel John Q. Burbridge (wounded October
21); Lt. Col. William J. Preston [subsequently commanded
Burbridge's 4th Mo. Cav.], (mortally wounded and taken prisoner)
7th Missouri Cavalry, Colonel Solomon G. Kitchen (wounded October 23)
8th Missouri Cavalry, Colonel William L. Jeffers
10th Missouri Cavalry, Colonel Robert R. Lawther
14th Missouri Cavalry Battalion, Lieutenant Colonel Robert C. Wood
Davies' Missouri Cavalry Battalion, Lt. Col. J. F. Davies
Hogane's Engineer Company, Captain James T. Hogane

Artillery: Major Joseph H. Pratt
Harris' Missouri Battery (3 guns), Lieutenant T. J. Williams
Hynson's Texas Battery (3 guns), Captain Henry C. Hynson

Appendix

Freeman's Brigade—Colonel Thomas R. Freeman
  Ford's Arkansas Cavalry Battalion, Lieutenant Colonel Barney Ford
  Freeman's Missouri Cavalry, Lieutenant Colonel Joseph R. Love (taken
    prisoner October 23); Major William Cook
  Fristoe's Missouri Cavalry, Colonel Edward T. Fristoe

SHELBY'S DIVISION
Brigadier General Joseph O. Shelby

Shelby's Iron Brigade—Brigadier General M. Jeff Thompson
  5th Missouri Cavalry, Colonel Frank B. Gordon
  11th Missouri Cavalry, Colonel Moses W. Smith
  12th Missouri Cavalry, Lieutenant Colonel William H. Erwin
  Elliott's Missouri Cavalry, Colonel Benjamin F. Elliott
  Johnson's Cavalry Battalion, Major Rector Johnson
  Slayback's Missouri Cavalry Battalion, Lieutenant Colonel Alonzo
    Slayback
  Collins' Missouri Battery (2 guns), Captain Richard A. Collins

Jackman's Brigade—Colonel Sidney D. Jackman
  Crisp's Cavalry Battalion, Lieutenant Colonel John T. Crisp
  Hunter's Missouri Cavalry, Colonel DeWitt C. Hunter
  Jackman's Missouri Cavalry, Lieutenant Colonel C. H. Nichols
  Schnable's Missouri Cavalry Battalion, Lieutenant Colonel John
    A. Schnable
  Williams' Missouri Cavalry Battalion, Lieutenant Colonel D. A.
    Williams
  Collins' Missouri Battery (2 guns), Lieutenant Jacob D. Connor

Tyler's Brigade—Colonel Charles H. Tyler
  Coffee's Missouri Cavalry, Colonel J. T. Coffee
  Perkins' Missouri Cavalry, Colonel Caleb Perkins
  Searcey's Missouri Cavalry, Colonel James T. Searcey
  Unorganized recruits

Unattached
  46th Arkansas Infantry (mounted), Colonel W. O. Coleman

ORGANIZATION OF THE ARMY OF THE BORDER
MAJOR GENERAL SAMUEL R. CURTIS COMMANDING,
DEPARTMENT OF KANSAS

Escort: Co. G, 11th Kansas Cavalry, Captain G. L. Gove
and Two-Gun Battery, Lieutenant Edward Gill

Major Robert H. Hunt, Chief of Artillery

PROVISIONAL CAVALRY DIVISION
Major General James G. Blunt

First Brigade—Colonel Charles R. Jennison, 15th Kansas Cavalry
   3rd Wisconsin Cavalry (Detachment), Captain Robert Carpenter
   15th Kansas Cavalry, Lieutenant Colonel George H. Hoyt
   Foster's Missouri Cavalry Battalion, Captain George S. Grover
   Battery (5 guns) manned by 15th Kansas Cavalry, Lieutenant Henry
      L. Barker

Second Brigade—Colonel Thomas Moonlight, 11th Kansas Cavalry
   5th Kansas Cavalry (Companies L and M), Captain James H. Young
   11th Kansas Cavalry, Lieutenant Colonel Preston B. Plumb
   16th Kansas Cavalry (Companies A and D), Lieutenant Colonel Samuel
      Walker
   Battery (4 guns) manned by Co. E, 11th Kansas Cavalry

Third Brigade—Colonel Charles W. Blair, 14th Kansas Cavalry
   4th Kansas Militia, Colonel W. D. McCain
   5th Kansas Militia, Colonel G. A. Colton
   6th Kansas Militia, Colonel James D. Snoddy (arrested October 16);
      Colonel James Montgomery
   10th Kansas Militia, Colonel William Pennock
   14th Kansas Cavalry (Company E), Lieutenant William B. Clark
   19th Kansas Militia, Colonel A. C. Hogan
   24th Kansas Militia Battalion, Lieutenant Colonel George Eaves
   2nd Kansas State Artillery (2 guns), Lieutenant Daniel C. Knowles
   9th Wisconsin Battery (4 guns), Captain James H. Dodge

Fourth Brigade—Colonel James H. Ford, 2nd Colorado Cavalry
    2nd Colorado Cavalry, Major J. Nelson Smith (killed October 21);
        Major J. H. Pritchard
    16th Kansas Cavalry (Detachment), Major James Ketner
    McLain's Indep. Colorado Battery (6 guns), Captain W. D. McLain

KANSAS STATE MILITIA DIVISION
Major General George W. Dietzler

Brigadier General M. S. Grant
Brigadier General William H. M. Fishback

Units (not brigaded)
    1st Kansas Militia, Colonel Charles H. Robinson
    2nd Kansas Militia, Colonel George W. Veale
    2nd Kansas Colored Militia, Captain James L. Rafferty, Captain Rich-
        ard J. Hinton
    3rd Kansas Militia, Colonel Charles Willemsen
    7th Kansas Militia, Colonel Peter McFarland
    9th Kansas Militia, Colonel Frank M. Tracy
    12th Kansas Militia, Colonel L. S. Treat
    13th Kansas Militia, Colonel Alexander S. Johnson
    14th Kansas Militia, Colonel William Gordon
    18th Kansas Militia, Colonel Matthew Quigg
    20th Kansas Militia, Colonel J. B. Hubbell
    21st Kansas Militia, Colonel Sandy Lowe
    22nd Kansas Militia, Colonel William Weer

Artillery
    Independent Colored Battery (2 guns), Lieutenant Patrick H. Minor
    Leavenworth Battery, Kansas Militia Light Artillery (2 guns), Captain
        Gustavus Zesch (assumed command October 20)
    Topeka Battery of 2nd Kansas Militia (1 gun), Captain Ross Burns
        (wounded; taken prisoner October 22)
    Cracklin's Battery of 3rd Kansas Militia (2 guns), Captain Joseph
        Cracklin
    Grover's Battery of 3rd Kansas Militia (2 guns), Captain Joel Grover

UNATTACHED UNIT
Kansas City Home Guards, Colonel Kersey Coates

ORGANIZATION OF THE ARMY OF THE DEPARTMENT OF MISSOURI
MAJOR GENERAL WILLIAM S. ROSECRANS, COMMANDING

PROVISIONAL CAVALRY DIVISION
Major General Alfred S. Pleasonton

First Brigade—Brigadier General Egbert B. Brown (arrested October 23); Colonel John F. Philips, 7th Missouri Militia Cavalry
1st Iowa Cavalry (Detachment), Major John McDermott
1st Missouri Militia Cavalry, Colonel James McFerran (arrested October 23); Lieutenant Colonel Bazel Lazear
4th Missouri Militia Cavalry, Major George W. Kelly
7th Missouri Militia Cavalry, Colonel John F. Philips, Lieutenant Colonel Thomas T. Crittenden

Second Brigade—Brigadier General John McNeil
2nd Missouri Cavalry (Detachment), Captain George M. Houston
3rd Missouri Militia Cavalry (Detachment), Lieutenant Colonel Henry M. Matthews
5th Missouri Militia Cavalry, Lieutenant Colonel Joseph Eppstein
7th Kansas Cavalry, Major Francis Malone
9th Missouri Militia Cavalry (Detachment), Lieutenant Colonel Daniel M. Draper
13th Missouri Cavalry, Colonel Edwin C. Catherwood
17th Illinois Cavalry, Colonel John C. Beveridge

Third Brigade—Brigadier General John B. Sanborn
2nd Arkansas Cavalry, Colonel John E. Phelps
6th Missouri Militia Cavalry (Detachment), Major William Plumb
6th Enrolled Mo. Militia Cavalry (Detach.), Lieutenant Colonel John F. McMahan
7th Enrolled Mo. Militia Cavalry (Detach.), Major W. B. Mitchell
8th Missouri Militia Cavalry, Colonel Joseph J. Gravely

Fourth Brigade—Colonel Edward F. Winslow, 4th Iowa Cavalry (wounded October 23); Lieutenant Colonel Frederick W. Benteen, 10th Missouri Cavlary
   3rd Iowa Cavalry, Major Benjamin S. Jones
   4th Iowa Cavalry, Major Abial R. Pierce
   4th Missouri Cavalry (Detachment), Captain George D. Knispel
   7th Indiana Cavalry (Detachment), Major S. W. Simonson
   10th Missouri Cavalry, Lieutenant Colonel Frederick W. Benteen, Major William H. Lusk

Artillery—Colonel Nelson Cole, 2nd Missouri Light Artillery
   Co. H, 2nd Mo. Light Artillery (2 guns), Captain William C. F. Montgomery and (2 guns), Lieutenant Philip Smiley
   Co. L, 2nd Mo. Light Artillery (4 guns), Captain Charles H. Thurber
   Battery (2 guns) of 5th Mo. Militia Cavalry, Lieutenant Adam Hillerich

Unassigned
   2nd New Jersey Cavalry (Detachment), Captain Michael Gallagher
   19th Pennsylvania Cavalry (Detachment)

ORGANIZATION OF THE 16TH ARMY CORP
(A DETACHMENT OF THE FIRST AND THIRD DIVISIONS)
MAJOR GENERAL A. J. SMITH COMMANDING

FIRST DIVISION
Colonel Joseph J. Woods

Second Brigade—Colonel Lucius F. Hubbard, 5th Minnesota Infantry
   5th Minnesota Infantry
   7th Minnesota Infantry
   8th Wisconsin Infantry
   9th Minnesota Infantry
   10th Minnesota Infantry
   12th Iowa Infantry
   47th Illinois Infantry
   Battery G, 2nd Illinois Light Artillery (6 guns)

Third Brigade—Colonel Sylvester G. Hill, 35th Iowa Infantry
33rd Missouri Infantry
35th Iowa Infantry

THIRD DIVISION
Colonel David Moore

First Brigade—Colonel T. J. Kinney, 119th Illinois Infantry
58th Illinois Infantry
89th Indiana Infantry
119th Illinois Infantry

Second Brigade—Colonel James I. Gilbert, 27th Iowa Infantry
14th Iowa Infantry
24th Missouri Infantry
27th Iowa Infantry
32nd Iowa Infantry

Third Brigade—Colonel Edward H. Wolfe, 52nd Indiana Infantry
49th Illinois Infantry
52nd Indiana Infantry
117th Illinois Infantry
178th New York Infantry
3rd Indiana Battery (4 guns)
9th Indiana Battery (4 guns)

Notes

I. THE ADVANCE TO WESTPORT

1. Prelude to Battle

1. United States War Department, *The War of the Rebellion: A Compilation of the Official Records of the Union and Confederate Armies*, (128 volumes, Washington, D. C., 1880-1901), Series 1, Volume XLI, Part 1, 484-485. Hereinafter cited *O.R.*

2. W. L. Webb, *Battles and Biographies of Missourians, or, the Civil War Period of Our State*, (Kansas City, Mo., 1900), 223.

3. Lucien Carr, *Missouri: A Bone of Contention*, (Boston and New York, 1888), 360.

4. Webb, *Battles and Biographies of Missourians*, 227.

5. *O.R.*, Series 1, Vol. XLI, Part 1, Colonel C. R. Jennison's Report, 585.

2. "This May Seem a Wild Plan"

Much of this chapter first appeared in the *Bulletin of the Missouri Historical Society*, Volume XVIII, Number 1, under the title of "The Origin of the Confederate Invasion of Missouri, 1864."

1. *O.R.*, Series 1, Vol. XLI, Part 2, 1022.

2. *Ibid.*, 1024.

3. *Ibid.*, 1026.

4. *Ibid.*, 1022.

5. *Idem.*

6. *Idem.*

7. *Idem.*

8. *Ibid.*, 1023.

9. *Idem.*

10. *O.R.*, Series 1, Vol. XLI, Part 1, Major General William S. Rosecrans' Report, 307.

11. *Ibid.*, Dispatch to General Richard Taylor from General W. R. Boggs, 90.

12. *Ibid.*, 89-90.

13. *Ibid.*, Letter of Jefferson Davis to General E. Kirby Smith, 123.

14. *O.R.*, Series 1, Vol. XLV, Part 2, Letter of General Simon B. Buckner dated January 5, 1865, 765-766. Confederate correspondence covering this proposed movement across the Mississippi can be found in *O.R.*, Series 1, Vol. XLI, Part 1, 88-123. This controversy certainly reveals the folly of attempting to exercise detailed control of troop movements at a great distance—an error often committed by Jefferson Davis and the Confederate high command.

15. *O.R., Series* 1, Vol. XLI, Part 2, Letter of General J. G. Walker, August 3, 1864, 1038.

16. Webb, *Battles and Biographies of Missourians*, 209.

17. *O.R.*, Series 1, Vol. XLI, Part 2, Letter of General J. O. Shelby, August 15, 1864, 1067.

18. Dunbar Rowland, Editor, *Jefferson Davis, Constitutionalist, His Letters, Papers, and Speeches*, 10 volumes (Jackson, Miss., 1923), Vol. V, 552.

19. *O.R.*, Series 1, Vol. XLI, Part 2, Letter of Governor Harris Flanigan to Jefferson Davis, August 11, 1864, 1054-1055.

20. *Ibid.*, Letter of Senator A. H. Garland, August 8, 1864, 1048.

21. *O.R.*, Series 1, Vol. XLI, Part 1, Letter of General S. B. Buckner, September 3, 1864, 120; Letter of General E. Kirby Smith, December 6, 1864, 122.

22. Webb, *Battles and Biographies of Missourians*, 209.

23. Richard Taylor, *Destruction and Reconstruction* (New York, 1955), 240-241.

24. *O.R.*, Series 1, Vol. XLI, Part 1, Letter dated August 21, 1864, 113-117.

25. *Ibid.*, 116.

26. *Idem.*

27. Douglas Southall Freeman, *Lee's Lieutenants*, 3 volumes, (New York, 1943), Vol. II, 248.

28. *Ibid.*, Vol. III, 305.

29. *O.R.*, Series 1, Vol. XXXIV, Part 2, Letter of General E. Kirby Smith, January 15, 1864, 870.

30. *Snead Papers, 1826-1864*, Old Army Branch of the National Archives, Washington, D. C.

31. *Ibid.;* General Dabney H. Maury, "Recollections of the Elkhorn Campaign," *Southern Historical Society Papers*, Vol. 2, No. 4, (October, 1876), 183-184.

32. *O.R.*, Series 1, Vol. XLI, Part 2, Letter of General Sterling Price to Governor Thomas C. Reynolds, July 22, 1864, 1020.

33. *Ibid.*, 1011.

34. *Ibid.*, 1020.

35. *Ibid.*, Letter of General Sterling Price to General E. Kirby Smith, July 23, 1864, 1023-1024.

36. *Ibid.*, 1023.

37. As early as March 8, 1864, General Price had proposed to Kirby Smith an invasion of Missouri, suggesting that such a move would relieve the pressure upon Generals Lee and Johnston. See *O.R.*, Series 1, Vol. XXXIV, Part 2, 1029.

38. *O.R.*, Series 1, Vol. XLI, Part 2, 1015.

39. *Idem.*

40. *O.R.*, Series 1, Vol. XXXIV, Page 2, 869-870.

41. *O.R.*, Series 1, Vol. XLI, Part 1, 105.

42. R. U. Johnson and Clarence C. Buel, Editors, *Battles and Leaders of the Civil War*, 4 Volumes, (New York, 1884-1887), Vol. II, 724.

43. Governor Thomas C. Reynolds' *Memoir* in the (Marshall) *Texas Republican*, December 17, 1864.

44. See Reynolds' *Manuscript* in Paul Jenkins, *The Battle of Westport* (Kansas City, Mo., 1906), 181.

3. "In a Just and Holy Cause"

Much of this chapter first appeared in the *Bulletin of the Missouri Historical Society*, Volume XIX, Number 3, under the title of "The Confederate Advance to Lexington, 1864."

1. *O.R.*, Series 1, Vol. XLI, Part 2, 1040-1041.

2. These troops failed to join General Price. See *O.R.*, Series 1, Vol. XLI, Part 4, 1007.

3. *O.R.*, Series 1, Vol. XLI, Part 2, 1040.

4. *Idem.*

5. *O.R.*, Series 1, Vol. XLI, Part 1, 643.

6. *Ibid.*, General Sterling Price's Report, 627.

7. *Idem.*

8. *Dictionary of American Biography*, 20 Volumes and supplement, (New York, 1928-1944), Vol. VI, 243-244.

9. *O.R.*, Series 1, Vol. XLI, Part 1, 641-642.

10. *Dictionary of American Biography*, Vol. XII, 290-291.

11. *O.R.*, Series 1, Vol. XLI, Part 1, 642.

12. Excellent accounts of this famous Confederate brigade are to be found in Bennett H. Young, *Confederate Wizards of the Saddle*, (Boston, 1914); John N. Edwards, *Shelby and His Men; or, The War in the West*, (Kansas City, Mo., 1897); and Daniel O'Flaherty, *General Jo Shelby, Undefeated Rebel*, (Chapel Hill, N. C., 1954).

13. O'Flaherty, *General Jo Shelby*, vii.

14. John N. Edwards, *Shelby's Expedition to Mexico, An Unwritten Leaf of the War*, (Kansas City, Mo., 1889), 232.

15. *O.R.*, Series 1, Vol. XLI, Part 3, 940.

16. *O.R.*, Series 1, Vol. XLI, Part 1, General Price's Report, 623.

17. *Ibid.*, 627-628.

18. *Ibid.*, 628.

19. Cyrus A. Peterson and Joseph M. Hanson, *Pilot Knob, The Thermopylae of the West*, (New York, 1914), 107.

20. William Forse Scott, *The Story of a Cavalry Regiment: The Career of the Fourth Iowa Veteran Volunteers, from Kansas to Georgia, 1861-1865*, (New York, 1893), 307, 309; *O.R.*, Series 1, Vol. XLI, Part 1, 318.

21. *Idem.*

22. *O.R.*, Series 1, Vol. XLI, Part 3, 174.

23. *O.R.*, Series 1, Vol. XLI, Part 1, General Rosecrans' Report, 307.

24. Peterson and Hanson, *Pilot Knob*, 103; Birdie H. Cole, "The Battle of Pilot Knob," *Confederate Veteran*, Vol. XXII, (Septem-

Notes

ber, 1914), 417; David Murphy, *My Recollections of Pilot Knob, Mo., Sept. 27, 1864,* a manuscript in Missouri Historical Society, St. Louis, Mo.

25. *O.R.,* Series 1, Vol. XLI, Part 1, Report of General Thomas Ewing, Jr., 445-452; Part 3, 358, 381.

26. W. L. Cabell, *Report of General W. L. Cabell's Brigade in Price's Raid in Missouri and Kansas in 1864,* (Dallas, Texas, 1900), 5-6. (Hereafter cited as *Cabell's Report.)* *O.R.,* Series 1, Vol. XLI, Part 1, Report of General John B. Clark, Jr., 679. General Clark blamed the nature of the terrain for the uncoordinated attack.

27. *O.R.,* Series 1, Vol. XLI, Part 1, General Ewing's Report, 448; *Cabell's Report,* 6.

28. James H. Campbell, *Reminiscences of James H. Campbell's Experience During the Civil War, 1861 to 1865,* 10-11, a manuscript in the possession of E. Taylor Campbell, St. Joseph, Missouri. Campbell served in Clark's brigade of Marmaduke's division during Price's expedition. *O.R.* Series 1, Vol. XLI, Part 1, 629, 709.

29. Clement A. Evans, Editor, *Confederate Military History,* 12 Volumes, (Atlanta, Ga., 1899), Vol. IX, "Missouri," 182; *Cabell's Report,* 6; *James H. Campbell Manuscript,* 12.

30. *O.R.,* Series 1, Vol. XLI, Part 1, General Ewing's Report, 451.

31. *Ibid.,* 449.

32. Peterson and Hanson, *Pilot Knob,* 100.

33. *Confederate Military History,* Vol. IX, "Missouri," 181.

34. Thomas C. Fletcher, "The Battle of Pilot Knob, and the Retreat to Leasburg," *War Papers and Personal Reminiscences, 1861-1865,* Commandery of the State of Missouri, Military Order of the Loyal Legion of the United States, (St. Louis, Mo., 1892), 45-46.

35. *O.R.,* Series 1, Vol. XLI, Part 1, General Ewing's Report, 450.

36. Peterson and Hanson, *Pilot Knob,* 289.

37. Fletcher, *War Papers and Reminiscences,* 49.

38. John Thomas Scharf, *History of St. Louis City and County from the Earliest Periods to the Present Day,* 2 Volumes, (Philadelphia, 1883), Vol. I, 441.

39. *O.R.,* Series 1, Vol. XLI, Part 1, General Price's Report, 630.

40. Webb, *Battles and Biographies of Missourians,* 215; Thomas Arvin Belser, Jr., *Military Operations in Missouri and Arkansas, 1861-*

1865, an unpublished Ph.D. dissertation, Vanderbilt University, June, 1958, 728.

41. Both Shelby and Price reported Shanks mortally wounded in this action. *O.R.,* Series 1, Vol. XLI, Part 1, 630, 654. Webb said he was dangerously but not mortally wounded. Webb, *Battles and Biographies of Missourians,* 214. John Scott, in his *The Story of the Thirty-second Iowa Infantry Volunteers,* (Nevada, Iowa, 1896), 302, says that Shelby forced his way over a natural ford in the Osage river near Castle Rock, a point guarded by two cavalry regiments and several companies of the 32nd Iowa Volunteer Infantry. The action was short but intense and Colonel Shanks was shot through the chest. Left behind to be nursed by Southern sympathizers, he was later captured and sent to a Union hospital in St. Louis where he recovered.

42. *O.R.,* Series 1, Vol. XLI, Part 1, 631.

43. *Ibid.,* 311, 345, 418.

44. Webb, *Battles and Biographies of Missourians,* 214.

45. On December 17, 1864, Thomas C. Reynolds brought charges of incompetence and drunkenness against General Price after the invasion had collapsed and the remnants of the expedition had returned to Arkansas. The statement of charges, as released to the press, was bitter in its denunciations. See Paul B. Jenkins, *The Battle of Westport,* 41-44.

These accusations combined with other circumstances led General Price to demand a Court of Inquiry to investigate the facts of his Missouri invasion. This Court convened on April 21, 1865, in Shreveport, Louisiana, but the war ended before its deliberations were completed. For the proceedings of the Court, see *O.R.,* Series 1, Vol. XLI, Part 1, 701-729.

Many years after the death of General Price, Thomas C. Reynolds wrote to a friend, confessing that he had brought these charges against Price because of his own crushing disappointment and "extreme irritation at the campaign's results." See MS Letter Thomas C. Reynolds to Thomas L. Snead, February 16, 1887, in *Snead Papers,* Missouri Historical Society, St. Louis.

46. *O.R.,* Series 1, Vol. XLI, Part 1, General Rosecrans' Report, 311.

47. Washington (D. C.) *Evening Star*, February 17, 1897.

48. *O.R.*, Series 1, Vol. XLI, Part 1, General Alfred Pleasonton's Report dated November 30, 1864, 340.

49. Evans, ed., *Confederate Military History*, Vol. IX, "Missouri," 182 ff.

50. *O.R.*, Series 1, Vol. XLI, Part 1, General Price's Report, 632.

51. *Ibid.*, General John B. Sanborn's Report, 388.

52. Most of these recruits were from north-central Missouri and particularly from the counties bordering the north bank of the Missouri river. One Missouri resident wrote to a relative soon after the Confederate army's sojourn at Boonville: "It seems that the presence of Price's army acted like wildfire on the boys and men, a good many went off with him." See Mary Gentry Clark Gordon, *Letter Diary*, in the State Historical Society of Missouri, Columbia: Mary G. C. Gordon to Jane Gentry Hudnall, October 25, 1864.

53. *O.R.*, Series 1, Vol. XLI, Part 1, General Price's Report, 632.

54. M. Jeff Thompson Reminiscences (1864 section), a MS in *M. Jeff Thompson Papers*, No. 1566 in Southern Historical Collection, University of North Carolina Library, Chapel Hill, N. C., 31.

55. General Mower's veteran infantry division, after reorganizing in St. Louis, had been sent by river steamer to Jefferson City, and then by rail to a point near Sedalia, where it joined General A. J. Smith's command as it marched into Sedalia on October 20. N. D. Starr and T. W. Holman, compilers, *The 21st Missouri Regiment Infantry Veteran Volunteers*, (Ft. Madison, Iowa, 1899), 31-32; A. T. Bartlett, *Reminiscences of Dr. A. T. Bartlett, Surgeon, Thirty-third Missouri Infantry Volunteers in Missouri and Elsewhere*, a MS in the *Bartlett Collection*, Missouri Historical Society, St. Louis, 43-44.

56. *O.R.*, Series 1, Vol. XLI, Part 1, General John B. Sanborn's Report, 388; Richard J. Hinton, *Rebel Invasion of Missouri and Kansas, and the Campaign of the Army of the Border Against Sterling Price, in October and November, 1864*, (Chicago, Illinois, 1865), 113.

57. *James H. Campbell Manuscript*, 16.

58. *O.R.*, Series 1, Vol. XLI, Part 1, General Price's Report, 632; Evans, Ed., *Confederate Military History*, Vol. IX, "Missouri," 184; Peterson and Hanson, *Pilot Knob*, 58-59.

59. *M. Jeff Thompson Reminiscences*, 32-33; *O.R.*, Series 1, Vol. XLI, Part 1, Brigadier General M. Jeff Thompson's Report, 665; Jay Monaghan, *Swamp Fox of the Confederacy: The Life and Military Services of M. Jeff Thompson*, (Tuscaloosa, Alabama, 1956), 81.

60. *O.R.*, Series 1, Vol. XLI, Part 1, 665.

61. *M. Jeff Thompson Reminiscences*, 36-37.

62. *O.R.*, Series 1, Vol. XLI, Part 1, General Price's Report, 633.

II. THE ACTION BEFORE WESTPORT

1. "Kansas, Rally! To Arms, and the Tented Field"

1. John M. Schofield, *Forty-Six Years in the Army*, (New York, 1897), 68-69.

2. *O.R.*, Series 1, Vol. XLI, Part 2, 980.

3. *O.R.*, Series 1, Vol. XLI, Part 1, General Curtis' Report, 464.

4. *Ibid.*, 465.

5. *O.R.*, Series 1, Vol. XLI, Part 3, Dispatch from General Curtis to Governor Carney, dated Sept. 20, 1864, 279.

6. *Ibid.*, Dispatch from General Curtis to Governor Carney, dated Sept. 21, 1864, 291.

7. *O.R.*, Series 1, Vol. XLI, General Curtis' Report, 465.

8. Albert Castel, *A Frontier State at War: Kansas, 1861-1865*, (Ithaca, New York, 1958), 180-181.

9. *O.R.*, Series 1, Vol. XLI, Part 3, Dispatch from General Curtis to Governor Carney, dated October 8, 1864, 713.

10. *Idem.*

11. *Ibid.*, Telegram from Governor Carney to General Rosecrans, dated October 9, 1864—3:20 p.m., 724.

12. *O.R.*, Series 1, Vol. XLI, Part 1, General Curtis' Report, 468-469.

13. *Ibid.*, 469.

14. *Leavenworth Times*, October 9, 1864.

15. *White Cloud Chief*, October 9, 1864.

16. *O.R.* Series 1, Vol. XLI, Part 1, General Curtis' Report, 471.

17. *Idem.*

18. Hinton, *Rebel Invasion of Missouri and Kansas*, 41-43; Wiley Britton, *The Civil War on the Border*, 2 volumes, (New York, 1891), Vol. II, 437.

Notes

19. *Congregational Record*, Vol. 6, No. 10, (October, 1864), 117; *The Battle of the Blue of the Second Regiment, K.S.M.,* October 22, 1864. *The Fight, the Captivity, the Escape, as Remembered by Survivors and Commemorated by the Gage Monument at Topeka, Kansas,* (Chicago, 1896), 15-16; *Kansas City Journal,* October 23, 1902.

2. A Dark and Dangerous Man

1. James G. Blunt, "General Blunt's Account of His Civil War Experiences," *Kansas Historical Quarterly,* Vol. I, No. 3, (May, 1932), 251.

2. *Dictionary of American Biography,* Vol. II, 399; Howard N. Monnett, "A Yankee Cavalryman Views the Battle of Prairie Grove," *Arkansas Historical Quarterly,* Vol. XXI, No. 4, (Winter, 1962), 287-304.

3. *O.R.,* Series 1, Vol. XLI, Part 3, 717.

4. In his memoir General Blunt claims to have been the one who urged Curtis to force Governor Carney to call out the militia and that it was only due to his (Blunt's) insistence that Curtis declared martial law and forced the governor's hand. See *Blunt's War Experiences,* 252. There is no evidence whatsoever to support Blunt's contention. This is just another example of the man's boastfulness.

5. General Sykes was an old regular, commanding a division at Malvern Hill, Second Bull Run, Antietam, Fredericksburg and a corps at Gettysburg. He had been sent to Kansas in April, 1864. His health was not good and Curtis feared he would not be able to stand field duty. See Hinton, *Rebel Invasion of Missouri and Kansas,* 37-38. However, there is no doubt that behind General Sykes' removal was Senator James Lane, maneuvering to get Blunt in command of the Kansas troops.

6. Letter from Colonel James H. Ford to General Samuel R. Curtis, dated October 12, 1864, in *Samuel Ryan Curtis Papers,* Iowa Department of History and Archives, Des Moines, Iowa.

7. *O.R.,* Series 1, Vol. XLI, Part 1, General James G. Blunt's Report, 572.

8. *Ibid.,* 572-573.

9. "The Civil War Diary of John Howard Kitts," *Collections of the Kansas State Historical Society, 1915-1918,* Vol. XIV, 331.

10. Hinton, *Rebel Invasion of Missouri and Kansas*, 65.

11. *O.R.*, Series 1, Vol. XLI, Part 1, 571, 596, 618 and Part 4, 57.

12. Now Kansas City, Kansas.

13. *Samuel J. Reader Diary, 1864-1869*, Vol. 6. A MS. diary in the Kansas State Historical Society, Topeka, Kansas.

14. *Lawrence Journal*, October 15, 17, 1864; *White Cloud Chief*, October 13, 20, 1864; *Leavenworth Daily Times*, October 17, 18, 1864; *Oskaloosa Independent*, October 15, 1864.

15. *Samuel J. Reader Diary*, Vol. 6.

16. Hinton, *Rebel Invasion of Missouri and Kanas*, 60.

17. *Ibid.*, 67; *O.R.*, Series 1, Vol. XLI, Part 1, General Curtis' Report, 472-473.

18. George S. Grover, "The Price Campaign of 1864," *Missouri Historical Review*, Vol. VI, No. 4, (July, 1912), 168.

19. On October 20 after the 2nd Colorado and the 16th Kansas had joined General Blunt, he organized them into the Fourth Brigade of his division with Colonel James H. Ford of the 2nd Colorado in command.

20. In his memoir Blunt states that after the junction had been made he would assume command of all the troops in the field. See *Blunt's Civil War Experiences*, 254.

21. *O.R.*, Series 1, Vol. XLI, Part 1, General Blunt's Report, 573.

22. Hinton, *Rebel Invasion of Missouri and Kansas*, 79.

23. *O.R.*, Series 1, Vol. XLI, Part 1, General Blunt's Report, 573.

3. *"This Is the Place to Make the Fight"*

1. H. E. Palmer, "Company A, Eleventh Kansas Regiment, In the Price Raid," *Transactions of the Kansas State Historical Society, 1905-1906*, Vol. IX, 435.

2. *O.R.*, Series 1, Vol. XLI, Part 1, Colonel Thomas Moonlight's Report, 591.

3. *O.R.*, Series 1, Vol. XLI, Part 4, General Field Orders No. 6, Army of the Border, 118.

4. *O.R.*, Series 1, Vol. XLI, Part 1, General Price's Report, 633.

5. Hinton, *Rebel Invasion of Missouri and Kansas*, 86.

6. Grover, *The Price Campaign of 1864*, 171.

7. Palmer, *Company A, Eleventh Kansas Regiment, In the Price Raid*, 436.

8. *O.R.*, Series 1, Vol. XLI, Part 4, Dispatch from General Blunt to General Curtis, dated October 20, 1864—8 a.m., 144-145.

9. *Ibid.*, Dispatch from General Curtis to General Blunt, dated October 20, 1864, 145.

10. *Ibid.*, Dispatch from General Blunt to General Curtis, dated October 20, 1864, 145-146.

11. *Ibid.*, Dispatch from General U. S. Grant to General Henry W. Halleck, dated October 20, 1864—7:30 p.m., 126.

12. *Blunt's Civil War Experiences*, 256.

4. "They Fought Us on the Blue Grass Ridges"

1. *James H. Campbell Manuscript*, 15.

2. *O.R.*, Series 1, Vol. XLI, Part 1, General John B. Clark, Jr.'s Report, 682.

3. Hinton, *Rebel Invasion of Missouri and Kansas*, 93.

4. *O.R.*, Series 1, Vol. XLI, Part 1, General Clark's Report, 682.

5. Palmer, *Company A, Eleventh Kansas Regiment, In the Price Raid*, 439; Archer S. Childers, *Recitals and Reminiscences*. A type-written MS. in Kansas State Historical Society.

6. Grover, *The Price Campaign of 1864*, 174.

7. *O.R.*, Series 1, Vol. XLI, Part 1, General Clark's Report, 682.

8. Hinton, *Rebel Invasion of Missouri and Kansas*, 94-95.

9. *O.R.*, Series 1, Vol. XLI, Part 1, General Jo Shelby's Report, 657.

10. *Ibid.*, General Blunt's Report, 575.

11. Hinton, *Rebel Invasion of Missouri and Kansas*, 95-96.

12. *James H. Campbell Manuscript*, 16.

13. Edwards, *Shelby and His Men*, 345.

14. Hinton, *Rebel Invasion of Missouri and Kansas*, 97.

15. *O.R.*, Series 1, Vol. XLI, Part 1, General Curtis' Report, 476-477.

16. *Blunt's Civil War Experiences*, 256.

17. *O.R.*, Series 1, Vol. XLI, Part 1, General Curtis' Report, 477.

18. *Ibid.*, General Shelby's Report, 657.

19. Major Edmund G. Ross of the 11th Kansas Cavalry was later

to become United States Senator Edmund G. Ross of Kansas and to cast the vote which saved President Andrew Johnson from impeachment.

20. Palmer, *Company A, Eleventh Kansas Regiment*, 439-440.

21. Letter of General Joseph O. Shelby in *Kansas City Journal*, November 24, 1881.

22. Grover, *The Price Campaign of 1864*, 172-173.

23. Hinton, *Rebel Invasion of Missouri and Kansas*, 97.

24. *Blunt's Civil War Experiences*, 256-257.

25. This incident is recorded by Col. Moonlight in his official report, *O.R.*, Series 1, Vol. XLI, Part 1, 592; by Hinton, *Rebel Invasion of Missouri and Kansas*, 97-98; by Capt. Clad Hamilton, "A Colonel of Kansas," *Kansas Historical Collections*, Vol. XII, (1911-1912), 286; and by William E. Connelley, *The Life of Preston B. Plumb*, (Chicago, 1913), 186.

26. *O.R.*, Series 1, Vol. XLI, Part 1, Colonel C. R. Jennison's Report, 583.

27. *James H. Campbell Manuscript*, 17-18.

28. Hinton, *Rebel Invasion of Missouri and Kansas*, 100.

29. *Ibid.*, 101.

30. Connelley, *Life of Preston B. Plumb*, 187.

31. *O.R.*, Series 1, Vol. XLI, Part 1, General Blunt's Report, 575.

32. *Ibid.*, Colonel Moonlight's Report, 593.

5. "I Can Stop Price at This Crossing"

1. *O.R.*, Series 1, Vol. XLI, Part 4, Telegram from General Curtis to General Blunt, 165.

2. *Ibid.*, 169.

3. *Samuel J. Reader Diary*, Vol. 6.

4. *O.R.*, Series 1, Vol. XLI, Part 4, Telegram from General Curtis to General Rosecrans, 164.

5. *Blunt's Civil War Experiences*, 257.

6. *O.R.*, Series 1, Vol. XLI, Part 1, Colonel James H. Ford's Report, 608.

7. *Ibid.*, Colonel Jennison's Report, 584.

8. Hinton, *Rebel Invasion of Missouri and Kansas*, 126; *Samuel J. Reader Diary*, Vol. 6, entry for October 21, 1864.

Notes

9. *O.R.*, Series 1, Vol. XLI, Part 1, General Curtis' Report, 479; Hinton, *Rebel Invasion of Missouri and Kansas*, 117.

10. "Price's Invasion," *Congregational Record*, Vol. 6, No. 10, (November, 1864), 123; Gage, *The Battle of the Blue of the Second Regiment*, K.S.M., 34.

11. *O.R.*, Series 1, Vol. XLI, Part 4, Dispatches of General Pleasonton to General Rosecrans, 183; Letter of General John B. Sanborn to Rev. J. J. Lutz dated St. Paul, Minn., July 12, 1895, in Kansas State Historical Society.

12. Hinton, *Rebel Invasion of Missouri and Kansas*, 119.

13. *O.R.*, Series 1, Vol. XLI, Part 1, General Pleasonton's Report, 340.

14. *Ibid.*, General Rosecrans' Report, 312.

15. *O.R.*, Series 1, Vol. XLI, Part 4, 145, 158, 183.

16. Stephen E. Ambrose, editor, *A Wisconsin Boy In Dixie. The Selected Letters of James K. Newton*, (Madison, Wisconsin, 1961), 123-124; H. Warren Phelps' Diary in *Journal of History*, Vol. XVII, No. 3, (July, 1924), 261.

17. General A. J. Smith and his infantry marched back across the state of Missouri following General Price's defeat at Westport, were placed on transports at St. Louis and sent to General George H. Thomas in Nashville. They arrived in time to turn the tide at the battle of Nashville, December 15, 1864. See Francis F. McKinney, *Education In Violence*, (Detroit, Mich., 1961), 398.

6. "Death Was Everywhere—"

1. Edwards, *Shelby and His Men*, 349.

2. *O.R.*, Series 1, Vol. XLI, Part 1, Colonel Sidney Jackman's Report, 675.

3. *Ibid.*, General Curtis' Report, 479.

4. *Idem.*

5. *Ibid.*, Colonel Jackman's Report, 675.

6. Hinton, *Rebel Invasion of Missouri and Kansas*, 128.

7. *O.R.*, Series 1, Vol. XLI, Part 1, Colonel Jennison's Report, 584; M. Jeff Thompson's *Reminiscences*, 41; General Joseph O. Shelby's Letter in *Kansas City Journal*, Nov. 24, 1881.

8. *O.R.*, Series 1, Vol. XLI, Part 1, Colonel Moonlight's Report, 593.

9. Hinton, *Rebel Invasion of Missouri and Kansas*, 135.

10. *O.R.*, Series 1, Vol. XLI, Part 1, Colonel Jackman's Report, 675.

11. Hinton, *Rebel Invasion of Missouri and Kansas*, 136.

12. *Ibid.*, 137.

13. Edwards, *Shelby and His Men*, 350.

14. P. I. Bonebrake, "Recollections of the Second Day's Fight in the Battle of Westport," *Westport 1812-1912*, (Kansas City, Mo., 1912), 71-72; Hinton, *Rebel Invasion of Missouri and Kansas*, 140.

15. *Samuel J. Reader Diary*, Vol. 6, entry for October 22, 1864.

16. *O.R.*, Series 1, Vol. XLI, Part 1, Colonel Jennison's Report, 585.

17. *Blunt's Civil War Experiences*, 258.

18. Hinton, *Rebel Invasion of Missouri and Kansas*, 144-145; *O.R.*, Series 1, Vol. XLI, Part 1, General Deitzler's Report, 615-616.

19. Hinton, *Rebel Invasion of Missouri and Kansas*, 144; *Blunt's Civil War Experiences*, 258; *O.R.*, Series 1, Vol. XLI, Part 1, Colonel Jennison's Report, 585; Colonel Moonlight's Report, 593.

20. *Ibid.*, General Pleasonton's Report, 340.

21. *Ibid.*, General John McNeil's Report, 371; Hinton, *Rebel Invasion of Missouri and Kansas*, 115.

22. *Idem.*

23. *Cabell's Report*, 11.

24. *O.R.*, Series 1, Vol. XLI, Part 1, General McNeil's Report, 371; Hinton, *Rebel Invasion of Missouri and Kansas*, 115.

25. *O.R.*, Series 1, Vol. XLI, Part 1, Colonel Phelps' Report, 403.

26. *Cabell's Report*, 11.

27. Simeon M. Fox, *The Seventh Kansas Cavalry: Its Services in the Civil War*, (Topeka, Kansas, 1908), 54.

28. *O.R.*, Series 1, Vol. XLI, Part 1, General McNeil's Report, 371.

29. Letter by Mrs. Robert Hill to Mrs. Kate S. Doneghy, dated October 23, 1864, in *Reminiscences of the Women of Missouri During the Sixties*, compiled by Missouri Division, United Daughters of the Confederacy, (n.p.,n.d.), 188.

30. *Idem.*

31. Hinton, *Rebel Invasion of Missouri and Kansas*, 115.
32. *O.R.*, Series 1, Vol. XLI, Part 1, General E. B. Brown's Report, 347.
33. Scott, *The Story of a Cavalry Regiment*, 320.
34. *O.R.*, Series 1, Vol. XLI, Part 1, General Clark's Report, 683.
35. *Ibid.*, Colonel Winslow's Report, 329.
36. *James H. Campbell Manuscript*, 18.

7. *"I Am Preparing to Renew the Attack"*

1. Connelley, *The Life of Preston B. Plumb*, 189. After the war Major Smith's remains were removed by his brother, Major Samuel D. Smith, Brigade Surgeon of the 1st Kansas, to Greenwood Cemetery near Leavenworth, Kansas.
2. Connelley in his *Life of Preston B. Plumb*, 189, claims that General Curtis went to Kansas after Major Smith's funeral and established a camp at the "Six-mile House" on the Leavenworth road. Because of this action, confidence in Curtis was shattered. However, there is no solid evidence to substantiate this claim. Connelley bases his assertion on the word of a single militia musician who did not tell his story until June 21, 1910—almost forty years after the event was alleged to have occurred. Such evidence is questionable.
3. *O.R.*, Series 1, Vol. XLI, Part 4, 190.
4. Richard S. Brownlee, *Gray Ghosts of the Confederacy: Guerrilla Warfare in the West, 1861-1865*, (Baton Rouge, La., 1958), 128-129.
5. *O.R.*, Series 1, Vol. XLI, Part 4, 189.
6. *Ibid.*, 183-184.
7. *Ibid.*, 203.
8. *O.R.*, Series 1, Vol. XLI, Part 1, 484-485, 700; *Cabell's Report*, 11.
9. *Congregational Record*, Vol. 6, No. 10, 124.
10. W. L. Cabell, "Capture of Cabell and Marmaduke," *Confederate Veteran*, VIII, (1900), 153.
11. *O.R.*, Series 1, Vol. XLI, Part 4, 203.
12. *Ibid.*, 203-204.
13. Samuel H. M. Byers, *Iowa in War Times*, (Des Moines, Ia., 1888), 574.

14. *O.R.*, Series 1, Vol. XLI, Part 1, General Pleasonton's Report, 341.

15. *Idem.*

16. Colonel Samuel J. Crawford in his book, *Kansas in the Sixties,* (Chicago, Ill., 1911), 148-149, states that in this conference General Curtis advocated a withdrawal of the Army of the Border to Kansas and that the other officers present urged General Blunt to place General Curtis under arrest and assume command of the army. Before doing so, however, General Blunt asked Curtis what he proposed to do and Curtis left the decision to Blunt. General Blunt then made the decision to stand and fight at Westport.
It is very doubtful that anything of the kind ever occurred. Nowhere in any reliable source is there to be found any evidence whatsoever substantiating Colonel Crawford's claim. General Blunt makes no mention of it in his memoirs and General Blunt certainly was not a modest man.

17. *O.R.*, Series 1, Vol. XLI, Part 1, General Curtis' Report, 484-485.

8. Sunday, October 23, 1864

1. *O.R.*, Series 1, Vol. XLI, Part 1, General Curtis' Report, 485.

2. Hinton, *Rebel Invasion of Missouri and Kansas,* 152-153; Britton, *Civil War on the Border, 1863-1865,* Vol. II, 483.

3. *Report of the Adjutant General of the State of Kansas, 1861-'65,* (Topeka, Kansas, 1896), 239.

4. *O.R.*, Series 1, Vol. XLI, Part 1, Colonel Moonlight's Report, 593-594.

5. Hinton, *Rebel Invasion of Missouri and Kansas,* 153; *Blunt's Civil War Experiences,* 259.

6. *Kansas Adjutant General's Report,* 239.

7. Edwards, *Shelby and His Men,* 353.

8. *O.R.*, Series 1, Vol. XLI, Part 1, General Price's Report, 635; *M. Jeff Thompson's Reminiscences,* 42.

9. *Archer S. Childers Manuscript.*

10. *M. Jeff Thompson's Reminiscences,* 42.

11. Hinton, *Rebel Invasion of Missouri and Kansas,* 154-157.

12. *Kansas Adjutant General's Report,* 240.

13. *M. Jeff Thompson's Reminiscences*, 43.

14. Hinton, *Rebel Invasion of Missouri and Kansas*, 158.

15. *O.R.*, Series 1, Vol. XLI, Part 1, General Curtis' Report, 485.

16. *Ibid.*, General Blunt's Report, 576; *Blunt's Civil War Experiences*, 259.

17. Hinton, *Rebel Invasion of Missouri and Kansas*, 158-159.

18. *O.R.*, Series 1, Vol. XLI, Part 1, Colonel Charles W. Blair's Report, 598.

19. Hinton, *Rebel Invasion of Missouri and Kansas*, 155.

20. *Ibid.*, 159; *O.R.*, Series 1, Vol. XLI, Part 1, General Curtis' Report, 485; *Letter of James Campbell* to his brother, Charles Campbell, dated Linn County, Kansas, November 9, 1864, in Kansas State Historical Society.

21. Hinton, *Rebel Invasion of Missouri and Kansas*, 159; *O.R.*, series 1, Vol. XLI, Part 1, Colonel Blair's Report, 598-599.

22. *Ibid.*, Colonel Moonlight's Report, 594.

23. Major General Samuel R. Curtis' *Campaign Book of the Army of the Border October and November 1864*, a MS. in Kansas State Historical Society.

24. The identity of George Thoman as the local citizen who led General Curtis to a flanking position was established through the family records of Miss Doris Jean Mabry, a great-granddaughter of George Thoman. During the years of research for this book, Thoman's name came up several times as General Curtis' benefactor, but the proof was lacking until Miss Mabry and her aunt, Mrs. Fred H. Reinhardt, supplied the evidence by means of family records. George Thoman lived out his life in and around Shawnee Mission and is buried in Forest Hill Cemetery, Kansas City, Mo., across the drive southeast of the Confederate Monument to General Joseph Shelby and his men.

25. *O.R.*, Series 1, Vol. XLI, Part 1, General Curtis' Report, 486.

26. *Idem.*; *Blunt's Civil War Experiences*, 259; *Kansas Adjutant General's Report*, 240; Britton, *Civil War on the Border*, Vol. II, 483.

27. Edwards, *Shelby and His Men*, 354; *O.R.*, Series 1, Vol. XLI, Part 1, General M. Jeff Thompson's Report, 667.

28 Wiley Britton, "Resume of Military Operations in Arkansas

and Missouri, 1864-65," *Battles and Leaders of the Civil War*, Vol. IV, 377.

29. *O.R.*, Series 1, Vol. XLI, Part 1, General Shelby's Report, 658.

30. *M. Jeff Thompson's Reminiscences*, 43.

31. *O.R.*, Series 1, Vol. XLI, Part 1, General Curtis' Report, 486.

32. *Ibid.*, Colonel Sidney Jackman's Report, 676.

33. *Ibid.*, Colonel Jennison's Report, 586.

34. *Idem.*

35. *Idem.; M. Jeff Thompson's Reminiscences*, 44; Hinton, *Rebel Invasion of Missouri and Kansas*, 160-161; Britton, *Civil War on the Border*, Vol. II, 483-484.

36. *O.R.*, Series 1, Vol. XLI, Part 1, General Shelby's Report, 658.

37. *Ibid.*, 659; *Kansas Adjutant General's Report*, 240; *M. Jeff Thompson's Reminiscences*, 44.

38. *O.R.*, Series 1, Vol. XLI, Part 1, General Shelby's Report, 659; Edwards, *Shelby and His Men*, 356-357; *M. Jeff Thompson's Reminiscences*, 44-45.

39. *O.R.*, Series 1, Vol. XLI, Part 1, General E. B. Brown's Report, 347; Diary of Colonel John F. Philips, *The Annals of Kansas City*, Vol. 1, No. 3, (December, 1923), entry dated Sunday, Oct. 23, 268.

40. *O.R.*, Series 1, Vol. XLI, Part 1, General Pleasonton's Report, 340-341.

41. *Ibid.*, Colonel John F. Philips' Report, 350; Scott, *The Story of a Cavalry Regiment*, 321; *Diary of Col. John F. Philips*, 268. General Brown was later tried by a Court Martial in St. Louis on charges preferred by General Pleasonton and was acquitted.

42. *O.R.*, Series 1, Vol. XLI, Part 1, Colonel Winslow's Report, 328; Colonel Philips' Report, 350; Scott, *The Story of a Cavalry Regiment*, 322; Hinton, *Rebel Invasion of Missouri and Kansas*, 170-171.

43. *Idem.; O.R.*, Series 1, Vol. XLI, Part 1, Colonel Philips' Report, 350.

44. *Ibid.*, 351; Hinton, *Rebel Invasion of Missouri and Kansas*, 170.

45. *Ibid.*, 171.

46. *O.R.*, Series 1, Vol. XLI, Part 1, Colonel Philips' Report, 351.

47. *Diary of Colonel John F. Philips*, 269.

48. Scott, *The Story of a Cavalry Regiment*, 324.

Notes

49. *Ibid.*, 324-325; *O.R.*, Series 1, Vol. XLI, Part 1, Colonel John F. Philips' Report, 351; Major George W. Kelly's Report, 363; *Diary of Colonel John F. Philips,* 269; Hinton, *Rebel Invasion of Missouri and Kansas,* 171-173.

50. *Ibid.*, 173.

51. *Diary of Colonel John F. Philips,* 269.

52. Hinton, *Rebel Invasion of Missouri and Kansas,* 173-174; *O.R.*, Series 1, Vol. XLI, Part 1, General Sanborn's Report, 390; Scott, *The Story of a Cavalry Regiment,* 326-327.

53. Edwards, *Shelby and His Men,* 356-357; *M. Jeff Thompson's Reminiscences,* 44-45; *O.R.*, Series 1, Vol. XLI, Part 1, General Shelby's Report, 659.

54. Edwards, *Shelby and His Men,* 357.

55. Dr. J. H. P. Baker *Diary, 1864-1865,* in State Historical Society of Missouri, entry for October 23, 1864.

56. Hinton, *Rebel Invasion of Missouri and Kansas,* 174-175.

57. *M. Jeff Thompson's Reminiscences,* 46.

58. *O.R.*, Series 1, Vol. XLI, Part 1, General John McNeil's Report, 372.

59. *Idem.*

60. *Ibid.*, Colonel Charles H. Tyler's Report, 700; Cabell, "Capture of Cabell and Marmaduke," *Confederate Veteran,* VIII, (1900), 153.

61. John Darr, "Price's Raid Into Missouri," *Confederate Veteran,* XI, (1903), 361-362; *Cabell's Report,* 11.

62. *O.R.*, Series 1, Vol. XLI, Part 1, General McNeil's Report, 372.

63. *Ibid., General Price's Report,* 635-636.

64. *Idem.;* Darr, *Price's Raid Into Missouri,* 361.

65. *O.R.*, Series 1, Vol. XLI, Part 1, Colonel John L. Beveridge's Report, 379.

66. *Cabell's Report,* 11; Darr, *Price's Raid Into Missouri,* 361.

67. Hinton, *Rebel Invasion of Missouri and Kansas,* 347. The case was later brought before the Judge Advocate General because of irregularities in the trial. The finding of the court was revoked and General McNeil was restored to rank and pay.

68. "Erastus B. Soper's History of Company D, 12th Iowa Infantry, 1861-1866," edited by Mildred Throne, *Iowa Journal of History,* Vol. 56, No. 3, (July, 1958), 270.

69. *O.R.*, Series 1, Vol. XLI, Part 1, Surgeon Ferdinand V. Drayton's Report, 343.

70. *Ibid.*, General Curtis' Report, 491.

71. *Ibid.*, General Price's Report, 640.

72. H. Warren Phelps' Diary printed in *Journal of History*, Vol. XVII, No. 3, (July, 1924), under the title "A Military Campaign," 262.

73. *Henry Klinge Diary*, a MS. diary in possession of Miss Jeanette Klinge of Marshall, Missouri, entry for Monday, October 24, 1864.

74. Edwards, *Shelby and His Men*, 357.

75. *O.R.*, Series 1, Vol. XLI, Part 1, General Curtis' Report, 491.

76. *Ibid.*, Colonel Jackman's Report, 676.

77. These casualties are to be found in the *O.R.*, Series 1, Vol. XLI, Part 1, scattered throughout brigade and regimental reports, 338, 361, 377, 393, 670, 686, 692, 693, 697, 699, 700; also in Britton, *Civil War on the Border*, Vol. II, 504-505; also in Byers, *Iowa in War Times*, 583.
Report of the Adjutant General of the State of Kansas for the Year 1864, (Leavenworth, Kansas, 1865), contains many Kansas Militia casualty lists as does Alfred T. Andreas, *History of the State of Kansas*, (Chicago, 1883), 179-211.

78. Hinton, *Rebel Invasion of Missouri and Kansas*, 181.

79. *Kansas City Western Journal of Commerce*, October 25, 1864.

80. *O.R.*, Series 1, Vol. XLI, Part 1, Surgeon Drayton's Report, 343; Major Samuel B. Davis' Report, 551.

81. *The Leavenworth Daily Times*, October 27, 1864; Hinton, *Rebel Invasion of Missouri and Kansas*, 182.

82. *O.R.*, Series 1, Vol. XLI, Part 1, Surgeon Drayton's Report, 343; Major Davis' Report, 551-552.

III. The Retreat from Westport

1. "A Vigorous Pursuit Was Necessary"

1. *O.R.*, Series 1, Vol. XLI, Part 1, General Curtis' Report, 491.

2. *Idem.*

3. *Idem.*; Hinton, *Rebel Invasion of Missouri and Kansas*, 175-176.

4. *O.R.*, Series 1, Vol. XLI, Part 1, General Field Order dated October 23, 1864—3 p.m., 492.

5. *Ibid.*, General Curtis' Report, 492; Hinton, *Rebel Invasion of Missouri and Kansas*, 176-177.

6. *O.R.*, Series 1, Vol. XLI, Part 1, Colonel Moonlight's Report, 594.

7. *Ibid.*, Itinerary of Price's Army, 646.

8. *M. Jeff Thompson's Reminiscences*, 62.

9. Evans, ed., *Confederate Military History*, Vol. IX, "Missouri," 191-192.

10. Hinton, *Rebel Invasion of Missouri and Kansas*, 183.

11. *M. Jeff Thompson's Reminiscences*, 45-46; Hinton, *Rebel Invasion of Missouri and Kansas*, 183.

12. *M. Jeff Thompson's Reminiscences*, 46.

13. *James H. Campbell Manuscript*, 19-20.

14. *Ibid.*, 21.

15. *Colonel Philips' Diary*, entry for October 24, 1864.

16. *Ibid.*, entry for October 25, 1864.

17. *O.R.*, Series 1, Vol. XLI, Part 1, General Pleasonton's Report, 341; General Curtis' Report, 493-494.

18. Hinton, *Rebel Invasion of Missouri and Kansas*, 206.

19. *Ibid.*, 208-209; *O.R.*, Series 1, Vol. XLI, Part 1, General Curtis' Report, 496; Colonel Benteen's Report, 332; Colonel Philips' Report, 352; *Colonel Philips' Diary*, entry for October 25, 1864.

20. *James H. Campbell Manuscript*, 20-21.

21. *Cabell's Report*, 12-13; Cabell, *Capture of Cabell and Marmaduke*, 153-154.

22. *O.R.*, Series 1, Vol. XLI, Part 1, General Price's Report, 637.

23. *Ibid.*, 636-637.

24. *M. Jeff Thompson's Reminiscences*, 47.

25. *O.R.*, Series 1, Vol. XLI, Part 1, General Shelby's Report, 659-660.

26. *M. Jeff Thompson's Reminiscences*, 48.

27. *O.R.*, Series 1, Vol. XLI, Part 1, General McNeil's Report, 373.

28. *James H. Campbell Manuscript*, 22.

29. *O.R.*, Series 1, Vol. XLI, Part 4, General Price's General Order No. 22, 1013-1014.

30. Hinton, *Rebel Invasion of Missouri and Kansas*, 235; *O.R.*, Series 1, Vol. XLI, Part 1, Colonel Benteen's Report, 333; General Curtis' Report, 502-503.

31. *Ibid.*, General Pleasonton's Report, 338.

32. *Ibid.*, General Blunt's Report, 577. In his Memoir General Blunt contradicts his official report and states that he moved to Fort Scott because General Curtis quit the field without leaving any orders. See *Blunt's Civil War Experiences*, 261.

33. *O.R.*, Series 1, Vol. XLI, Part 1, General Curtis' Report, 502.

34. Secretary of War, *Official Army Register for 1863*, (Washington, D. C., 1863), 65-66.

35. *Diary of Colonel John F. Philips*, entries for October 26 and 27, 1864.

36. *O.R.*, Series 1, Vol. XLI, Part 1, General Rosecrans' Report, 314.

37. *Ibid.*, General Curtis' Report, 506-507.

38. *Ibid.*, Letter from General Pleasonton to General Curtis, dated October 27, 1864, 506.

39. *Ibid.*, General Curtis' Report, 505, 507.

40. *Ibid.*, 507-508.

41. *Blunt's Civil War Experiences*, 262.

42. *M. Jeff Thompson's Reminiscences*, 57-58.

43. Scott, *The Story of a Cavalry Regiment*, 342; *Blunt's Civil War Experiences*, 262-263.

44. *O.R.*, Series 1, Vol. XLI, Part 1, General Sanborn's Report, 392; Hinton, *Rebel Invasion of Missouri and Kansas*, 270-271.

45. *Ibid.*, 275.

46. *Ibid.*, 276; *O.R.*, Series 1, Vol. XLI, Part 1, General Curtis' Report, 510.

47. Colonel Charles W. Blair's Third Brigade of Blunt's division had been made up almost entirely of Kansas State militia. Some of his militiamen had been sent home after the battle of Westport and the remainder had simply melted away after the first long march of sixty miles. What was left of the Third Brigade was combined with the other three brigades of Blunt's division and Colonel Blair became an aide-de-camp on General Curtis' staff. See *O.R.*, Series 1, Vol. XLI, Part 1, Colonel Blair's Reports, 599-606.

Notes

48. *Ibid.*, General Curtis' Report, 511.

49. *Idem.*

50. *Ibid.*, 512; General Rosecrans was the senior major-general and should have been present to assume command of the combined Missouri and Kansas forces at Westport and in the pursuit of Price's army. See *Official Army Register for 1863*, 3, 64. General Rosecrans was later removed from command in Missouri because of his improper handling of affairs during Price's invasion.

51. *O.R.*, Series 1, Vol. XLI, Part 4, 334.

52. *O.R.*, Series 1, Vol. XLI, Part 1, General Price's Report, 639.

53. William G. Hazen Letter to Alex R. Hazen dated December 21, 1864, in State Historical Society of Missouri, Columbia, Mo.

54. *Dr. J. H. P. Baker Diary, 1864-1865*, entry for November 1-5, 1864. A MS. in the State Historical Society of Missouri, Columbia, Mo.

Bibliography

I. Manuscripts, Diaries, Letters

Dr. J. H. P. Baker Diary, 1864-1865. State Historical Society of Missouri, Columbia, Missouri.

Bartlett Collection. Reminiscences of Dr. A. T. Bartlett, surgeon, Thirty-third Missouri Infantry Volunteers in Missouri and elsewhere. Missouri Historical Society, Jefferson Memorial Library, St. Louis, Missouri.

Army Journal of R. L. Brown, October 16-December 31, 1864. Missouri Historical Society, Jefferson Memorial Library, St. Louis, Missouri.

Archer S. Childers, *Recitals and Reminiscences*. Kansas State Historical Society, Topeka, Kansas.

Correspondence of General John S. Marmaduke, 1863-1864. Old Army Branch of the National Archives, Washington, D. C.

Major General Samuel R. Curtis, *Campaign Book of the Army of the Border October and November 1864*. Kansas State Historical Society, Topeka, Kansas.

Reverend J. B. Fuller Letter dated October 24, 1864, in the Robert M. Snyder Collection, University of Missouri at Kansas City Library.

Mary Gentry Clark Gordon Letter Diary. Mary G. C. Gordon to Jane Gentry Hudnall, October 7, 8, 9, 10, 13, 15, 16, 17, 19, 20, 24, 25, 1864. State Historical Society of Missouri, Columbia, Missouri.

Bibliography

Henry M. Greene, *My Big Blue Experience.* Kansas State Historical Society, Topeka, Kansas.

William G. Hazen Letter to Alex R. Hazen, December 21, 1864. State Historical Society of Missouri, Columbia, Missouri.

James Campbell Letter dated November 9, 1864. Kansas State Historical Society, Topeka, Kansas.

Jefferson Davis Papers. Duke University Library, Durham, North Carolina.

John Kemp, *What I Remember of the Battle of the Blue and Incidents Connected With It.* Kansas State Historical Society, Topeka, Kansas.

Joseph Mason Kern Scrapbook and Diary. Southern Historical Collection, University of North Carolina Library, Chapel Hill, North Carolina.

James Henry Lane Papers. Kansas State Historical Society, Topeka, Kansas.

Henry Klinge Diary. In possession of Miss Jeanette Klinge of Marshall, Missouri.

M. Jeff Thompson Papers, Southern Historical Collection. University of North Carolina Library, Chapel Hill, North Carolina.

Diary of Monroe J. Miller, July 1, 1864-November 16, 1864, in Monroe Joshua Miller Papers. Missouri Historical Society, Jefferson Memorial Library, St. Louis, Missouri.

James Montgomery Letter to George Stearns dated Mound City, Kansas, December 10, 1864. Kansas State Historical Society, Topeka, Kansas.

Dr. Peter McVicar. Sermon preached at the funeral of those who fell at the battle of the Big Blue, October 22, 1864; reinterred at a Topeka cemetery on December 10, 1864. Kansas State Historical Society, Topeka, Kansas.

Sterling Miles, *Reminiscences of the Battle of the Big Blue.* Kansas Historical Society, Topeka, Kansas.

David Murphy, *My Recollections of Pilot Knob, Mo., Sept. 27th, 1864.* Missouri Historical Society, Jefferson Memorial Library, St. Louis, Missouri.

Orders and Circulars, Sterling Price's Command, 1864-1865. Old Army Branch of the National Archives, Washington, D. C.

Captain H. E. Palmer, Price's Raid. *My Collections of Stirring Events Which Happened Forty Years Ago.* Kansas State Historical Society, Topeka, Kansas.

General Sterling Price Letter Book, August 28, 1863-March 9, 1865. National Archives, Washington, D. C.

Reminiscences of James H. Campbell's Experiences During the Civil War, 1861 to 1865. In the possession of E. Taylor Campbell, St. Joseph, Missouri.

Thomas C. Reynolds, *General Sterling Price and the Confederacy,* St. Louis Public Library, St. Louis, Missouri.

Richard Josiah Hinton Papers. Kansas State Historical Society, Topeka, Kansas.

Harvey D. Rice, *Reminiscences of the Battle of the Blue.* Kansas State Historical Society, Topeka, Kansas.

John B. Sanborn Letter dated July 12, 1895. Kansas State Historical Society, Topeka, Kansas.

Samuel J. Reader's Private Journal or Diary. Kansas State Historical Society, Topeka, Kansas.

Samuel Ryan Curtis Papers. Iowa Department of History and Archives, Des Moines, Iowa.

Simeon M. Fox Papers. Kansas State Historical Society, Topeka, Kansas.

Thomas L. Snead Papers. Missouri Historical Society, Jefferson Memorial Library, St. Louis, Missouri.

Thomas L. Snead Papers, 1862-1864. Old Army Branch of the National Archives, Washington, D. C.

Special Letters and Orders of General Jo Shelby's Command, 1864. Old Army Branch of the National Archives, Washington, D. C.

T. C. Stevens Collection. Kansas State Historical Society, Topeka, Kansas.

Thomas Moonlight Papers. Kansas State Historical Society, Topeka, Kansas.

Thomas C. Reynolds Papers. Manuscript Division, Library of Congress.

Thomas C. Reynolds Papers. Missouri Historical Society, Jefferson Memorial Library, St. Louis, Missouri.

John Utt, A military history of the Seventh Kansas Cavalry regiment. Kansas Historical Society, Topeka, Kansas.

Bibliography

Levi Williams, *My Recollections of the Battle of the Blue.* Kansas Historical Society, Topeka, Kansas.

H. K. Winans, A description of the burial of the dead of the Second regiment, Kansas State Militia, who fell at the Battle of the Blue, October 22, 1864. Kansas State Historical Society, Topeka, Kansas.

II. Printed Primary Sources

Adjutant General, State of Missouri, *General Orders, 1861-1865,* (n.p., n.d.)

Stephen E. Ambrose, editor, *A Wisconsin Boy in Dixie. The Selected Letters of James K. Newton,* Madison, Wisconsin, 1961.

The Battle of the Blue of the Second Regiment, K.S.M., October 22, 1864. The Fight, the Captivity, the Escape, as Remembered by Survivors and Commemorated by the Gage Monument at Topeka, Kansas, Chicago, (1896).

James G. Blunt, "General Blunt's Account of his Civil War Experiences," *Kansas Historical Quarterly,* I, No. 3, (May, 1932).

Parkison I. Bonebrake, *Recollections of the Second Day's Fight in the Battle of Westport,* (n.p., n.n., n.d.)

August Bondi, *Autobiography of August Bondi, 1833-1907,* Galesburg, Illinois, 1910.

Wiley Britton, *The Civil War on the Border,* 2 Volumes, New York, 1891.

Wiley Britton, *The Union Indian Brigade in the Civil War,* Kansas City, Missouri, 1922.

Wiley Britton, "Resume of Military Operations in Missouri and Arkansas, 1864-65," *Battles and Leaders of the Civil War,* IV, New York, 1884.

Cloyd Bryner, *Bugle Echoes: The Story of the Illinois 47th,* Springfield, Illinois, 1905.

Lathrop Bullene, *Lathrop Bullene, 1826-1915,* (n.p., n.n.), 1916.

William L. Cabell, "Capture of Cabell and Marmaduke," *Confederate Veteran,* VIII, 1900.

William L. Cabell, *Report of General W. L. Cabell's Brigade in Price's Raid in Missouri and Kansas in 1864,* Dallas, Texas, 1900.

"The Campaign in Missouri Against Price," *United States Service Magazine*, Vol. I, (January, 1865).

Samuel J. Crawford, *Kansas in the Sixties*, Chicago, 1911.

Frederic A. Culmer, editor, "Brigadier Surgeon John W. Trader's Recollections of the Civil War in Missouri," *Missouri Historical Review*, Vol. XLVI, No. 4, (July, 1952).

John Darr, "Price's Raid into Missouri," *Confederate Veteran*, XI, (August, 1903).

Albert N. Doerschuk, "Extracts From War-Time Letters, 1861-1864," *Missouri Historical Review*, Vol. XXIII, No. 1, (October, 1928).

Frederick Dyer (comp.) *A Compendium of the War of the Rebellion*, Des Moines, Iowa, 1908.

John N. Edwards, *Shelby and His Men: or, The War in the West*, Cincinnati, 1867.

Clement A. Evans, editor, *Confederate Military History*, 12 volumes, Atlanta, Georgia, 1899.

Thomas C. Fletcher, "The Battle of Pilot Knob, and the Retreat to Leasburg," *War Papers and Personal Reminiscences, Missouri Military Order of the Loyal Legion*, I, St. Louis, Missouri, 1892.

Adjutant General Simeon M. Fox, *The Story of the Seventh Kansas*, (n.p., n.d.)

Simeon M. Fox, *The Seventh Kansas Cavalry: Its Services in the Civil War*, Topeka, Kansas, 1908.

Simeon M. Fox, "The Early History of the Seventh Kansas Cavalry," *Collections of the Kansas State Historical Society*, XI, 1909-1910.

George S. Grover, "The Price Campaign of 1864," *Missouri Historical Review*, Vol. VI, No. 4, (July, 1912).

Richard J. Hinton, *Rebel Invasion of Missouri and Kansas and the Campaign of the Army of the Border Against General Sterling Price, in October and November, 1864*, Chicago, Illinois, 1865.

Warner Lewis, "Civil War Reminiscences," *Missouri Historical Review*, Vol. 2, (April, 1908).

Vivian Kirkpatrick McLarty, editor, "The Civil War Letters of Colonel Bazel F. Lazear," *Missouri Historical Review*, Vol. XLV, No. 1, (October, 1950).

General Dabney H. Maury, "Recollections of the Elkhorn Cam-

Bibliography

paign," *Southern Historical Society Papers*, Vol. II, No. 4, (October, 1876).

Frank Moore, editor, *The Rebellion Record: A Diary of American Events*, 12 volumes, 1861-1871.

Adela E. Orpen, *Memories of Old Emigrant Days in Kansas, 1862-1865*, London, 1926.

Henry E. Palmer, "Company A, Eleventh Kansas Regiment in the Price Raid," *Transactions of the Kansas State Historical Society*, IX, 1905-1906.

H. Warren Phelps, "A Military Campaign. A Campaign Through Arkansas, Missouri and into Kansas, September 2 to October 27, 1864," *Journal of History*, Vol. 17, (July, 1924).

John F. Philips, "Diary of Acting Brig. Genl. Jno. F. Philips," *The Annals of Kansas City, Missouri*, I, No. 3, (December, 1923).

"Price's Invasion," *Congregational Record*, Vol. 6, (October-November, 1864).

Stephen H. Ragan, *Battle of Westport*, Kansas City, Missouri, 1910.

Stephen H. Ragan, "The Battle of Westport," *Annals of Kansas City, Missouri*, I, No. 3, (December, 1923).

Reminiscences of the Women of Missouri During the Sixties, compiled by Missouri Division, United Daughters of the Confederacy. (n.p., n.d.)

Report of the Adjutant General of the State of Kansas for the Year 1864, Leavenworth, Kansas, 1865.

Report of the Adjutant General of the State of Kansas, 1861-65, Topeka, Kansas, 1896.

Peter D. Ridenour, *Autobiography*, Kansas City, Missouri, 1908.

John B. Sanborn, "The Campaign in Missouri in September and October, 1864," *Glimpses of the Nation's Struggle. Third Series. Minnesota Commandery of the Military Order of the Loyal Legion*, New York, 1893.

John M. Schofield, *Forty-Six Years in the Army*, New York, 1897.

John Scott, *The Story of the Thirty-second Iowa Infantry Volunteers*, Nevada, Iowa, 1896.

William Forse Scott, "The Last Fight for Missouri," *Personal Recollections of the War of the Rebellion. New York Military Order of the Loyal Legion*, III, New York, 1907.

ACTION BEFORE WESTPORT, 1864

William Forse Scott, *The Story of a Cavalry Regiment—4th Iowa Veteran Volunteers from Kansas to Georgia 1861-1865*, New York, 1893.

"Second Regiment Kansas State Militia," *Congregational Record*, Vol. 6, (December 10, 1864).

Joseph O. Shelby, "Price's Raid," *Kansas City Journal*, November 24, 1881.

Erastus B. Soper, "History of Company D, 12th Iowa Infantry, 1861-1866," edited by Mildred Throne, *Iowa Journal of History*, Vol. 56, No. 3, (July, 1958).

Speech of Governor Thomas Carney, Leavenworth, Kansas, 1864.

N. D. Starr and T. W. Holman (Comp.), *The 21st Missouri Regiment Infantry Veteran Volunteers*, Fort Madison, Iowa, 1899.

"The Civil War Diary of John Howard Kitts," *Collections of the Kansas State Historical Society*, Vol. XIV, 1915-1918.

War of the Rebellion: A Compilation of the Official Records of the Union and Confederate Armies, 128 volumes, Washington, D.C., 1880-1901.

W. L. Webb, *Battles and Biographies of Missourians, or, the Civil War Period of our State*, Kansas City, Missouri, 1900.

William S. Burke (Comp.), *Official Military History of Kansas Regiments During the War for the Suppression of the Great Rebellion*, Leavenworth, Kansas, 1870.

III. Newspapers and Scrapbooks

The October and November, 1864 issues of the following newspapers were consulted:

Atchison Champion and Press, Atchison, Kansas.
Burlingame Chronicle, Burlingame, Kansas.
Congregational Record, Lawrence, Kansas.
Weekly California News, California, Missouri.
Columbia, Missouri Statesman, Columbia, Missouri.
Emporia News, Emporia, Kansas.
Freedom's Champion, Atchison, Kansas.
Hiawatha Union-Sentinel, Hiawatha, Kansas.
Junction City Union, Junction City, Kansas.
Kansas Chief, Troy, Kansas.

176

Bibliography

Kansas Farmer, Topeka, Kansas.
Kansas Press, Council Grove, Kansas.
Kansas State Journal, Lawrence, Kansas.
Kansas Tribune, Lawrence, Kansas.
Western Journal of Commerce, Kansas City, Missouri.
Daily Kansas City Western Journal of Commerce, Kansas City, Missouri.
Leavenworth Daily Conservative, Leavenworth, Kansas.
Leavenworth Evening Bulletin, Leavenworth, Kansas.
Leavenworth Daily Times, Leavenworth, Kansas.
Lexington Weekly Union, Lexington, Missouri.
The Liberty Tribune, Liberty, Missouri.
Manhattan Weekly Independent, Manhattan, Kansas.
Olathe Mirror, Olathe, Kansas.
Oskaloosa Independent, Oskaloosa, Kansas.
Southern Kansas Herald, Paola, Kansas.
Topeka State Journal, Topeka, Kansas.
Topeka Daily Tribune, Topeka, Kansas.
White Cloud Kansas Chief, White Cloud, Kansas.
Wyandotte Weekly Gazette, Wyandotte, Kansas.
Washington, D. C. Evening Star, (Issue of February 17, 1897).
Kansas in the Civil War—Scrapbook in 3 volumes, Kansas State Historical Society, Topeka, Kansas.
Native Sons of Kansas City Scrapbook, the Native Sons of Kansas City, Missouri.

IV. Secondary Sources

"Army Leaders Honor Heroic Southerner," *Kansas City Journal*, April 6, 1939.
Virginia H. Asbury, "An Anomaly of Written History," *Confederate Veteran*, Vol. 22, (March, 1914).
A. B. Barnes, "Horrid Times of the War in Kansas," *Confederate Veteran*, Vol. 18, (October, 1910).
"Battle of Westport," *Confederate Veteran*, Vol. 34, (October, 1926).
"Battle of Westport," *Kansas City Journal*, October 23, 1902.
Thomas Arvin Belser, Jr., *Military Operations in Missouri and*

Arkansas, 1861-1865. An unpublished Ph.D. dissertation, Vanderbilt University, Nashville, Tennessee, June, 1958.

A. Birdsall, *The History of Jackson County, Missouri,* Kansas City, Missouri, 1881.

William P. Borland, "General Jo Shelby," *Missouri Historical Review,* VII, No. 1, (October, 1912).

Richard S. Brownlee, *Gray Ghosts of the Confederacy: Guerrilla Warfare in the West, 1861-1865,* Baton Rouge, Louisiana, 1958.

————"The Battle of Pilot Knob," *State of Missouri Official Manual for the Years 1961-1962,* Jefferson City, Missouri.

Edward Bumgardner, *The Life of Edmund G. Ross,* Kansas City, Missouri, 1949.

Samuel H. M. Byers, *Iowa in War Times,* Des Moines, Iowa, 1888.

Lucien Carr, *Missouri: A Bone of Contention,* Boston and New York, 1888.

Theodore S. Case, editor, *History of Kansas City, Missouri,* Syracuse, New York, 1888.

Albert Castell, *A Frontier State at War: Kansas, 1861-1865,* Ithaca, New York, 1958.

————"War and Politics: The Price Raid of 1864," *Kansas Historical Quarterly,* Vol. XXIV, No. 2, (Summer, 1958).

Birdie H. Cole, "The Battle of Pilot Knob," *Confederate Veteran,* Vol. 22, (September, 1914).

William E. Connelley, *The Life of Preston B. Plum, 1837-1891,* Chicago, Illinois, 1913.

————*Standard History of Kansas and Kansans,* 5 volumes, Chicago, Illinois, 1918.

H. H. Crittenden, *The Battle of Westport and National Memorial Park,* Kansas City, Missouri, 1938.

G. W. Cullum et al., *Biographical Register of the Officers and Graduates of the U. S. Military Academy at West Point, N. Y.,* New York, 1891-1940.

Dictionary of American Biography, edited by Allen Johnson, Dumas Malone, and Harris E. Starr, 20 volumes and supplement, New York, 1928-1944.

Jennie Edwards, *John N. Edwards,* Kansas City, Missouri, 1889.

Eli G. Foster, *The Civil War by Campaigns,* Topeka, Kansas, 1899.

Bibliography

Harrison Hannahs, "General Thomas Ewing, Jr." *Collections of the Kansas State Historical Society,* XII, 1911-1912.

Emanuel F. Heisler, *The Battle of the Big Blue,* (n.p., n.n., n.d.)

Wilfred R. Hollister and Harry Norman, *Five Famous Missourians,* Kansas City, Missouri, 1900.

Louis O. Honig, *Westport, Gateway to the Early West,* Kansas City, Missouri, 1950.

Paul B. Jenkins, *The Battle of Westport,* Kansas City, Missouri, 1906.

Arthur Roy Kirkpatrick, "Missouri's Secessionist Government, 1861-1865," *Missouri Historical Review,* Vol. XLV, No. 2, (January, 1951).

————"Missouri, the Twelfth Confederate State," unpublished Ph.D. dissertation, University of Missouri, Columbia, Missouri, 1954.

William T. McClure, "The Fourth Kansas Militia in the Price Raid," *Transactions of the Kansas State Historical Society,* Vol. VIII, 1903-1904.

George Miller, *Missouri's Memorable Decade,* 1860-1870, Columbia, Missouri, 1896.

Jay Monaghan, *Civil War on the Western Border 1854-1865,* Boston, 1955.

————*Swamp Fox of the Confederacy: The Life and Military Services of M. Jeff Thompson,* Tuscaloosa, Alabama, 1956.

Howard N. Monnett, "Decisive Conflict: The Battle of Westport," *Kansas City Star,* April 23, 1961.

————"The Origin of the Confederate Invasion of Missouri, 1864," *Bulletin of the Missouri Historical Society,* Vol. XVIII, No. 1, (October, 1961).

————"The Confederate Advance to Lexington, 1864," *Bulletin of the Missouri Historical Society,* Vol. XIX, No. 3, (April, 1963).

————"A Yankee Cavalryman Views the Battle of Prairie Grove," *Arkansas Historical Quarterly,* Vol. XXI, No. 4, (Winter, 1962).

Norman Potter Morrow, *Price's Missouri Expedition, 1864,* an unpublished M.A. thesis, University of Texas, 1949.

Stephen B. Oates, *Confederate Cavalry West of the River*, Austin, Texas, 1961.

Daniel O'Flaherty, *General Jo Shelby, Undefeated Rebel*, Chapel Hill, North Carolina, 1954.

Joseph Howard Parks, *General Edmund Kirby Smith, C.S.A.*, Baton Rouge, Louisiana, 1954.

J. R. Perkins, "Jefferson Davis and General Sterling Price," *Confederate Veteran*, Vol. XIX, (October, 1911).

Cyrus A. Peterson and Joseph M. Hanson, *Pilot Knob, The Thermopylae of the West*, New York, 1914.

Jesse C. Petherbridge (Comp.), *Kansas State Militia, 1864*, Kansas City, Missouri, 1907.

Ezra J. Warner, *Generals In Gray*, Baton Rouge, Louisiana, 1959.

Westport, 1812-1912, Kansas City, Missouri, 1912.

Daniel W. Wilder, *The Annals of Kansas*, Topeka, Kansas, 1875.

Index

A

Anderson, Bloody Bill, 4, 13, 29.
Anderson, Major Martin, 54, 58.
Arkansas river, 19, 138.
Army of the Border, 47, 72, 73, 77, 80,
  84, 92, 103, 128, 134.
  strength of, 36.
  organization of, 43-46.
  position at Westport, 95.
Army of the Cumberland, 22.
Army of the Department of the Missouri, 22.
  organization of, 28, 75.
Army of Missouri, 21, 27, 29, 30, 32, 40.
  47, 51, 56, 65, 68, 74, 85, 127, 129, 133.
  136, 138.
  attacks Pilot Knob, 23-24.
  organization of, 19.
  organized by Gen. Price, 19.
  order of march, 21.
  losses, 122, 123-124.
  retreat of, 127-138.
Army of Northern Virginia, 8.
Army of the Potomac, 27.
Atchison, Kansas, 39.
Atlanta, Georgia, 3, 8, 9, 22.
Aubry, Kansas, 128.

B

Baker, Dr. J. H., 117.
Barker, Lt. H. L., 44, 81, 98.
Barker's Battery, 44, 60, 65, 79, 105.
Baxter Springs, Kansas, 92.
Beef herd, Confederate, 26, 86, 93, 94,
  119.
Behan, Capt. J. Henry, 5, 6, 7, 8, 9, 11,
  13.
  letters to Jeff Davis, 5-7.
Bent house, 99, 106.
Benteen, Lt. Col. Frederick W., 89, 116,
  132, 133, 136.
  takes command at Byram's Ford,
  115.
  at Mine Creek, 131-132.
  rejoins Curtis, 137.
Beveridge, Col. J. L., 86, 120.
Big Blue, Battle of, 77-85.
Big Blue river, 47, 48, 67, 68, 69, 72, 73,
  76, 78, 79, 82, 84, 87, 111, 117.
Blair, Col. Charles W., 43, 44, 45, 48,
  95, 102, 103.
Blocher's Arkansas Confederate Battery, 106, 116.
Bloomfield, Missouri, 21.
Blunt, Gen. James G., 36, 44, 47, 49,

First Arkansas Infantry—Confederate, 19.
First Iowa Cavalry, 94
First Missouri State Militia Cavalry, 111, 113, 114.
Fishback, Gen. W. H. M., 43, 44, 45, 47.
Fisk, Gen. Clinton B., 26, 27.
Flanigan, Governor Harris, 10.
Ford, Col. James H., 43, 47, 59, 63, 78, 95, 98.
Fort Davidson, 25.
  description of, 23.
  defense of, 24.
  assault on, 23-24.
  fall of, 24.
  magazine explosion, 24.
Fort Larned, 41.
Fort Leavenworth, 3, 36, 37, 41, 42, 124.
Fort Scott, 37, 39, 47, 132, 133.
Fort Smith, 92, 138.
Forty-ninth Illinois Infantry, 123.
Foster, Maj. Emory S., 48.
Foster's Cavalry Battalion, 48, 52.
Fourteenth Iowa Infantry, 23.
Fourteenth Kansas Cavalry, 44.
Fourteenth Missouri Cavalry—Confederate, 65, 133.
Fourth Iowa Cavalry, 89, 112, 114, 115.
Fourth Kansas State Militia, 44, 47, 72, 102.
Fourth Missouri Cavalry—Confederate, 58.
Fourth Missouri State Militia Cavalry, 111, 114.
Fredericktown, Missouri, 21, 22.
Freeman, Col. T. R., 131.
Freeman's Brigade, 59, 131, 138.

G

Garland, Senator Augustus H., 10.
Gasconade river, 26.
Georgetown-Lexington road, 30.
Gill, Lt. Edward, 103.
Gillis House, 85, 91, 95.

Glasgow, Attack on, 30-31.
Glasgow, Missouri, 30.
Gordon, Col. Frank B., 79, 81, 82, 84, 105.
Grand river, 117, 129.
Grant, Gen. M. S., 46, 47, 72, 78, 81, 82, 83, 84.
Grant, Gen. Ulysses S., 55, 136.
Green, Capt. Louis F., 51, 71.
Greene, Col. Colton, 57.
Greenville, Missouri, 21.
Greer, Capt. James E., 54.
Greer, Judge, 83.
Grover, Capt. George S., 48.
Guilford, Lt. Col., 81.

H

Halleck, Gen. Henry W., 22, 55, 92, 122, 136.
Hannibal and St. Joseph Railroad, 29.
Harris House, 4, 101.
Harrison, Col. Isaac F., 18.
Harrisonville road, 81, 82, 99, 106, 108, 116.
Helena, Arkansas, 20, 35.
Hermann, Missouri, 26.
Hickman Mills Crossing, 72, 81.
Hickman Mills, Missouri, 43, 45, 47, 48, 59, 69, 78, 118.
Hickman Mills road, 94.
Hicks, Lt. Henry A., 71.
Hill, Mrs. Robert, 88.
Hinkle's ford, 72, 80, 81.
Hinkle's Grove, 110, 116.
Hogan, Col. A. C., 71, 85.
Holden, Missouri, 48.
Holmes, Gen. T. W., 16.
Home Guards, 49, 95.
Hood, Gen. John B., 6, 9.
Hoyt, Lt. Col. George H., 44.
Hughey's Arkansas Confederate Battery, 86, 119.
Hughey, Capt. W. M., 86.
Hunt, Maj. R. H., 63, 66.
Huntoon, Capt. Joel, 54.

Index

Hynson's Texas Battery, 113, 114.

I

Independence-Kansas City road, 69, 70, 71.
Independence-Lexington road, 48, 53, 54, 55.
Independence-Little Santa Fe road, 78, 86, 94, 118.
Independence, Missouri, 47, 53, 60, 65, 66, 67, 69, 77, 78, 86, 121, 124, 128.
Independence-Westport road, 88.
Independent Colorado Battery, 44, 60, 62, 63, 71, 85, 98, 100, 105, 106, 135.
Indian Creek, 117, 127.
Indian Territory, 18-19, 138.
Iron Brigade, 21, 100, 116.
    reputation of, 20.
    organized, 20.
    at the Osage river, 26.
    M. Jeff Thompson assumes command of, 29.
    attack on Sedalia, Mo., 31-32.
    in advance at Lexington, Mo., 51.
    advance into Independence, Mo., 67.
    attack at Byram's ford, 80.
    assault on Westport, 84.
    defense of Brush Creek, 108.
    last stand at Westport, 110.
    defense on the Little Osage, 132.
    in the Battle of Newtonia, Mo., 135-136.
Iuka, Battle of, 13.

J

Jackman, Col. Sidney, 78, 79, 82, 84, 116, 123, 132.
Jackman's Brigade, 21, 78, 100, 108.
Jackman's Missouri Cavalry, 63.
Jackson, Governor Claiborne Fox, 20.
James, Jesse, 13.
Jeffers, Col. William L., 89.
Jefferson Barracks, 22.
Jefferson City, Missouri, 26, 27, 28, 49.

Jefferson County, Kansas, 40.
Jennison, Col. Charles R., 43, 65, 72, 79, 80, 81, 84, 85, 95, 107, 108.
Jennison's Brigade, 48, 65, 95, 98, 108, 117.
Johnson, Capt. Curtis, 107, 108.
Johnson County, Kansas, 70.
Johnson, Senator Robert W., 16.
Johnston, Gen. Joseph E., 8, 9.
Jones Hotel, 88.
Jonesborough, Missouri, 31.

K

Kansas City Home Guards, 49, 95.
Kansas City, Missouri, 49, 71, 84, 95, 99, 124.
Kansas-Nebraska Bill, 3.
Kansas Redlegs, 43.
Kansas river, 92, 128.
Kansas State Militia, 49, 54, 69, 71, 99, 102, 128, 134.
Kelly, Maj. George W., 114.
Kendall, Lt. W. H., 44.
Ketner, Maj. James, 59.
Kirby Smithdom, 15.
Klinge, Pvt. Henry, 123.
Knowles' Battery, 44, 105.
Knowles, Lt. D. C., 44.

L

Lafayette County, Missouri, 51.
La Mine river, 31.
Lane, Senator James H., 39, 42, 51.
Laynesport, Arkansas, 138.
Lawrence, Kansas, 37, 40.
Lawther, Col. Robert R., 57, 58.
Lazear, Lt. Col. B. F., 113.
Leasburg, Missouri, 25.
Leavenworth, Kansas, 38, 42.
Lee, Gen. Robert E., 8.
Lee, Gen. Stephen D., 9.
Lexington, Battle of, 13, 20.
Lexington, Missouri, 32, 47, 48, 49, 75.
    fairgrounds in, 50.
    Masonic College in, 50.

Index

LaVergne, TN USA
14 March 2011
220047LV00007B/47/A